Teach
Them ALL
to Read

In memory of Cliff Schimmels—Teacher, friend, and mentor
May 11, 1937–May 9, 2001

Teach Them ALL to Read

Catching the Kids Who Fall Through the Cracks

Elaine K. McEwan

CORWIN PRESS, INC.
A Sage Publications Company
Thousand Oaks, California

For information:

Corwin Press, Inc.
A Sage Publications Company
2455 Teller Road
Thousand Oaks, California 91320
www.corwinpress.com

Sage Publications Ltd.
6 Bonhill Street
London EC2A 4PU
United Kingdom

Sage Publications India Pvt. Ltd.
M-32 Market
Greater Kailash I
New Delhi 110 048 India

Printed in the United States of America

Library of Congress Cataloging-in-Publication Data

McEwan, Elaine K., 1941–
    Teach them ALL to read: Catching the kids who fall through the cracks / Elaine McEwan.
        p. cm.
    Includes bibliographical references and index.
    ISBN 0–7619–4502–4 (c) — ISBN 0–7619–4503–2 (p)
    1. Reading (Elementary) 2. Language arts (Elementary) I. Title: Catching the kids who fall through the cracks. II. Title.
    LB1573 .M1667 2002
        372.4—dc21   2001008016

This book is printed on acid-free paper.

    03 04 05 10 9 8 7 6 5 4 3

Acquisitions Editor:	Robb Clouse
Editorial Assistant:	Erin Buchanan
Copy Editor:	Marilyn Power Scott
Production Editor:	Diane S. Foster
Typesetter:	Graphicraft, Ltd., Hong Kong
Indexer:	Molly Hall
Cover Designer:	Michael Dubowe

Contents

Preface

*W*hy do so many students fall through the cracks in reading? *What* can educators do to prevent this widespread academic free fall? Finding answers to these tough questions has consumed much of my professional career. In the early 1980s, I took a principalship in a failing school, where nearly 75% of the students were below grade level in reading. Although we were privileged to raise reading achievement from the 20th to the 70th percentile overall, many of our students continued to fall through the cracks. For them, learning to read was an agonizing process, and if help came at all, it was often too little and too late to overcome the cumulative effects of failure.

I wish I had known then what I know now. Today, there is a growing body of high-quality research to inform our instructional practices—particularly what we do with those students who are most at-risk of reading failure. Now we know that early identification and intensive intervention are essential. Waiting for students to "bloom" like Leo, the winsome Leo Lionni (1971) character, is an exercise in futility. Now we know, that for those students at risk of reading failure, immersion in well-written literature, although important, isn't nearly enough. We have discovered some essential pieces of the reading puzzle that we knew very little about 20 or 30 years ago.

If I could only travel back in time and offer answers to those students who fell through the cracks while I was a teacher, media specialist, and principal! Ron Edmonds (1981) believed that

> We can, whenever and wherever we choose, successfully teach all children whose schooling is of interest to us. We already know more than we need to do that. Whether or not we do it must finally depend on how we feel about the fact that we haven't so far. (p. 53)

Although Edmonds was writing in the broad sense about student achievement, his statement could well be paraphrased to describe the current status of reading instruction: *We can, whenever and wherever we choose, successfully teach all children to read. We already know more than we need to do that. Whether or not we do it must finally depend on how we feel about the fact that we haven't so far.*

THE GOALS OF THIS BOOK

In 1998, I wrote *The Principal's Guide to Raising Reading Achievement* and developed a workshop for principals based on my personal experiences with raising reading achievement. My goal was to share the very latest in reading research with practitioners to help them make literacy a reality for more of their students. I recently heard from one of those principals, Kathie Dobberteen, the principal of La Mesa Dale Elementary School in the San Diego, California, area.

Here is an excerpt from Kathie's message:

> I haven't written to you in several years, but I went to one of your workshops in 1998. You emailed me a number of times as I was exploring what else we could do to raise our literacy levels, especially in first grade. You talked to me about the importance of phonemic awareness, reading a lot, and spending more time on reading instruction. Last year, because of your help [and Kathie's outstanding instructional leadership and powerful vision for what her school could become], we finally have 90% of our students reading at and above grade level at our Title I school (up from 42% in 1996). Ninety-four percent of our fifth graders went on to middle school reading at and above grade level, with 33% of them reading at 8th and 9th grade levels. (K. Dobberteen, personal communication, August, 2001)

Kathie and her staff have received three major awards for their significant instructional accomplishments: Title I Distinguished School, California Distinguished School, and one of six Chase School Change Awards given yearly by Fordham University and the Chase Manhattan Foundation.

Although the workshop that Kathie attended was designed for elementary school principals, there were always a number of middle and high school principals who came, looking for ways to increase literacy in their schools. To meet their needs more specifically, I developed a workshop for secondary administrators, and in 2001, I followed up with a book: *Raising Reading Achievement in Middle and High Schools: Five Simple-to-Follow Strategies for Principals.* Although my workshops were primarily intended for principals, many administrators brought teams of teachers or invited me back to present to their staff members. I discovered that many new teachers knew very little about how to teach reading. Their preservice training had given short shrift to reading instruction. Even remedial and special education teachers were frustrated at their lack of exposure to current research, best practices, and strategies that worked with their difficult-to-reach students. They eagerly pored through the roller-bag of resources I bring to each workshop, asked questions, and stayed "after class" to talk about their most challenging students. I soon realized that a book about reading instruction was needed, not only for teachers—classroom, special education, and reading—but also for the many administrators who lead schools and supervise special programs.

I have written this book with the following goals in mind:

- To give you a short course in the most current reading research regarding how students learn to read, regardless of age or grade, so that you can make informed decisions about curriculum and instruction
- To help you understand that *learning to read* is only the first step; students must also develop fluency, acquire cognitive strategies, and continue to read a lot to deepen their knowledge and understanding
- To focus your attention on the variables at work in your school and district that can be altered to create a reading culture and make a huge difference in reading achievement—especially for those students who are currently falling through the cracks
- To convince you of the power that rests in you and your colleagues to teach every child to read

WHO THIS BOOK IS FOR

This book has been written for a broad audience. There are few, if any, educators today who are not deeply concerned with literacy levels in their schools. From superintendents to the most recently hired teachers—everyone is feeling the relentless pressure of high-stakes tests combined with a growing population of at-risk students and resources that are spread too thin. This book is intended for the following groups:

- Teachers of all kinds and levels—regular classroom, special education, bilingual education, and remedial reading—who are looking for ways to teach reading more effectively
- Special education, bilingual, and Title I administrators who need assistance in evaluating and improving their district reading programs
- Superintendents and principals who need specific and timely information about how to raise reading achievement in their district and schools
- Central office administrators (e.g., those responsible for school improvement, grant writing, staff development, and curriculum selection) who need a quick-reading and practical compendium of the best practices and programs in reading instruction
- College and university professors who are looking for a beginning-level but comprehensive book on reading instruction

WHAT THIS BOOK IS NOT

Although the reader will certainly gain a great deal that will be of practical value in the classroom from reading this book, it is not intended to be a comprehensive instructional guide, nor does it contain a recommended and "guaranteed to work for every child" program. Many children require a customized package of instruction based on their unique learning needs. Professional educators need not only a variety of successful methods and approaches in their tool kits, but they also need the freedom to make informed professional judgments.

Although I do use the terms *literate* and *literacy* throughout the book when referring to the abilities to read, write, and speak at or above the expectations held for a particular age or grade level, this book is primarily about reading. Of course, if one is teaching reading effectively, one's students *must* talk and write about what they are reading every day, in every subject, and at every grade level. This book, however, is only about reading.

READING TO LEARN

Most authors write books hoping that somebody, anybody, will actually read them. I have much higher expectations than that. My hope is that you will not merely read this book but "read to learn" from this book. And my further hope is that you will take what you have learned and put it to work in your school, classroom, or district. To that end, and because this is a book about reading, I have included a number of features to help you more readily understand and remember what you read.

I have chosen a simple jigsaw puzzle to illustrate the essential components of reading instruction. Figure P.1, The Reading Puzzle, shows the assembled

Figure P.1   The Reading Puzzle

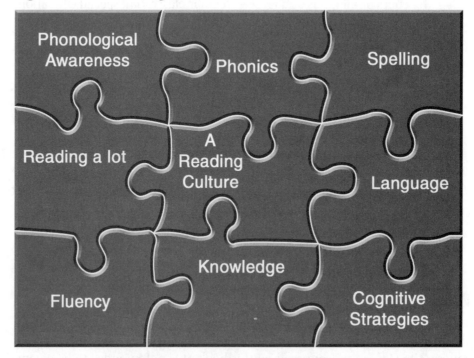

puzzle. Throughout the book, individual pieces of the puzzle will provide visual cues regarding the subject under discussion.

You will also find other features to help you read to learn:

- *Graphic organizers* that provide visual representations or summaries of various aspects of the text
- *Short sidebars* that offer you a breather from reading to learn and give you the opportunity for reflection
- *A glossary* that defines the many technical terms that are needed to understand the complexities of reading instruction
- *A variety of resources*, including a comprehensive list of phonics readers, a set of lesson plans for teaching the four essential cognitive strategies to students, and sample forms and templates to help you set goals and plan for reading instruction
- A checklist of 50 strategies to build a reading culture

OVERVIEW OF THE CONTENTS

Chapter 1 describes the students who are falling through the cracks. You will learn who these students are and why there are so many of them. You will also have an opportunity to meet some parents whose children have fallen through the cracks as well as adults who are living with illiteracy. Chapter 2 is packed with information and ideas to get you started, including

- Brief definitions of each of the nine pieces of the reading puzzle (i.e., the components of a reading program that are essential for students to become literate at every grade level)
- A list of 10 alterable variables that when changed in research-based ways will affect the literacy levels of your students
- Twelve fallacies about reading instruction that frequently fool us and often contribute to the reading failure of at-risk students

Chapters 3 through 7 provide in-depth discussions of each of the puzzle pieces. Chapter 3 explains the pieces that are crucial to unlocking the written code: *phonological awareness*, *phonics*, and *spelling*. These three pieces, when solidly put into place, will give students the foundation they need to acquire literacy.

Chapter 4 adds another piece, albeit an often forgotten one, to the reading puzzle: *fluency*. When students do not read fluently, they do whatever they can to avoid reading. Yet students will not develop fluency without reading a lot. What is the answer to this conundrum? You will find out in Chapter 4. Chapter 5 discusses the three puzzle pieces that are essential to gaining meaning from text for the purposes of both learning and enjoyment—*language*, *knowledge*, and *cognitive strategies*.

Chapter 6 describes my favorite piece of the puzzle: *reading a lot*. As a former media specialist and voracious reader myself, I have a passion for putting students and books together. I know the importance of reading in my own life, as well as the lives of my two children, and I won't rest until every student learns to love reading a lot.

Chapter 7 shows you how to put the final and centerpiece of the puzzle—*a reading culture*—in place in classrooms, schools, and districts. A reading culture is a schoolwide way of doing things that supports the development of literacy for every student. A highly persuasive and pervasive reading culture is characterized by 12 traits, and in Chapter 8 you will find 50 site-tested strategies for developing each of these traits in your own setting.

THE CHALLENGE

Be ready to be challenged as you read. You will be asked to examine your long-standing beliefs about reading; evaluate the results you are currently achieving; and then determine what needs to be changed in your classroom, school, or district. I am confident that *Teach Them ALL to Read: Catching the Kids Who Fall Through the Cracks* will give you the tools you need to do just that!

ACKNOWLEDGMENTS

Although I am the author of *Teach Them ALL to Read: Catching the Kids who Fall Through the Cracks*, writing this book would not have been possible without the help of others. I gratefully acknowledge the contributions and suggestions of the following educators who read all or portions of this manuscript, made substantive comments and suggestions for improvement, answered specific questions I had about various pieces of the reading puzzle, or shared their down-in-the-trenches experiences: Joseph Torgesen, Mary Damer, William Bursuck, Dennis Munk, Nettie Griffin, Kathie Dobberteen, Jan Antrim, Marcia Davidson, Becky Rosenthal, John Correll, Kathy Ryan, Jeanne Wanzek, Jan Rauth, Linda Thomas, and the thousands of teachers, principals, and central office administrators who have attended my reading workshops and *asked* all of the questions that I have attempted to answer in this book.

I must credit Ann Walker, Assistant Executive Director of the National Association of Elementary School Principals, and Gracia Alkema, the Founding President and Publisher Emerita of Corwin Press, for originally conceiving the idea of a workshop for principals on raising reading achievement. I am especially appreciative to Ann for the feedback she gave to me during the development and piloting of those early workshops and for her continued support and encouragement.

My profound thanks are extended to Larche Farrill, former administrator and now director of Outreach for the Missouri Council of School Administrators, for inviting me to be a part of the Readership Academy in Missouri over the past 3 years. Larche and a roundtable of principals conceived the idea of a program for principals focused on reading improvement, obtained grant funding, and then invited principals to five sites around the state to learn, share, and network with their colleagues. The principals and teachers of Missouri have taught me much about both leadership and reading; I now count many of them as good friends.

I am, as always, grateful and lovingly indebted to my husband and business partner, E. Raymond Adkins. He plays a variety of roles during the writing of all of my books—copy editor, sounding board, encourager, supporter, and even nursemaid. He anticipates my every need, he is always there when I need him, and his advice is unfailingly sound. He is the unsung coauthor of this book.

About the Author

 **Elaine K. McEwan** is a partner and educational consultant with The McEwan-Adkins Group offering workshops in instructional leadership, team building, raising achievement, reading improvement K-12, and school-community relations. A former teacher, librarian, principal, and assistant superintendent for instruction in a suburban Chicago school district, she is the author of more than two dozen books for parents and educators. Her Corwin Press titles include *Leading Your Team to Excellence: Making Quality Decisions* (1997); *Seven Steps to Effective Instructional Leadership* (1998); *The Principal's Guide to Attention Deficit Hyperactivity Disorder* (1998); *How to Deal With Parents Who Are Angry, Troubled, Afraid, or Just Plain Crazy* (1998); *The Principal's Guide to Raising Reading Achievement* (1998); *Counseling Tips for Elementary School Principals* (1999), with Jeffrey A. Kottler; *Managing Unmanageable Students: Practical Solutions for Educators* (2000), with Mary Damer; *The Principal's Guide to Raising Math Achievement* (2000); *Raising Reading Achievement in Middle and High Schools: Five Simple-to-Follow Strategies for Principals* (2001); and *Ten Traits of Highly Effective Teachers: How to Hire, Mentor, and Coach Successful Teachers* (2001).

McEwan is the education columnist for the *Northwest Explorer* newspaper, is a contributing author to several online Web sites for parents, and can be heard on a variety of syndicated radio programs helping parents solve schooling problems. She was honored by the Illinois Principals Association as an outstanding instructional leader, by the Illinois State Board of Education with an Award of Excellence in the Those Who Excel Program, and by the National Association of Elementary School Principals as the National Distinguished Principal from Illinois for 1991. She received her undergraduate degree in education from Wheaton College and advanced degrees in library science (MA) and educational administration (EdD) from Northern Illinois University. McEwan lives with her husband and business partner E. Raymond Adkins in Oro Valley, Arizona. Visit her Web site at www.elainemcewan.com where you can learn more about her books and workshops, or contact her directly at emcewan@mindspring.com.

1

Falling Through the Cracks

Of all the things that children have to learn when they get to school, reading and writing are the most basic, the most central and the most essential. Practically everything else that they do there will be permeated by these two skills. Hardly a lesson can be understood, hardly a project finished unless the children can read the books in front of them and write about what they have done. They must read and write or their time at school will be largely wasted.

—Bryant and Bradley (1985, p. 1)

No one wants to fail. Failure has the power to paralyze with fear, enrage with frustration, and demoralize with despair. We have all experienced failure—as learners ourselves (e.g., unlocking the mysteries of computers or mastering the intricacies of golf), as teachers working with students for whom we had no instructional answers, and sometimes even as parents and grandparents, watching our children or grandchildren struggle with learning to read. Failure is particularly traumatic for children and adolescents because they have so few emotional, psychological, and intellectual resources on which to draw. Failure on the part of our students is the beginning of a downward spiral—falling through the cracks.

"Falling through the cracks" is by no means a scientific description. You won't find it in reading textbooks along with terms such as *dyslexia, reading disability, learning disability, unexpected underachiever, slow learner,* or *backward reader.* "Falling through the cracks" is not an officially sanctioned label requiring a lengthy "wait and see" period to determine if a child will outgrow the problem or develop the skills that are lacking. To qualify for falling through the cracks, a student does not have to go through a prereferral process, interminable testing, and then display a 25-point discrepancy between his or her nonverbal IQ and achievement. A good teacher knows almost immediately when a student is falling through the cracks. It only takes a few days—or at the most, a couple of weeks—to figure it out.

FALLING THROUGH THE CRACKS: THE DEFINITION

Falling through the cracks simply means falling behind when everyone else is moving forward. Stanovich (1986) captured the essence of this educational free fall when he applied the term, "Matthew effect," to the field of reading. The term was first coined by sociologist Robert Merton (1968) and later picked up by Walberg and Tsai (1983) to describe an educational phenomenon. The term has its origins in the New Testament parable of the talents in Matthew 25:29 in which, according to Merton's (1968) initial interpretation, the "rich get richer and the poor get poorer." As used by Stanovich (1986), the term describes the effect of reading deficits from which poor readers almost never recover—despite our most valiant efforts to remediate, accommodate, and compensate.

Stanovich (1986) eloquently describes what happens to children when they fall through the cracks in terms of learning to read.

> Slow reading acquisition has cognitive, behavioral, and motivational consequences that slow the development of other cognitive skills and inhibit performance on many academic tasks. In short, as reading develops, other cognitive processes linked to it track the level of reading skill. Knowledge bases that are in reciprocal relationships with reading are also inhibited from further development. The longer this developmental sequence is allowed to continue, the more generalized the deficits will become, seeping into more and more areas of cognition and behavior. Or to put it more simply and sadly—in the words of a tearful 9-year-old, already falling frustratingly behind his peers in reading progress, "Reading affects everything you do." (p. 390)

I frequently appear on radio call-in shows devoted to educational topics. A program devoted to reading problems is always a favorite of producers because the phone lines light up almost immediately and stay lit throughout the hour. On one occasion, I offered my e-mail address to the listening audience if they had questions that weren't answered during the show. By the time I returned home a few days later, I had received over 70 e-mails from parents whose children were experiencing reading difficulties and from adults whose lives had been adversely affected by their inability to read well. Their poignant cries for help define falling through the cracks in ways that research and statistics can never do. You will have an opportunity to read some of their notes to me in the sidebars.

Individuals who fall through the cracks usually spend their school careers in remedial reading, special education, alternative education, or compensatory education and often drop out or graduate from high school still unable to "understand and use those written language forms required by society and/or valued by the individual" (Elley, 1992, p. 3). When children arrive in kindergarten, we are powerless to change the variables that have already affected their chances for reading success. We cannot raise their IQs, enhance their early childhood literacy experiences, increase their socioeconomic levels, or improve the educational attainment of their mothers. We *can*, however, teach them to read.

HOW MANY STUDENTS ARE FALLING THROUGH THE CRACKS?

One of the most heartbreaking sights in American schools today is that of children—once so eager to read—discovering that they are not learning how. There comes over those sparkling eyes a glaze of listless despair. We are not talking about a few children and scattered schools. We are talking about millions of children and every school in the nation. And the toll in young spirits is the least of it. The toll in the learning and thinking potential of our citizenry is beyond measure. (Sylvia Farnham-Diggory, as quoted in Spalding & Spalding, 1990, p. 10)

> ## MY HEART IS BREAKING
>
> [M]y daughter] cannot decode more than a few of the words in her second-grade reader. Her teacher put her in a reading program three times a week for half an hour sessions. However, he called me yesterday and recommended that she be tested for learning disabilities with their team of experts. Her comprehension is good and so is her vocabulary, but she can't blend three sounds together to make a word. She loves being read to, and I've been reading to her each night since she was a baby. She can tell you all about the life of Laura Ingalls Wilder, facts about whales, and things from all the books we have enjoyed together over the years. I know she wants to read but is finding the whole process so very difficult. She cried when I told her she was going to go through more testing. She just wants to fit in and be like everyone else, and my heart is breaking.[2]

There is general agreement among most researchers in the field of reading and learning disabilities that only about 5% of the children currently enrolled in school have genuine learning disabilities sufficiently severe to require placements in special education. These disabilities are pervasive and extraordinarily difficult to remediate without intensive and specialized training (Lyon, Fletcher, et al., 2000, p. 262). However, the total percentage of students in the United States (Grades K-12) who are currently enrolled in special education, remedial reading, or compensatory and alternative education programs for older students far exceeds this 5% figure.

Remedial reading and special education could easily be called growth industries in the United States. We are experiencing record Title I expenditures, burgeoning Reading Recovery programs,[1] statewide initiatives to improve reading achievement (Manzo, 1998), widespread accountability testing to raise reading achievement (Editorial Projects in Education, 2000, pp. 72–73), and mushrooming special education programs (Finn, Rotherham, & Hokanson, 2001). The educational toll of picking up the pieces after kids have fallen through the cracks represents only a fraction of the total costs of reading failure. There are also the social costs of funding juvenile homes (Allen-Hagen, 1991), prisons, adult education programs, and remedial college programs (Sandal, 2001), as well as the millions in lost earnings that adults who cannot read incur.

In his 1985 book, *Illiterate America*, Jonathan Kozol painted a bleak picture of literacy levels in the United States:

> Fifteen percent of recent graduates of urban high schools read at less than sixth grade level. One million teenage children between twelve and seventeen cannot read above the third grade level. Eighty-five percent of juveniles who come before the courts are functionally illiterate. Half the heads of households classified below the poverty line by federal standards cannot read an eighth grade book. Over one third of mothers who receive support from welfare are functionally illiterate. Of 8 million unemployed adults, 4 to 6 million lack the skills to be retrained for hi-tech jobs. The United States ranks forty-ninth among 158 member nations of the United Nations in its literacy levels. (pp. 4–5)

A GOOD KID WITH BAD GRADES

My son is 17 years old. He was left back in first grade because he couldn't read and had a very hard time with the phonics. When he was in first grade the second time, he had the same teacher for reading, and she told me that he is one of those people that will never hear the different phonics. Now he is in high school and is having a very hard time getting good grades. I know he is studying because I see him do it. Please advise me on how to help him. It seems that the only thing that we do now is fight about his grades. He truly is a very good, loving person, but with bad grades. He is so discouraged that he is constantly saying that he is dumb and that he will never be able to go to college.

A 1987 report titled *The Subtle Danger: Reflections on the Literacy Abilities of America's Young Adults* (Venezky, Kaestle, & Sum) offered this caution:

> We will not collapse tomorrow from a lack of adequate literacy skills, but we may find that year by year, we continue to fall behind in international competitiveness, and that society becomes more divided between those who are skilled and those who are not. (p. 53)

Literacy levels have scarcely improved since these dire warnings and predictions of the mid-80s. Consider the following grim statistics:

A TOUGH CHILDHOOD

I had a very tough childhood and did not learn the skills I need to read like I wish I could. I remember all the words I can because I do not have . . . the sounds to sound out the words. [I]f I do not quickly bring up that word I see, I have a real problem. I would like to know where I might get help, to learn the sounds so I can decode the words. I believe that is my problem.

The National Institute for Literacy reports that although very few adults in the United States are truly illiterate, between 21% and 23% of the adult population, or approximately 44 million people, can read only a little —not well enough to fill out an application, read a food label, or read a simple story to a child. Another 45 to 50 million people (25% to 28% of the adult population) can perform more complex literacy tasks, such as comparing, contrasting, or integrating pieces of information, but cannot engage in higher-level reading and problem solving such as would be needed to attend a community college or hold a highly skilled job (Reder, 2001).

The International Adult Literacy Survey, which compared the literacy skills of adults in Australia, Belgium, Canada, Germany, Ireland, the Netherlands, New Zealand, Poland, Sweden, Switzerland, the United Kingdom, and the United States (National Literacy Secretariat of Canada, 1997), found that the United States has more adults in the bottom two levels of literacy (i.e., they lack a sufficient foundation of basic skills to function successfully in our society) than any of the other countries except Poland.

During the past 10 years, the number of students ages 6 through 21 identified as learning disabled has increased 38% with the largest increase (44%) among students between the ages of 12 and 17 (Lyon, Fletcher, et al., 2001, p. 262).

Reading achievement overall has failed to improve during the past 10 years as reported by the most recent report of the National Assessment of Educational Progress (National Center for Education Statistics, 2001). In the year 2000, the national administration of the reading test showed that 37% of fourth grade children demonstrated reading abilities below the basic level. This means that these children did not have sufficient reading skills to satisfactorily complete grade level assignments involving reading. One alarming aspect of the report is that, although overall reading levels did not change significantly from prior years, the gap between good and poor readers grew larger. Children classified as good readers actually performed better than they did in the previous assessment, but children classified as poor readers performed worse than they did previously. How many kids are falling through the cracks annually? Too many. Who these students are and why their numbers are growing will be explored just ahead.

> ## HOOKED ON PHONICS DIDN'T HELP
>
> I have a very dear friend who is an adult and is functionally illiterate. I desire greatly to assist her but need some direction on where to start. She has tried *Hooked on Phonics*, and it did not come as easy to her as it appeared on television. Furthermore, she has tried one-on-one tutoring, but that proved to be quite expensive. She has been tested, and based on the results, is functioning on a third-grade reading level. Please provide whatever assistance you can.

WHO ARE THE STUDENTS WHO ARE FALLING THROUGH THE CRACKS?

About 5% or even less of the total number of students nationwide who enroll in kindergarten each fall learn to read as if by magic. They arrive at school already reading fluently. They may announce one day that they have learned to read, or their teachers may discover them reading a faculty bulletin or newspaper during playtime. They weren't "taught" to read in the conventional sense of the word, but were able, by virtue of the ways in which nature and nurture blessed them, to figure out on their own how the English language works. These students are not distributed evenly among all of the kindergarten classes across the country. Many classes have none, whereas some may have as many as five or six fluent readers.

Another 20% to 30% of students overall learn to read with ease when exposed to any kind of formal instruction. These children seem almost teacher or curriculum proof. Again, there is no guarantee regarding how many of these students will show up in each classroom. Some classrooms may contain a majority of students who learn to read with ease; others may have as few as 5%, or even none.

A STRUGGLING READER

My daughter is in kindergarten. Fortunately, it is a small class, and the teacher can give her a lot of attention. She is in a phonics program and does know all of her sounds, her blends, and almost all of the special sounds they have learned so far, but when it comes to putting all the words together in a sentence, she clams up and really seems to struggle. How can I help her at home?

For about 60% of students overall, learning to read will be hard work. Success will depend largely on the effectiveness of instruction, the continuity and articulation of the curriculum, and the stability of the child's family and school environments. Some of the students in this cohort will fall through the cracks; others will sail through school. If one or more of the following traumas occurs, any one of the children has the unfortunate potential to fall through the cracks: (a) ineffective instruction or curriculum, (b) a poorly managed or disorganized classroom, (c) an unstable classroom (i.e., multiple teachers coming and going because of illnesses or maternity leaves), (d) an unsafe or poorly run school, or (e) family stress and difficulties (e.g., divorce, job loss, or serious illness).

About 15% to 25% of students will find reading to be one of the most difficult tasks they have ever undertaken. Even with the presence of specialized, intensive, and one-to-one instruction that begins as early in their school careers as possible, their progress will be slow and their need for practice and overlearning crucial. Last, about 5% of the total number of students overall will have a serious and pervasive reading disability and will likely be placed in special education. That is not to say that these two bottom cohorts of students *cannot* learn to read or *will* not learn to read eventually. To survive academically, however, they will require the very best in systematic and direct reading instruction from highly skilled and supportive teachers.

Although the goal of leaving no child behind is an admirable one, the expectation that *every* child will be on *grade level* by third or fourth grade seems a highly unrealistic one, even to those who specialize in early intervention programs for the prevention of reading difficulties. Torgesen (2000) explains:

> [If we were to set an absolute grade level reading comprehension standard for every child,] this would mean that we would be expecting all children to have at least average verbal ability. Since decades of cognitive research suggests that it is unrealistic to expect *all* children to attain verbal intelligence estimates within average range as a result of special instruction (Lee, Brooks-Gunn, Schnur, & Liaw, 1990), it also seems unrealistic to expect reading teachers to accomplish this goal starting as late as kindergarten or first grade. (pp. 55–56)

The harsh reality of Torgesen's (2000) statement often blurs our vision of what can be accomplished in schools, however. To focus on the impossibility of getting *every* student to grade level is one way to miss the fact that huge numbers of students are currently failing to learn to read at anywhere near their verbal abilities. We must lay aside the somewhat artificial and not altogether statistically sound concept of "grade level" (Spear-Swerling & Sternberg, 1998, p. 61), if our legislators and state boards of education will let us, while at the same time disabusing ourselves of the notion that raising reading achievement is a somehow suspect and politically motivated goal. We must focus instead on the vast numbers of students whose quality of academic life, to say nothing of their success as adults, would be immeasurably improved if they could read commensurate with their potential—whatever it may be. If we are to reach *that* goal, we will be busy for some time to come. We can save the grade-level debate for later.

The students who are most likely to fall through the cracks sort themselves into several categories. Many of them fit into multiple categories and present a variety of risk factors—further increasing their odds of reading failure. Students at risk of reading failure include (a) low-IQ, low-achieving students; (b) boys; (c) developmentally delayed students; (d) special education students; (e) low-socioeconomic (SES) students or students of racial and ethnic minorities; (f) non-native-English-speaking students; (g) students with speech and hearing impairments; (h) early intervention and remedial reading students; and (i) teacher- or school-disabled students. All kinds of students fall through the cracks—rich ones, poor ones, children with below-average IQs, and even gifted ones. Children from "good "schools can even fall through the cracks. A student can fall through the cracks anywhere.

DESPERATE FOR HELP

My son reads slowly. He guesses at some words, and he doesn't know the meanings of a lot of words. If he doesn't know a word, he tends to skip right over it. In the Standard Achievement Tests that he took last year, he scored way below normal. For the National Grade Percentile in the total reading, he scored at the 8th percentile, for vocabulary he scored at the 22nd percentile, and for comprehension he scored at the 5th percentile. I have asked to have him tested, but he hasn't been tested yet. I just want to know if there is a real problem or not. He does have a lot of trouble in school, and I feel really bad about that. I've tried to help him in every way that I possibly can, but nothing seems to work. I just don't know what to do anymore.

Low-IQ, Low-Achieving Students

Low-IQ, low-achieving students who fail to qualify for any kind of help or special services are prime candidates for falling through the cracks. Their IQs are below average but not low enough to qualify as mentally impaired. These students do not meet the criteria for learning disabilities either because the discrepancy between their ability and achievement is too small or even non-existent. Low-IQ, low-achieving students are often socially promoted despite a lack of literacy skills, and they rarely experience success in school. Sometimes, the rules are bent, and they *are* identified as learning disabled or EMI so they can receive services of some kind. If they are placed in effective special education programs that focus on student outcomes, they may receive the services they need to learn to read. But the majority, after repeated school failure and several grade retentions, often drop out of school when they can (Tynan & Latsha, 1999).

One very interesting finding from recent research on the prevention of reading disabilities is that, if children are given adequately intensive, explicit, and mastery-oriented instruction in early reading skills, IQ is not strongly related to how well they acquire *beginning* reading skills (Vellutino, Scanlon, &

Lyon, 2000). Other factors, such as specific language weaknesses, SES, and behavior disturbances are much stronger predictors of early reading failure than is general intelligence level.

Boys

Boys seem to fall through the cracks more readily than girls, not because they are overlooked or ignored by their teachers, but rather because of their teachers' heightened anticipation of problems as well as their increased awareness and attentiveness to boys' slightest departures from behavioral and academic norms. In a sense, one might say that some boys are "picked on" or "singled out." Teachers are more prone to identify learning and behavioral problems in boys than girls (Vogel, 1990). One longitudinal study of literacy acquisition among low-income children found that teachers were more likely to contact the parents of boys regarding academic problems than they were to contact girls' parents, even though there were no overall difference in academic performance between the boys and girls (Snow, Barnes, Chandler, Goodman, & Hemphill, 1991).

McGuinness (1985) points out that, in general, the male-female ratio in special reading classes is, at the most conservative estimate, 3:1; in other words; 75% of the reading-disabled group are males. The sex ratios for those students with identified reading disabilities, once hypothesized to be biologically based, with boys more likely to have disabilities than girls, have more recently been found to be nearly equal, so any actual imbalance between the sex ratios is less a function of actual differences in the distribution of reading disabilities in boys and girls and more a function of a referral bias on the part of teachers (Shaywitz, Shaywitz, Fletcher, & Escobar, 1990). Teachers, irrespective of their own gender, appear to respond differently to boys than they do to girls (Sadker, Sadker, & Klein, 1991).

We can only speculate at this point regarding the emotional and psychological repercussions, to say nothing of the academic fallout, for boys who are labeled as disabled, slow learners, and hyperactive, irrespective of their actual status. Their teachers are more likely to (a) have lowered academic expectations for them, (b) be hyperattentive to their perceived or actual departure from strict behavioral norms, and (c) experience a general lack of efficacy with regard to meeting their academic needs. If any of these factors are also combined with other risk factors (e.g., poverty or developmental delays), the odds of boys falling through the cracks increase exponentially.

HELP

My son is 16 years old and has ADHD and multiple learning differences. Needless to say, his reading has always been a problem. He cannot hear the sounds [that] letters and syllables make, and as a result, he struggles with reading to the point of giving up. We [his teachers and I] have tried, what seems to me, to be every reading program known to man. Help!

Developmentally Delayed Students

Students who are physically, emotionally, or cognitively immature when they arrive in kindergarten are often thought to be "late bloomers." Their teachers may mistakenly believe that time and maturation will solve all problems—that these students like desert plants, after a "rare sudden shower of rain . . . [will] spontaneously burst into bloom" (Ansara, 1969, p. 51). Unfortunately, this expected blooming seldom occurs, and the student becomes just another educational fatality. Juel (1994) warns educators of the dangers of this "wait and see" attitude:

> There is an unbounded optimism among teachers that children who are late in starting will indeed catch up. Given time, something will happen! In particular, there is a belief that the intelligent child who fails to learn to read well will catch up to his classmates once he has made a start. Do we have any evidence of accelerated progress in late starters? There may be isolated examples which support this hope, but correlations from a follow-up study of 100 children two to three years after school entry lead me to state rather dogmatically that where a child stood in relation to his age-mates at the end of his first year at school was roughly where one could expect to find him at age 7 or 8. (p. 120)

Special Education Students

Laurence Lieberman (2001) writes in an *Education Week* commentary that special education is neither alive nor special anymore. Lieberman has been a special education teacher, the learning disabilities coordinator in the former U.S. Office of Education, and the chairman of the special education doctoral program at Boston University. He speaks from experience. His reasons for making this shocking pronouncement are some of the same ones that I believe lead to so many learning disabled special education students falling through the cracks.

Many LD students disappear academically because the focus of special education is no longer on preparing students to return to regular education when they are able to read and write but, rather, to be included in the regular classroom while accommodations and modifications are made to their program. For students with physical or profound mental disabilities, inclusion has much to commend it. For the child with learning disabilities, inclusion often means giving up on learning to read and write.

In some classrooms, education for students with disabilities, particularly those with learning disabilities, resembles the way business is conducted with low-achieving students in urban schools—I pretend I'm really teaching you what you need to know to be successful in the real world, and you pretend that you're really learning it (Meichenbaum & Biemiller, 1998). In fact, recent analyses of the achievement of reading-disabled children within inclusion settings shows that most of them make very little progress in their reading ability from year to year. One study showed that 80% of the poorest readers made no measurable gain over the school year (Klinger, Vaughn, Hughes, Schumm, & Elbaum, 1998), and another (Zigmond & Baker, 1996) showed that LD students, as a whole, made no progress toward closing the gap in reading achievement that got them identified as learning disabled in the first place!

Low-SES[3] Students and Racial- and Ethnic-Minority Students

The lower overall reading achievement of low-SES students and ethnic-minority students as compared to their higher-SES counterparts, has been documented, discussed, and dissected for over 30 years. Coleman (1966) and his colleagues were among the first to report the academic deficits of students from low-income families. More recently, the results of the National Assessment of Educational Progress have shown the same disappointing achievement gap (National Center for Education Statistics, 2001). The reading achievement of affluent suburban students is significantly and consistently higher than that of students in urban schools in high-poverty areas (Hart & Risley, 1995).

Whether children from low-SES or ethnic-minority families fall through the cracks often has more to do with where and with whom they go to school than the fact that they are poor or from a racial or ethnic minority. There is a greater chance of low-SES or minority students achieving academic success if they attend a school in which the population contains a mix of moderate-SES and higher-SES students. High concentrations of low-SES students or ethnic minority students can create difficult and discouraging challenges for many educators.

In a homogeneous class of low-achieving students, for example, such as one might typically find in urban schools or suburban and rural schools with urban demographics, teachers can fall into an insidious low-expectations trap. Students who are skill deficient, have unproductive school behaviors, lack organization, and have low motivation need more than just fancy slogans or good intentions to engage them in learning. Over the years, lowered expectations for many low-income and minority students has resulted in a sense of educational powerlessness and debilitating meaninglessness (Fine, 1991). The greater the number of low performers in a classroom, the less certain teachers feel about their abilities to influence learning and achievement (Smylie, 1989), thus creating a vicious cycle of lowered expectations and concomitant achievement.

Low-SES and ethnic-minority students fall through the cracks in huge numbers not only because of educational variables—for instance, lowered classroom expectations (Ennis, 1998) and poorly staffed and administered schools (Edmonds, 1981)—but also because of environmental variables, such as fewer and often very different opportunities in the home for informal literacy learning (Baker, Serpell, & Sonnenschein, 1995; Goldenberg, Reese, & Gallimore, 1992). We know that students from low-SES backgrounds come to school less prepared to learn to read than their more affluent counterparts in two broad areas. First, they have had less exposure to print and so their knowledge of letters and how print can be used to convey meaning is less well developed than it is in their middle-class counterparts (Adams, 1990). They have also not had as many opportunities to play certain types of language games with their parents (i.e., learning nursery rhymes), so they are less sensitive to the sounds in language (Hecht, Burgess, Torgesen, Wagner, & Rashotte, 2000). Lack of experience and knowledge in these areas make it difficult for children from low-SES backgrounds to acquire the early word-reading skills that are the foundation of later fluent reading and comprehension. The other broad area in which children from low-SES environments have fewer opportunities to learn is in general verbal knowledge, particularly vocabulary, which is so important for good reading comprehension once children begin reading more difficult texts in third grade and up.

Non-Native-English-Speaking Students

One of the largest groups of students at risk of reading failure in the United States currently is non-native-English-speaking students, and when these students are also poor, their odds of limited literacy attainment are very high. The United States is not the only country that experiences this problem; African (Postlewaite & Ross, 1992) and European (Tosi, 1979) countries experience early school dropout and high failure rates where immigrant children are immersed in second-language instruction. Canada offers the most successful model of dual-language literacy, but the cultural, economic, academic, and familial resources that are available to support students there are vastly different from those that face the majority of immigrants to the United States.

The debate of how and when to teach English reading to non-English-speaking or limited-English-proficient students is a rancorous one at times. Unfortunately, there are no easy or sufficiently research-based answers available. The joint report from the National Research Council, the Commission on Behavioral and Social Sciences and Education, and the Committee on the Prevention of Reading Difficulties in Young Children (Snow, Burns, & Griffin, 1998) summarizes the current state of affairs as follows:

> The accumulated wisdom of research in the field of bilinguals and literacy tends to converge on the conclusion that initial literacy instruction in a second language can be successful, that it carries with it a higher risk of reading problems and of lower ultimate literacy attainment than initial literacy instruction in a first language, and that this risk may compound the risks associated with poverty, low levels of parental education, poor schooling, and other such factors. (p. 234)

Students With Speech and Hearing Impairments

Students with speech and hearing impairments are at a very high risk for reading failure. Their inability to hear and manipulate the sounds of the English language inhibits phonological skill development—a critical prerequisite to learning to read (Torgesen & Mathes, 2000). Between 40% and 75% of preschoolers with early speech difficulties develop reading problems later on (Aram & Hall, 1989; Bashir & Scavuzzo, 1992). Even when students' speech difficulties are mild to moderate and are easily remediated by speech therapy, they remain at greater risk for reading problems than other students (Scarborough & Dobrich, 1990).

Hearing impairment and deafness are also highly associated with reading difficulty (Conrad, 1979; Karchmer, 1978; Waters & Doehring, 1990). Even when students have no documented hearing impairments, a history of chronic ear infections leading to intermittent hearing loss during preschool years can be associated with reading difficulties (Wallace & Hooper, 1997).

CAN'T HEAR THE SOUNDS

My daughter, age 11, has had speech therapy for three years on a one-to-one basis for one hour, four times a week. It was a phonics-based program and didn't work. Her teacher says that she doesn't hear sounds. Her hearing is perfect, although she has had five sets of ear tubes and numerous ear infections. I'm lost. I cannot afford to waste any time or for her to lose her self-esteem. She is bright (IQ is 105), gets along with everybody, and is very well behaved. She just cannot read or spell.

Early Intervention and Remedial Reading Students

Students with reading difficulties are like the hot potato in that game teachers sometimes play with students when it is too cold or rainy to go out for recess. A readily available object, such as an eraser, becomes the "hot potato," and students pass it quickly around the classroom or circle hoping *they* won't get caught with the potato when the signal is given and thus be forced out of the game.

So it is with students who are failing to learn to read. Teachers pass these students from an after-school program to Reading Recovery to special education, hoping against hope that someone else will have an answer—any answer—as to why this child is failing. There is frequently no rationale to the methods that are chosen. Each teacher does his or her "own thing," whether it be guided reading in predictable books, a structured phonics program, comprehension strategies—or a little bit of everything all mixed in together. Failing students are the hot potatoes; when they fail in one location, they are dropped into another pair of hands. Meanwhile, their parents naively assume that their child is learning to read.

Many schools have begun to provide something called preventive instruction to children who seem to be falling through the cracks from their first day in kindergarten. However, most current efforts to help students in the early elementary grades lack sufficient intensity and consistency. They are often taught for too little time with too many other children in their instructional groups. Sometimes, they are taught by volunteers who have little training in teaching the specific skills that are so difficult for many children to acquire. Reading instruction for these children is often more fragmented than that of other children who learn to read more easily, and at-risk students sometimes end up actually receiving less instruction than those who are learning normally (Allington & Shake, 1986).

The remedial reading instruction provided to older children who do not qualify for special education but who continue to have reading difficulties suffers from many of the same problems as current preventive approaches. Instruction is often not targeted on the needed skills, children are frequently taught in groups that are much too large, and often, not enough instruction is provided to accelerate reading development to average levels. Problems in providing effective remedial instruction are compounded by the extreme diversity of poor readers in late elementary, middle, and high school. Many students are still struggling to acquire beginning level skills, whereas others need to expand their current reading skills so they can more effectively use reading as a tool for learning. If these students are mixed together in large groups, it is unlikely that the needs of individual students will ever be adequately met.

Teacher-, Curriculum-, or School-Disabled Students

Most students who fall through the cracks arrive in kindergarten with a built-in set of challenging learning and demographic characteristics. But sometimes, we further diminish their learning opportunities once they are in school. Teachers who are discouraged and demoralized by lack of instructional leadership, peeling paint, tattered textbooks, and few staff development opportunities are less likely to marshal the enormous energy and will that are needed to make a difference in the lives of challenging students. Teachers whose preservice training has been limited to collecting resources for thematic units rather than learning how to teach blending and segmenting don't know how to *teach them all to read* (N. Griffin, personal communication, September 23, 2001).

SUMMARIZING CHAPTER 1

There are many factors that put students at risk for falling through the cracks in reading—their environmental demographics (e.g., lack of early literacy experiences, poverty, or limited English proficiency), their genetic characteristics (e.g., lack of phonological awareness skills, learning disabilities, or speech and hearing difficulties), or their educational experiences (e.g., ineffective schools, teachers, or methods).

LOOKING AHEAD

You are no doubt growing somewhat impatient. You picked up this book to find answers, and thus far, you have only encountered more problems. I can hear you saying to yourself, "I already know all of the reasons kids can't read. I can't change any of that. Give me some solutions."

Help is on the way. In Chapter 2, you will find out what to do first, second, and third: (a) Read to learn as much as you can about reading instruction; (b) focus on the instructional variables that, when altered in your classroom, school, or district, can help you to teach all of your students to read; and (c) reflect on 12 fallacies regarding reading instruction that often fool us and frequently lead to even more students falling through the cracks.

NOTES

1. Since its establishment in 1995, over 8,000 individuals have become members of the Reading Recovery Council of North America (Reading Recovery Council of North America, 2001. Retrieved from the World Wide Web, August 2001.) Reading

Recovery in this country was established at Ohio State University in the 1990s. Since then, it has been implemented in 38 states, the District of Columbia, four Canadian provinces, Australia, England, and New Zealand (Ohio State University, 1992–1993).

2. The names of the individuals who sent E-mails to me have been omitted to protect their privacy.

3. The acronym SES stands for the term *socioeconomic status*. Low-SES students are those who are eligible for free and reduced lunch or breakfast (or both) because of their family's low income. The presence of large numbers of low-SES students makes a school eligible for Title I funding. Schools with large numbers of Title I students are designated as Title I schools.

2

Developing an Action Plan

Read, Focus, and Reflect

C an you identify the students who are falling through the cracks in your classroom, school, or district? Some of them are easy to spot. They are daydreaming, sleeping, or just plain misbehaving. Others with reading difficulties are still valiantly going through the motions, paying attention to lessons that are irrelevant to their instructional needs or pretending to read what they can't understand. What can you do to rescue these students from their academic free fall? Read, focus, and reflect before you do anything.

First, *read to learn about reading*. Learn as much as you can about the essential pieces of the reading puzzle. I have included multiple references to the critical reading instruction research from the world's most respected scholars to support the assertions and recommendations I have made. I invite you to read widely for yourself in the must-read books I've included for each puzzle piece so that you can make informed decisions about reading instruction.

Second, forget about all of the usual reasons that are given for why so many students fall through the cracks—the inalterable variables over which educators have no control. *Focus instead on the alterable instructional variables*. When changed in research-based ways, these variables can make a huge difference in the literacy levels of your students.

Third, *reflect on the fallacies that have fooled many of us at one time or another*. Examine your personal beliefs about reading instruction to determine if any of them fall into a category I have titled, *Twelve Fallacies That Fool Us and Fail Our Students*.

READ TO LEARN ABOUT READING

Your first task is to learn all you can about reading instruction. There are a variety of perspectives, theories, stages, and models advanced by theorists and researchers that explain reading and describe how individuals learn to read (Chall, 1996; Perfetti, 1985; Pressley, 1998). I have chosen a simple nine-piece jigsaw puzzle to illustrate the critical components of *teaching all students to read.* Everyone has assembled (or at least tried to assemble) a jigsaw puzzle at least once and knows that if even one piece of a puzzle is missing or out of place, the final picture will be incomplete. Those who are putting it together are frustrated by the missing piece(s), much like students are frustrated when they sense they are missing key pieces of the reading puzzle. Figure 2.1 displays the nine reading puzzle pieces paired with their definitions. We will put these pieces together in Chapters 3 through 7.

If you are a jigsaw puzzle aficionado, you know that the process of assembling a puzzle, particularly a very complicated one, goes more quickly when several people are involved. The process can proceed even more expeditiously when all of the members of that team are on the same page, so to speak, using the same assembly strategies and communicating readily with one another.

Figure 2.1 The Reading Puzzle Explained

Puzzle Piece	Description
Phonological Awareness	The ability to hear and manipulate sounds (e.g., words, syllables, and phonemes).
Phonics	A teaching method aimed at matching the specific sounds of the English language with individual letter(s).
Spelling	The ability to recognize, recall, reproduce, or obtain orally or in written form the correct sequence of letters in words.
Fluency	Automaticity and flow in the act of reading.
Language	Speech and sound system; the meanings of words; how words are put together to construct a message; and how discourse of various kinds is carried out.
Knowledge	What an individual knows about a specific discipline or domain.
Cognitive Strategies	Mental tools, tricks, or shortcuts to gain meaning, understanding, and knowledge.
Reading a lot	Reading a lot of text, at increasing levels of difficulty with accountability
A Reading Culture	The collective attitudes, beliefs, and behaviors of all of the stakeholders in a school regarding any and all of the activities associated with enabling all students to read at the highest level of attainment possible for both their academic and personal gain.
	• Definitions are taken from the glossary. Cited sources (if applicable) can be found there.

The basic assembly team of the reading puzzle consists of the teacher, the student, and the parent(s). However, if catching the kids who are falling through the cracks is not a schoolwide or districtwide priority, individual teachers will shoulder a disproportionate share of the responsibility.

I firmly believe in teacher accountability, but I know from experience that when students are falling through the cracks, the principal, business manager, curriculum supervisor, special education director, and even the superintendent must also be there to catch them. Strong instructional leadership, adequate resources, and comprehensive staff development are essential. Although a single teacher *can* do amazing things, catching the kids who fall through the cracks takes teamwork and collaboration.

FOCUS ON THE ALTERABLE VARIABLES

The second task at hand is to consider what needs to change in your classroom, school, or district. When I assumed the principalship of a suburban Chicago elementary school in the early 1980s, reading achievement was at an all-time low—the 20th percentile for Grades 2 through 6 on the Iowa Test of Basic Skills. I was brand new to administration and knew nothing about raising test scores. My teaching experience was in communities similar to the imaginary Lake Wobegon, Minnesota, where all of the students are above average. At the first faculty meeting, I asked the teachers why *they* thought achievement was so low. They had plenty of reasons for the dismal state of affairs: the students, the parents, and the school board, to name just a few. Too many of the students were on free lunch, too many of the parents didn't speak English, and the school board didn't care. The teachers didn't mention any role they might have personally played in the test results, but their reactions were not unlike those of most teachers faced with failing students. In retrospect, my staff fit the following description to a T: "We say we believe that all children can learn, but few of us really believe it" (Delpit, 1995, p. 172). Faced with what may appear to be insurmountable obstacles, teachers often feel powerless to make a difference, and unfortunately, they frequently communicate their low expectations to each other and their students.

I decided that what the staff needed was a good dose of Benjamin Bloom. At the time, Bloom (1980) was writing about what he called "alterable variables." He scolded his readers for whining about things over which they had no control (e.g., characteristics of students and their parents). He urged them to focus their energies and creativity on the context or environmental variables that affect student learning (Weinstein & Hume, 1998, p. 101). As we brainstormed what those variables might be at Lincoln School, the list began to grow—so did our excitement and motivation to change the way we conducted the business of schooling. During the 8 years we worked together as a team, reading achievement climbed to between the 70th and 80th percentiles. There were few individuals on the staff, in the student body, or among our parent community who were not profoundly changed by the process. We discovered that we were all capable of achieving far more than we imagined. We stopped making excuses and started changing what we had the power to change. We stopped acting defensive, argumentative, and hopeless. Instead, we became focused, optimistic, and empowered. And together, as educators, parents, and students, we celebrated our successes.

The 10 variables that we altered in the early 1980s are still germane to raising reading or any other kind of achievement today. The challenge lies in determining just which ones need to be altered in your school and *how* they need to be changed. No one can give you a guaranteed-to-work recipe. As Dorothy and her comrades in *The Wizard of Oz* discovered, *The wizard is within you.* Here follow just a few of the things you have the power to change to make literacy a reality for all of your students.

Change How You State Your Goals

Write goals that are meaningful and measurable. Basketball coach John Wooden (as quoted in Wahl, 2001), winner of many national championships at UCLA, says, "Never mistake activity for achievement" (p. 38). If you write goals that are meaningful and measurable, you will be far less likely to mistake curricular fluff for data-based accomplishments. Daily, weekly, and monthly progress (no matter how small) for every child will lead to solid schoolwide achievement gains (Schmoker, 1999).

Change How You Choose What to Teach

Choose teaching methods and materials that are research based and have been shown to get results, particularly with students at risk of reading failure. Don't make decisions based on glitzy sales presentations, the recommendation of a consultant, or the fact that another district is doing it. Do you know if the programs you are currently using actually get results with the students who are at risk of falling through the cracks?

Change the Alignment of What You Teach

All staff members in a school need to be "on the same page" instructionally. Students who are at risk of falling through the cracks need consistency in their instructional programs. They need to hear the same message, be taught the same strategies, and receive the same high expectations from *every* teacher with whom they spend time (English, 1992). Children who come to school poorly prepared to learn to read are totally dependent on their teachers to gradually build their knowledge and skills in a systematic and sequential fashion. This requires kindergarten, first-grade, and second-grade teachers in particular to have a shared vision of the strategies and knowledge they expect their students to master.

Change What You Teach

If your classroom, school, or district is missing one or more of the critical pieces of the reading puzzle as they are described in Chapters 3 through 7, add the pieces that are missing to what you are already doing that works. A well-conceived beginning reading program is just that—*a beginning*. There must also be a consistent effort on the part of every teacher to build fluency and to motivate students to read a lot. But, reading a lot, without regard for the quality of what is read or for students' understanding of what they have read misses the whole point of reading a lot in school—learning! But how can students acquire knowledge from what they read if they are not taught the essential cognitive strategies? There are many ways a student can fail to become literate. Find the students who cannot read, and teach them how to read. Then, build fluency and automaticity in reading through reading a lot. Last, teach every student how to read to learn. Without the *complete* package, students can fall through the cracks at many points along the way.

Change How You Use Instructional Time

Every minute of instructional time is precious. Make this time count for learning. Examine the time-on-task data for your most at-risk students and determine how you can increase their academic learning time (e.g., through small-group direct instruction, preferred seating at desks rather than at tables or on the floor, the use of more advanced organizers and activation of prior knowledge before beginning a lesson, and clearly stated learning objectives). Protect teaching time. Be ruthless in pruning curricular frills and unnecessary interruptions that distract teachers and students from achieving literacy.

Change When and How You Teach the Critical Components of Reading

Don't wait until students are failing and then rush in to recover and remediate them. In accordance with recent recommendations from the National Research Council (Snow et al., 1998) and the National Reading Panel (2000), many districts are determining that for many students, especially those who are at risk of reading failure, a first step (although certainly not the only one or the all-sufficient one) to reducing reading failure must include programs of early identification and prevention. When students with weak phonological processing skills are systematically taught those skills as well as knowledge about letters in kindergarten and first grade (National Reading Panel, 2000, pp. 7–8; Snow et al., 1998, pp. 151–152), their likelihood of falling through the cracks is greatly diminished.

Change the Amount of Time Students Spend Practicing What You Teach

To become a *successful* reader, students must *read a lot successfully*. The time-on-task literature amply demonstrates that when students are academically engaged at a high success rate, achievement goes up (Fisher & Berliner, 1985). Make sure that your students are reading a lot on a level that is as closely matched to their abilities and interests as possible. If what they are reading is *too easy*, they will fail to acquire the new knowledge and vocabulary that is well within their grasp. If what students are reading is *too difficult*, they will become frustrated and give up.

Change How You Assess What You Teach

If students are not making incremental progress (no matter how small) every week, find out why. Many teachers find it useful to administer brief objective assessments each week that target the specific skills they are teaching. Others are able to objectively monitor the progress of their students through brief assessments that occur as a natural part of instruction. This latter strategy is often combined with more formal assessments of progress administered three times a year (beginning, middle, and end). Teachers and administrators must have timely and objective information about student progress from the very beginning of reading instruction in kindergarten and continuing through high school.

Change Your Expectations for Students

The research regarding the power of expectations is voluminous. If teachers expect students to fail, they will (Ennis, 1998). Educators are often unaware of the countless things they say and do in the classroom that communicate their beliefs regarding students' inability to learn (Armor et al., 1976; Ashton & Webb, 1986). Investigate a staff development program, such as Teacher Expectations and Student Achievement, in which teachers are trained to recognize and use teaching behaviors that communicate high expectations (Kerman, 1979).

Change How You Group to Teach

Use a variety of grouping strategies and plans in classrooms. No grouping strategy should be used exclusively (Mosteller, Light, & Sachs, 1996). For some purposes, such as teaching basic phonemic awareness or beginning word-reading strategies that require very focused teaching and practice, it is helpful to have groups composed of children with similar skills. In contrast, when working on comprehension strategies or engaging in critical discussions of text, it can be helpful to children with weaker skills to observe more advanced children model higher-level skills.

REFLECT ON THE FALLACIES THAT FOOL US AND FAIL OUR STUDENTS

Achievement test results show that the statistically average child, normally endowed and normally taught, learns to read only with considerable difficulty. He does not learn to read naturally. That is, despite his evident facility

*at learning and despite having previously mastered what would seem to be the
hardest part of reading (i.e., learning an unknown language), children almost
never learn to read without instruction. And even when given explicit,
devoted, daily instruction, the average child learns to read very slowly and
with great difficulty.* (Gough & Hillinger, 1980, p. 179)

The third and last task at hand is to reflect regarding your personal beliefs
about reading instruction. The ease with which a very few children acquire
reading proficiency and the effortless way in which skilled readers construct
meaning and gain understanding from what they read have led some to theorize
that learning to read and the teaching of reading are relatively easy things to
do (Goodman, 1986, 1996; Smith, 1971). This seductive notion has been an
appealing one to teachers who have, at the same time, watched countless students fall through the cracks. To facilitate the development of literacy by sur-
rounding children with a print-rich environment is both a loftier sounding goal
and a far less demanding and complex task than to directly and systematically
teach children the skills and knowledge they need in order to read. Although
some children do learn to read effortlessly, the majority of students need a
highly skilled and knowledgeable reading teacher. I share Louisa Moats's belief
that "teaching reading is rocket science" (Moats, 1999).

There are few more contentious curricular forums than that of reading
instruction.[1] In no other instructional arena, save perhaps math or bilingual
education, are the issues as hotly debated and the proponents more political in
their rhetoric. *Phonics* and *whole language* are the terms around which the proponents have rallied in the past,[2] but more recently, research by the National
Institute of Child Health and Human Development (e.g., Foorman, Fletcher,
Francis, Schatschneider, & Mehta, 1998) has become a proxy for phonics.[3]
Those educators who are serious about catching their students who are falling
through the cracks could easily become confused and disillusioned by the arguments, claims, and counterclaims of those currently on the leading edge of this
controversy. Leaving aside the nuances and specific technical concerns about
this individual study or that particular statement, we need to focus our attention on the basic facts about reading instruction that have emerged most clearly
from the past 20 years of intensive research in this area.

Unfortunately, there are a substantial number of instructional and curricular fallacies on both sides of the "great debate" (Chall, 1996) that continue to
deter progress in reading achievement. Here, in my view, are the top 12 fallacies about reading and reading instruction that often fool educators and frequently lead them to shortchange their students instructionally.

The Either-Or Fallacy

The either-or fallacy can be stated thus: One must choose *between* the code-
based approach to reading instruction (phonics) and a meaning-based emphasis (whole language). One is seemingly not permitted to have a foot in both
instructional camps—choosing the best from each. I was a first-year teacher
when Russell and Fea (1963) made the following statement:

Thinking in the field has moved away somewhat from an either-or point of view about one method or set of books to a realization that different children learn in different ways, that the processes of learning to read and reading are more complex than we once thought, and that the issues in reading instruction are many sided. (p. 867)

I have now retired from public education, and regrettably, the "either-or" point of view that Russell and Fea thought was long gone almost three decades ago is still alive and well. Pressley (1998) describes the lines in the sand that are still being drawn by some, as the two sides of the reading wars exchange verbal darts. The whole-language camp believes that "teachers who use published materials or teach skills are being deskilled themselves. Moreover, they are in political conspiracy with right-wing elements determined to maintain the social, economic, and political status quo," whereas "the phonics camp believes that whole language does not promote literacy" (pp. 276–277).

To take an either-or stance denies the synergistic relationship between code instruction and meaning. Without the ability to accurately and automatically identify words, students are denied the whole point of reading—meaning. On the other hand, if teachers and their students do not realize that code instruction is merely the means to gain understanding of the text and not the essence of reading—if students are stuck too long with flash cards and word drills—we risk undermining their motivation to read and their active involvement in constructing meaning from connected text. Code knowledge is wasted on those who do not use it regularly to read compelling narratives, read to learn in expository text, and navigate the complexities of our technological world. Those who can read but don't are only marginally more literate than those who cannot read at all.

Phonics Is All We Need, and If It Says It's Phonics, It Must Be Phonics

The persuasive infomercials for programs such as *Hooked on Phonics* and the *Phonics Game* have many parents and politicians believing that phonics is the *only* answer to declining literacy levels. There are many students, especially those at risk of reading failure, whose prerequisite phonological awareness skills are weak to nonexistent. They are sure to flounder in phonics unless the program also includes a strong phonological-awareness instructional component.

Many educators believe that if the word *phonics* appears anywhere in a program, teachers are teaching phonics. Many phonics programs are poorly written, untested, and impossible to teach. There are many recently developed phonics programs that contain just enough phonics to be dangerous, especially for at-risk students who need explicit, systematic instruction in the sound-spelling correspondences. The phonics strands in many popular reading series are often a morass of poor sequencing, uncoordinated tasks, and little decodable text in which students can actually practice and automatize their phonics skills (Felton, 1993; Iversen & Tunmer, 1993; Juel & Roper-Schneider, 1985).

Although there is no *perfect* phonics program, there *is* ample research that demonstrates what aspects of phonics instruction get results (Foorman, Fletcher, Francis, Schatschneider, 1998). Phonics, although a necessary piece of the reading puzzle, is nevertheless only one piece. Literacy is absolutely dependent on students' mastery of sound-spelling correspondences as an aid to accurate independent reading. However, without daily reading and writing opportunities, constant exposure to and reading of a wide variety of well-written narrative and expository texts, and systematic and well-designed cognitive strategy instruction, literacy will not become a reality for students (Chall & Popp, 1996).

Meaning Trumps Everything

Trump is a card-playing term. Certain cards have the power to "take" other cards and are said to "trump" them. The "meaning trumps everything" fallacy discounts the importance of knowing how to break the code (i.e., being able to use information about letter-sound correspondences to sound-out unknown words in text). One of the most common arguments from the meaning-trumps-everything position is that the best way for children to learn to read words is to first guess what the words are from their understanding of the passage they are reading and then to confirm their guesses with as little phonemic analysis as possible (Goodman, 1986; Smith, 1971).

The current understanding of the way that children become accurate and fluent readers (Ehri, 1998; Share and Stanovich, 1995) supports just the *opposite* position. Guessing at words from the context is just too unreliable to use as a frontline clue to the identity of words in text (Gough, 1983). One of the sturdiest conclusions from recent research on reading is that skilled reading depends critically on fluent and accurate identification of words *on the basis of their written spellings* (Adams, 1990). Good readers rely much less on context to help them identify words than do poor readers, because good readers are skilled at identifying words by looking at the letters used to represent them in text. Thus it is important for children to pay attention to the specific letters in words from the beginning of reading instruction.

Decoding Without Meaning

There is an often-repeated urban school myth that there are thousands of students who are able to "word call" (i.e., absolutely nail the correct pronunciation of every word they encounter) but have no idea of the meaning of what they are reading. The usual argument is that these students are so-called word callers because they had too much phonics instruction and too few opportunities to engage in meaningful literacy activities. This fallacy is often used, along with the fallacy of meaning trumps everything, to convince teachers not to waste their valuable time teaching decoding strategies when other compensating strategies (such as using context to identify words) will work just as well with far less instructional effort.

An in-depth study of 361 students in the early elementary grades, 168 of whom were reading disabled, examined the kinds and frequency of various comprehension and decoding difficulties (Shankweiler et al., 1999). The students were given tests of word and nonword reading, reading and listening comprehension, and also measures of language and cognitive ability. Those who did comparatively well at decoding, but whose comprehension was lower than might be expected were not nearly as common as children who were low in *both* decoding and comprehension. Relatively low reading comprehension *can* occur in children with well-developed word-reading skills, but the most likely cause is *not* excellent and abundant instruction in phonics and basic word reading skills but, rather, ineffective or nonexistent instruction in vocabulary and reading comprehension strategies.

Meaning Without Decoding

Another fallacy that continues to undermine the case for phonics instruction is the idea that it is possible (and indeed even easy) to gain fluent word identification skills without learning how to decode. There have been a number of reports regarding well-educated adults who have managed to build up such a large sight vocabulary that they are able to read and comprehend well despite their poorly developed phonemic decoding skills (Campbell & Butterworth, 1985). A closer examination of their stories, however, reveals evidence of unusual educational opportunities and extraordinary motivation. Problems with phonemic decoding skills are strongly correlated with reading comprehension problems in both secondary school and college (Bruck, 1990, 1992; Perfetti, 1985; Shankweiler, 1996). After examining the relationships between decoding and comprehension skill in a large sample of children of varying general ability levels, Shankweiler et al. (1999) concluded that "skill in phonological decoding is critical in distinguishing readers at different levels of ability to comprehend text" (p. 91).

Reading Aloud Teaches Children to Read

There is a very popular fallacy that voluminous reading aloud by parents or teachers (or both) is a *sure* route to reading proficiency (Sulzby & Teale, 1991). Reading aloud is of course a critical aspect of early literacy experiences and, for most children, lays a strong foundation for learning to read by nurturing language development as well as the acquisition of vocabulary and domain knowledge. But reading aloud, whether at home or at school, cannot be depended on to *teach* students *how to read* (Scarborough & Dobrich, 1994; Snow et al., 1998).

Durkin (1966) found that children who were reading when they entered school came from homes where parents regularly read aloud, but these same parents also taught their children letter names and letter sounds as well as providing practice in writing letters. Therefore, one cannot assume with certainty which variable was most powerful: reading aloud, reading aloud in combination with direct teaching, or just the direct teaching.

In a 7-year longitudinal study of instructional practices in kindergarten and first-grade classrooms and their relationship to student achievement,

Meyer, Stahl, Wardrop, and Linn (1999) concluded, "It appears that children learn to read by being taught to read instead of being read to and that they need to practice reading text in order to enhance their achievement" (p. 60). The researchers also found that the "time [kindergarten] teachers spent reading to children correlated negatively with the children's performance on all of the tests administered except for a listening test and a measure of science know-ledge" (p. 59). The researchers found almost a zero correlation between the time first-grade teachers spent reading to children and their students' achievement in reading.

As seductive and attractive as reading aloud, shared reading of big books, and talking together about stories can be, these activities do not teach students to read. Teachers teach students to read. "For children from low-print environments, every minute of effective reading instruction in school counts" (Foorman, Fletcher, & Francis, 1998, p. 29).

Sustained Silent Reading Cures All Reading Ills and Raises Reading Achievement, Too!

There is an abundance of conventional wisdom *and* excellent correlational evidence regarding the benefits of reading a lot. Even though elementary educators have been arguing on and off since the turn of the century about which methodology is best for teaching students to read, they *have* agreed that the more students read, the better they will read. The National Assessment of Educational Progress found that at the high school level, those who read well spend more time reading and read more pages, and those who read poorly read the least (Donahue, Voelkl, Campbell, & Mazzeo, 1999).

Anderson, Wilson, and Fielding (1988) found that the amount of time a child spends reading books is related to the child's reading level in fifth grade and growth in reading proficiency from the second to fifth grade. They concluded,

> The case can be made that reading books is a cause, not merely a reflection, of reading proficiency. Although this case falls short of being conclusive, it is as strong as the case for any other practice in the field of reading, in or out of school. (p. 302)

The deep and abiding belief of educators in the benefits of reading has created a mini-industry around the concept of motivating students to read more books. Programs such as Scholastic's (2001a) *Reading Counts* and Advantage Learning Systems's (2001) *Accelerated Reader* are based on this premise. Millions of pizzas have been donated in the cause of getting kids to read more. I've met principals who have shaved their heads, eaten fried worms, and kissed pigs—all for the cause of reading. I even had the temerity to jog around my school in a 1920s bathing suit to celebrate the number of books my students had read.

So it comes as a bit of a surprise to those of us who have been preaching that reading a lot will result in increased achievement to find that the recent report of the National Reading Panel (2000) found no solid experimental evidence to support reading a lot as a method that was causally related to improvements in reading level. A large share of the evidence in support of reading a lot as a method to increase reading skill was discounted by the panel because it came from correlational studies. In a correlational study, we can never be sure exactly what causes what. Does reading a lot help children become better readers, or do they read a lot because they *are* good readers?

Other support for the efficacy of motivational reading programs to increase reading achievement has come from quasiexperimental studies that did not use control groups, were sloppy about collecting data, or used different achievement tests to determine differences between experimental and control groups. However, there are other interpretations of the evidence on this issue, some very supportive of the idea that we should work hard to increase the amount of time children spend actually reading books (Allington, 2001). See Chapter 6 for a comprehensive discussion of this topic.

Apart from the issue of weaknesses in the research on this topic, the answer to why there is not a greater abundance of evidence in support of reading a lot may have a great deal to do with *what* students are reading (e.g., an appropriate level of difficulty) and how *accountable* they are being held for understanding what they read. If students spend time reading books that are too easy (i.e., they are not learning new vocabulary or acquiring knowledge) or too hard (i.e., they can't understand what they read), the time they spend won't produce increased levels of literacy. Or if students are not held accountable for talking and writing about what they have read, they may not make the effort needed to comprehend difficult text or to look up the meanings of unknown words.

Skilled Readers Are Skippers

The view that children can become fluent readers only if they learn to skip words, to just sample the visual information in text to support their hypotheses about its meaning, is related to the view discussed earlier that meaning trumps everything. Within this view, teachers are supposed to encourage guessing about words to help children become free from their so-called bondage to print. In fact, the understanding of skilled reading that emerges from the past 20 years of scientific research is, again, just the *opposite* of the view of skilled readers as word skippers. Two important facts about the way that skilled readers process text are relevant to this new understanding. The first of these facts is that skilled readers fixate, or look directly at, almost every word in text as they read (Rayner & Pollatsek, 1989). Skilled readers read rapidly, not because they selectively sample words and letters as they construct the meaning of text, but because they read the individual words rapidly and with little effort.

A key piece of knowledge here, and the second important fact relevant to our new understanding of skilled reading, is that good readers use information about all the letters in the words, even when they recognize them at a single glance (Just & Carpenter, 1987; Patterson & Coltheart, 1987). Because many words are differentiated from one another by only one or two letters, a global, or gestalt image of a word is not sufficient to help recognize it reliably. Instead, the memory image used in reading words by sight must include information about all, or almost all, the letters in a word's spelling. Even when reading very rapidly, the good reader extracts information about all the letters in a word as part of the recognition process.

Adams (1991) summarizes these facts about word recognition processes in skilled readers this way:

> It has been proven beyond any shade of doubt that skillful readers process virtually each and every word and letter of text as they read. This is extremely counter-intuitive. For sure, skillful readers neither look nor feel as if that's what they do. But that's because they do it so quickly and effortlessly. Almost automatically; with almost no conscious attention whatsoever, skillful readers recognize words by drawing on deep and ready knowledge of spellings and their connections to speech and meaning. (p. 207)

This information about the nature of word recognition processes in skilled readers reinforces the information we have about the unreliability of passage context as a means to accurate word identification. Children must establish good phonemic decoding and sight-word-reading habits from the beginning of their journey in learning to read.

Guessing Is Good

This myth is related to ones we have already considered under meaning trumps everything, and skilled readers are skippers, but it is so pervasive and interferes so negatively with what otherwise might be very effective instruction that I decided to give it its own identity in this section. This is the misconception that skilled readers rely heavily on context clues to identify words; in fact, some educators intentionally teach "using context" as a strategy to students, and some reading series provide posters and bookmarks to further reinforce the strategy. There is a popular reading assessment, Reading Miscue Inventory, (Goodman & Burke, 1972; Goodman, Watson, & Burke, 1987) that gives students credit if a misidentified word in the text *would* make sense in the context of the reading. For example, if a student guessed the word *pony* instead of correctly reading the word as *horse*, credit would be given because the guessed word has grammatical similarity as well as syntactic and semantic acceptability.

Gough and Hillinger (1980) assert that

> the role of context in reading is . . . seriously exaggerated by most scholars. . . . Context will enable the reader to predict, at best, not more than one word in four. Moreover, the predictability of a word in context is correlated with its frequency. The words that are predictable will tend to be those words that the child already recognizes, and the novel words that he now must recognize are exactly the ones which context will not enable him to predict. (pp. 186–187)

They go on to conclude "that if the child is to become a fluent reader, he must learn to decode, more precisely, to decipher. He must internalize the orthographic cipher of English" (p. 187).

In reality, guessing by using context clues to identify words is the preferred strategy of *weak* readers. An extensive body of research shows that skilled readers do not guess. In fact, the ability to identify words in the absence of semantic cues is one of the defining characteristics of skilled readers (Share & Stanovich, 1995).

The Three-Cueing System: A Genuine Urban Myth

In the late 1970s and early 1980s, a great deal was written about the intersection of lexical, semantic, and syntactic cues and their importance to the reader in constructing meaning from text. A fourth cueing system was often included in the discussion as well: pragmatics (i.e., constructing meaning from text often depends on having some practical knowledge and common sense).

One might assume that the current three-cueing system, revered by so many teachers today as a word identification strategy, would bear some resemblance to the earlier model. Think again. Reading guru, Marilyn Adams, author of innumerable distinguished works on reading, has written widely on the critical importance of cueing systems (Adams, Anderson, & Durkin, 1978; Adams & Bruce, 1982; Adams & Bruck, 1993). Therefore, she was stunned to find that when she explained *her* interpretation of the three-cueing system in response to a question from a teacher in one of her presentations, those in attendance stared at her blankly.[4] Oh, they could draw the Venn diagram that has been a staple in guided-reading workshops for years. But the teachers had never heard of Marilyn Adams's (1998) scholarly interpretation of the diagram based on the theory and research of linguistics and cognitive science. Their understanding was limited to a trio of simple questions they were told to ask students who are unable to identify words during a guided-reading session. *Does it make sense? Does it sound right? Does it look right?* Professor Adams was as mystified by the three questions as the teachers were by her interpretation.

Intrigued, Adams (1998) set out to find the birthplace and lineage of this "new" interpretation of the three-cueing system, much like investigative reporters try to track down the validity of an urban myth. Who conceived the original Venn diagram that has produced enough variations and permutations to fill a book of its own, and how did it come to have an interpretation that was totally contradictory to what research tells us about the process of learning to read?

David Pearson eventually heard of Adams's (1998) search and sent an article he had written years earlier (Pearson, 1976) that contained the elusive diagram. Pearson had conceived it to illustrate his position that phonics not be *overemphasized* to the exclusion of comprehension. How had this very reasonable and logical interpretation of what we know about learning to read have evolved into the strong belief that syntax and semantics are *more* important to gaining meaning from text than the graphophonemic system? In fact, the diagram *and* the three-cueing system are often used as the rationale for *not* teaching phonics.

Adams (1998) concluded that the concept seemed to have been born and raised in workshops, chat rooms, and teachers' lounges. Although the Venn diagram as conceived by Pearson (1976) clearly meant that productive reading depends on the interworking, overlapping, and intersection of all three cueing systems, something had been lost in its translation to contemporary classrooms. Between Pearson's (1976) article and 1988 when the Venn diagram made its only other appearance in a published work (Routman, 1988), other than workshop handouts, training materials, or curriculum frameworks, the three-cueing system had taken on a life of its own—a true urban myth.

Even though reading research unequivocally demonstrates the critical role that sound-spelling relationships play in accurate and fluent word identification, a more contemporary version of the old parlor game of "telephone" had somehow swept the country, and teachers were taught and passed the word to each with an evangelistic fervor that *meaning cues* come first when readers don't know what a word is. The training materials put it this way: "Use meaning cues first! Help a young reader learn that meaning is the most important source for cues! Let's all work together to avoid the phrase 'sound it out' " (California Early Literacy Learning Project, 1996).

Adams (1998) points out that although most teachers who use these questions think the three-cueing system is research based and widely respected in the reading community, most reading researchers have never heard of it. She further asserts that the three-cueing belief system "has wreaked disaster on students and hardship on teachers" (p. 97). This fallacy has fooled us, big time!

The Fat Cat Sat on the Rat Is Bor-r-ring and Bad for Kids

Decodable readers with controlled vocabularies have been summarily dismissed as altogether useless and unnecessary in the teaching of beginning reading by some whole-language enthusiasts. Allington (2001) asserts that "claims about the utility of decodable text are sheer nonsense and not supported by research available" (p. 21).

As a former media specialist, however, I know the value of having a book, any book, that a novice reader can actually "read" on his or her own. Oh, I'm not talking about the predictable books that are readily memorized after multiple readings. Memorizing predictable text is a wonderful *prereading* skill, but it *isn't* reading! Reading is independently figuring out every word on the page—a challenge the beginning reader can easily handle when the text contains only those sound-spelling correspondences he or she has mastered along with a few *sight words*[5] (exception words) that have been introduced and explained by the teacher. There are several studies demonstrating an advantage for beginning reading programs that include decodable texts (Felton, 1993; Foorman, Fletcher, Francis, Schatschneider, et al., 1998; Iversen & Tunmer, 1993).

Whether a given piece of text is decodable can only be determined after an examination of what the teacher has already taught the students (and what the students have mastered). What is decodable text for one child in one classroom may well be indecipherable for another child in another classroom, depending on what sound-spelling correspondences have been taught and mastered. After an analysis of beginning reading programs to determine the relationship between decoding instruction and text, Stein et al. (1998) warned educators to carefully examine the kinds and amounts of decodable text that are available to beginning readers. "The long-term effects of poor decoding instruction and lack of applied practice are potentially devastating to students and difficult for the best of teachers to reverse" (p. 23). Juel and Roper-Schneider (1985) concluded, on the basis of a study of first-grade readers, that "the types of words which appear in beginning reading texts may well exert a more powerful influence in shaping children's word identification strategies than the method of reading instruction" (p. 151).

Unbalanced Balanced Literacy

The term *balanced literacy* is a deceptive one. The adjective *balanced* implies a tension between two fairly *equal* ideas or concepts and is defined by Webster's in several related ways: (a) an equality of weight or power advantage; (b) the equilibrium of various elements in a design; and (c) harmonious proportions (McKechnie, 1983, p. 140). However, there seems to be a wild imbalance in many purportedly balanced reading programs.

I can only assume that the term *balanced* to describe a literacy program was chosen, I do not know by whom, to convey a sense of equality in terms of both importance and classroom emphases to *meaning* and *decoding*. Much of what goes for *balanced literacy instruction* that I have observed in my travels from north to south and coast to coast, however, is no more balanced than the old wooden see-saw in the school yard was when I sat on one end and my baby sister, 10 years younger, sat on the other.

I saw a classic example recently of unbalanced balanced literacy recently. It purported to be a *balanced literacy checklist* containing the key components of early literacy instruction. *Sorting, analogies to onset rimes, word walls, and word games* were given top billing as word identification activities and strategies, but there was no mention of direct instruction in phonological or phonetic skills. *The provision of familiar reading opportunities* was listed, but decodable texts were strangely absent. *Running records* and *portfolios* were considered state-of-the-art assessment tools, but oral reading fluency, word reading efficiency, and phonological awareness screenings did not make the cut. Students were expected, yea, encouraged and prompted by their teachers, to use *cue integration*, but there was nary a mention of decoding. When some of the most important components for at-risk learners make only a token appearance in lesson plans, district documents, and state frameworks, we have fallen for the fallacy of balanced literacy in a big way. I want truly balanced literacy for at-risk students. I want them to read wonderful books, both fiction and nonfiction. I want them to become voracious, voluminous, and voluntary readers. But first, they have to learn to read.

Please don't let political rhetoric, petty turf wars, ineffective materials and methods, or misconceptions and myths keep you from your appointed mission —*teaching them all to read.*

SUMMARIZING CHAPTER 2

Ask yourself these three important questions before beginning Chapter 3:

1. Am I conversant with the critical components of the reading puzzle that need to be in place to achieve the goal of teaching them all to read?

2. Am I doing everything I can in my classroom, school, or district to make sure that all students reach expected or even higher levels of literacy?

3. Do I have any mistaken beliefs about reading instruction that may be standing in the way of my students achieving literacy?

LOOKING AHEAD

Chapters 3 through 7 will examine each of the puzzle pieces in more depth, providing research, best classroom practices, and resources to help you learn more about each of the reading puzzle pieces.

NOTES

1. Jeanne Chall and Marie Carbo debated phonics in the pages of *Phi Delta Kappan* in the late 1980s (Carbo, 1988; Chall, 1989). Carbo, however, later backed off her anti-phonics position (Carbo, 1996). Gerald Coles and Reid Lyon took up the debate in the late 1990s in *Education Week* (Coles, 1997; Lyon, quoted in Mathes & Torgesen, 1997). Gerald Coles (2000a) and Louise Spear-Swerling (2000) exchanged salvos when Spear-Swerling reviewed Coles's (2000b) book, *Misreading Science: The Bad Science That Hurts Children.*

2. See the glossary for comprehensive definitions of phonics and whole language.

3. See the discussion at http://cars.uth.tmc.edu/debate/debate.htm.

4. The discussion in this section has been adapted from Adams (1998). This book chapter makes fascinating reading for anyone involved in the administration of reading instruction or staff development in the area of reading instruction.

5. There are a number of different definitions of *sight words* circulating in reading instruction. The concept of sight words originated with the "Look-Say" method of reading instruction. Students were expected to memorize the most common words of the English language. The Dolch list was created for that reason. Other educators use *sight words* to refer to words that although originally decoded by the child have been read so frequently they are now read fluently and automatically (but not without attention to the letters in the word). Other educators use the term to refer to the exception words in the English language that cannot be sounded out (e.g., was, the one, of, shoe, said) but must be memorized (Wren, 2001b).

3

Putting the Code
Pieces in Place

*Useful knowledge of the spelling-to-speech correspondences of English does not
come naturally. For all children, it requires a great deal of practice, and for many
children, it is not easy. The acquisition of this knowledge depends on developing a
reflective appreciation of the phonemic structure of the spoken language; on learning about letter-sound correspondences and spelling conventions of the orthography; and on consolidating and extending this knowledge by using it in the course
of one's own reading and writing.*

—Adams, 1998, p. 74

What comes to *your* mind when you hear the word *code?* I think of my
father-in-law who was a master of the Morse code and ventured
behind enemy lines during World War II to transmit radio messages to Allied
intelligence officers. When the dots and dashes of a reply came clattering
through his headset, he was able to decode them instantaneously into the letters of our English alphabet. Jean-François Champollion, the Egyptologist who
broke the code of Egyptian hieroglyphics from studying the Rosetta stone,
comes to mind as well. Champollion had to figure out the hieroglyphic code all
on his own. He didn't have a first-grade teacher to help him.

The code that is most important to students who do not know how to read
is the English alphabet code. If these nonreaders are to experience the thrill
of deciphering the indecipherable and figuring out what those mysterious
marks on the page mean, they will need to acquire an intimate knowledge of
the code: the conventionally accepted way in which letters or groups of letters

correspond to spoken sounds in our language. *Your* knowledge of that code has enabled you to gain meaning as you have read this book.

Three pieces of the reading puzzle are needed to help students access code knowledge: (a) phonological awareness; (b) phonics; and (c) spelling. Each of these pieces is essential, for without phonological awareness skills to hear and manipulate sounds, students will struggle in phonics instruction. The majority of students will need phonics instruction to learn how to decode (blend sounds together to read the words on the printed page) and encode (translate spoken and thought words into correctly spelled words). Almost 40 years ago, Mathews (1966) concluded that

> No matter how a child is taught to read, he comes sooner or later to the strait gate and the narrow way: he has to learn letters and the sounds for which they stand. There is no evidence whatever that he will ultimtely do this better from at first not doing it all. (p. 208)

PHONOLOGICAL AWARENESS

Phonological
Awareness

What Is Phonological Awareness?

The term *phonological awareness* has only become a part of mainstream education's vocabulary during the past 5 years, but research investigating the role of this constellation of skills in learning to read has been ongoing for nearly two decades (Liberman & Shankweiler, 1985; Wagner & Torgesen, 1987). Phonological awareness is the "conscious ability to detect and manipulate (e.g., move, combine, and delete) sound, as well as the awareness of sounds in spoken words in contrast to written words" (Smith, Simmons, & Kame'enui, 1996, p. 3). Examples of such abilities include blending sounds together to build words, generating a list of rhyming words, or counting out the number of individual sounds (phonemes) that are heard in a given word.

Many children acquire these skills effortlessly, but there are many more, irrespective of their IQ's, for whom phonological awareness tasks are extraordinarily difficult. Without phonological awareness, a child will be unable to do seemingly simple tasks, such as generating some words that rhyme with *cat* or substituting the /h/ sound for the /k/ sound in *cat* and figuring out what the new word is. Before children can do those tasks, they must be able to hear and manipulate the individual phonemes in words. This skill is a critical prerequisite to acquiring the English language code that is needed in order to read. Deficient phonological awareness skills need instructional interventions to be remediated. Children do not outgrow phonological deficits or develop phonological awareness skills with physical maturation (Liberman & Shankweiler, 1985).

How Students Acquire Phonological Awareness

There are four ways in which students can acquire phonological awareness. They can be genetically blessed in such a way that they acquire these skills in a seemingly effortless way. They can be environmentally blessed with parents who have talked to them constantly, played word games incessantly, and read aloud nursery rhymes and poetry every night at bedtime. Students can even be doubly blessed with great genes *and* a fabulous environment. Or, failing the blessings of nature and nurture, they can acquire phonological awareness skills from a highly effective teacher using a research-based curriculum taught explicitly, systematically, and supportively.

The Importance of Phonological Awareness

When I asked one researcher about the importance of phonological awareness, he called it the "500-pound gorilla." That phrase is not terribly scientific, but it succinctly summarizes the monumental role that phonological awareness plays in reading success. If a 500-pound gorilla is all you need to convince you of the importance of phonological awareness instruction in your classroom, school, or district, read no further. However, if you would like to learn more, read on.

If you have ever taught a very bright student who had reading difficulties and were unable to solve the riddle of why nothing seemed to work, phonological awareness may well have been the answer. Because phonological abilities are relatively independent of overall intelligence (Vellutino & Scanlon, 1987; Wagner & Torgesen, 1987), a teacher can fairly assume that if a student with a normal IQ and satisfactory listening comprehension is floundering in reading, one highly probable explanation for the problem is a phonological awareness deficit. The student who cannot hear the individual phonemes in spoken words is unable to take the next step in acquiring the ability to read: learning how these sounds correspond to the letters of our alphabet.

Multiple studies have investigated the effects of phonemic awareness instruction (Ball & Blachman, 1991; Byrne & Fielding-Barnsley, 1989; Cunningham, 1990; Lie, 1991; Lundberg, Frost, & Peterson, 1988; O'Connor, Jenkins, & Slocum, 1993; Torgesen, Wagner, & Rashotte, 1997; Vellutino & Scanlon, 1987) and report positive effects on reading, spelling, and phonological development, not only for at-risk students but also for normal achievers.

Phonological Awareness Instruction

Effective preschool and kindergarten teachers have always included listening activities, word play, and rhyming games in their lesson plans. They have instinctively known that children need these language skills to be successful in learning to read. The difference between that kind of incidental instruction and the way we now know phonological awareness must be taught in order to catch students at risk of reading failure is huge. Our earlier conception of language skills as developmental in nature permitted us to explain away those students who didn't "get it" as "not ready" (Francis, Shaywitz, Stuebing, Shaywitz, & Fletcher, 1996). We believed that students who didn't readily catch on to natural and informal language activities just needed more time to bloom. We retained them in kindergarten to give them another year to mature or placed them in a developmental first grade or an ungraded primary class. Marilyn Adams (1990) reminds us that

> The key to phonemic awareness seems to lie more in training than in age or maturation. If these children have not received the proper exposure to print and sound in either their homes or their kindergarten classrooms by age five and a half, what is there to suggest that they will by the time they are six and a half? (p. 331)

Successful intervention studies tell us a great deal about what phonological awareness instruction should look like in preschool, kindergarten, and first-grade classrooms. It is most effective when the following conditions are present:

There are sufficient amounts of direct instruction and coaching before students are expected to do a task independently. The instructional sequence (I do it, we do it, you do it) is essential when teaching phonological awareness to at-risk students. See Resource D for a sample lesson using this sequence. Some phonological awareness instructional materials merely describe an activity. The teachers' manual may launch immediately into the "you do it" phase of a lesson without showing teachers how to model for and coach their students ("I do it" and "we do it").

Students have ample opportunities to practice the individual sounds after teachers have orally modeled the sounds. An important aspect of the practice phase for students is *feeling* the individual sounds when they say them. Some students may even need to see themselves or the teacher (or both) in a mirror to understand precisely what is happening to their lips and tongues when a specific sound is produced. Some programs (e.g., Lindamood & Lindamood, 1998) label the sounds that are made—for example, "lip-poppers," "lip coolers," and "tongue coolers"—to help children understand how a sound feels (p. 34).

Teachers frequently review and reinforce what has been taught previously. A 5-minute review session while waiting for a birthday treat or music class will pay enormous dividends for all students but especially for struggling students. Review sessions are not optional for those students who are seriously deficient. The most successful school intervention programs build in booster review sessions for students who need them, taught by the speech pathologist, special educators, or Title I teachers. See the descriptions of Project PRIDE in both Chapter 7 and Resource C for additional information.

WHAT IS EXPLICIT, SYSTEMATIC, SUPPORTIVE INSTRUCTION?

Explicit: *plain in language; distinctly expressed; clearly stated; not merely implied*

The sequences of teaching events and teacher actions in code instruction must be conspicuous (Dixon, Carnine, & Kame'enui, 1992). There must be adequate teacher modeling (I do it) in order for students to see, hear, and understand the task or the skill and ample opportunities for students to concretely represent sounds with manipulatives or say the sounds with teacher support (we do it), before moving to the final phase of the instructional sequence when students are able to demonstrate the task or skill on their own (you do it).

Systematic: *characterized by the use of a method or plan*

The skills that are needed to access the English language code cannot be taught sporadically with an enticing activity pulled from a magazine and planned on the spur of the moment. To be effective, code instruction must be organized and sequential.

Supportive: *to uphold by aid, encouragement, or countenance; to keep from failing or declining*

Instruction must be scaffolded (i.e., the tasks that students are asked to do must be graduated in difficulty, with each one being only slightly more difficult than the last). Scaffolded instruction ensures success and keeps students feeling confident and motivated to learn.

Instruction is systematic, explicit, and supportive. (See the Sidebar on p. 35 which defines explicit, systematic, and supportive instruction.)

The program has a defined scope and sequence that begins with the largest sound units and progresses to the smallest: words to syllables to phonemes. *Phonemic Awareness in Young Children: A Classroom Curriculum* (Adams, Foorman, Lundberg, & Beeler, 1998) is an example of one such program. Kindergarten teacher, Nettie Griffin, who tells her story in Chapter 7, has used the *Phonological Awareness Training for Reading* (Torgesen & Bryant, 1993) with great success.

A sound-spelling correspondence component (phonics) is gradually added to instruction as appropriate.

Adequate attention is given to *segmenting*, *blending*, and *detection*.

The Optimum Time to Teach Phonological Awareness

For those students who are deficient in phonological awareness skills as measured by an assessment or those students who exhibit other signs of disability or delay, the optimal time to begin training is *before* formal reading instruction is initiated (O'Connor, Jenkins, & Slocum, 1993). If students begin formal reading instruction and fail, which they are almost certain to do if they lack phonological awareness skills, both teacher and students will experience frustration. For students with overall low academic ability, the ideal time to begin phonological training is early in kindergarten or first grade at the latest (Lie, 1991). For students who are having reading difficulties in upper grades, the best time to teach phonological awareness skills, if assessments reveal a deficit, is immediately.

Implementing a Prevention-Intervention Phonological Awareness Program

Implementing a comprehensive prevention-intervention phonological awareness program in your classroom, school, or district should be undertaken only with careful planning, a thorough assessment of students, ample staff training, and comprehensive on-site coaching. Here follow some guidelines to ensure success.

Choose a program that focuses on the two most important goals of phonological training: (a) helping children to notice the phonemes in words (i.e., to discover their

---

ASSESSING AND TEACHING PHONEMIC AWARENESS

These are the phonemic-awareness skills that are most commonly assessed and taught:

- Phoneme isolation: recognizing individual sounds in words; for example, "Tell me the first sound in *paste*" (/p/).

- Phoneme identity: recognizing the common sound in different words; for example, "Tell me the sound that is the same in *bike*, *boy*, and *bell*" (/b/).

- Phoneme categorization: recognizing the word with the odd sound in a sequence of three or four words; for example, "Which word does not belong: *bus*, *bun*, *rug*? (rug).

- Phoneme blending: listening to a sequence of separately spoken sounds and combining them to form a recognizable word; for example, "What word is /s/ /k/ /u/ /l/?" (school).

- Phoneme segmentation: breaking down a word into its sounds by tapping out or counting the sounds or by pronouncing and positioning a marker for each sound; for example, "How many phonemes in *ship*? (three).

- Phoneme deletion: recognizing what word remains when a specified phoneme is removed; for example, "What is *smile* without the /s/? (mile).

existence and distinctness) and (b) helping children to make the connection between the phonemes in words and the letters of the alphabet (Torgesen & Mathes, 2000, p. 43). Be cautious about the use of activities that have not been field tested with students or activities that are purported to be literature based. These activities are often developed around a poem or story without regard for the importance of a specific instructional sequence; they can easily confuse at-risk students.

Assess all students being considered for a phonological awareness program. There are a variety of tests ranging from the quick and easy to administer *Yopp-Singer Test of Phoneme Segmentation* (Yopp, 1995) to the *Lindamood Auditory Conceptualization Test* (Lindamood & Lindamood, 1979), a more complex diagnostic battery that is recommended for second-grade through high school students. The *Dynamic Indicators of Basic Early Literacy* (Kaminski & Good, 1996) includes a fluency component to assess response speeds for all phonological skills, as well as multiple forms so that students can be tested periodically throughout the school year.

Provide quality training and ongoing support for teachers. Any phonological awareness instruction program will benefit from the presence of a literacy coach or, at the very least, classroom support from the speech pathologist, to achieve maximum effectiveness. Teachers will need intensive training in both hearing and saying the individual sounds, for few, if any, teachers have had adequate preservice training to prepare them for teaching phonological awareness skills.

Teachers will need opportunities to practice speaking more slowly and carefully so that students can hear the sounds. A trainer or supervisor should test all teachers on their competence with the sounds before the program is launched. To teach phonological awareness using materials provided in a major reading series, teachers will need expert help in adapting, supplementing, and choosing which of the myriad suggested teaching activities really *do* support the development of phonological awareness. Remember that the mere presence of the terms *phonological awareness* or *phonemic awareness* in a catalog or sales brochure does not guarantee that a program will get results.

Make sure that the sequence of activities moves from words to syllables to sounds and that students are also taught the letters of the alphabet, but only after the sounds have been mastered. Make sure that teachers are provided with adequate scripts and ample practice exercises. Beware of programs that do not offer alternatives and enhancements for children who need extra practice.

Anticipate that some children will not respond to whole-group instruction and will need more intense small-group or even one-to-one instruction. Be ready to catch those students *before* they fall.

Acknowledge frustration, and listen to teachers' concerns during the beginning weeks of instruction.

MUST-READ BOOKS ABOUT THE CODE

Carnine, D. W., Silbert, J., & Kame'enui, E. J. (1997). *Direct Instruction Reading* (3rd ed.). Upper Saddle River, NJ: Merrill.

Chall, J. S., & Popp, H. M. (1996). *Teaching and Assessing Phonics: Why, What, When, How: A Guide for Teachers*. Cambridge, MA: Educators Publishing Service.

Moats, L. C. (1995). *Spelling: Development, Disability, and Instruction*. Baltimore: York.

Moats, L. C. (2000). *Speech to Print: Language Essentials for Teachers*. Baltimore: Brookes.

Torgesen, J. K., & Mathes, P. G. (2000). *A Basic Guide to Understanding, Assessing, and Teaching Phonological Awareness*. Austin, TX: PRO-ED.

Torgesen & Mathes (2000) point out that "it is not easy to pronounce individual phonemes correctly without some careful practice" (p. 47). Teachers will need constant encouragement, frequent praise, and persistent reminders that their efforts *will* pay off because they are using *explicit, systematic, and supportive instruction*. Once teachers gain experience, however, they will be exhilarated by the competencies of their students.

Don't cut short the time you allocate for phonological awareness instruction. Spending too little time, especially for the students at risk of reading failure, may be no better than not teaching phonological awareness at all. Plan for up to 45 minutes daily. It was only when Nettie Griffin started teaching phonological awareness every day without fail that she achieved the goal she had been aiming for all along: sending all of her students on to first grade, reading. If you are serious about getting results, spend time teaching students what you want them to know.

PHONICS

Once students have acquired solid phonological awareness skills, they will be ready to add the piece of the reading puzzle that will enable them to rapidly and fluently identify words: *phonics*. Phonics is the "body of knowledge about the relationship between written and spoken words, skill in its use, and a positive attitude toward its application in reading and writing" (Chall, 1996, p. 1). Other terms that are often used interchangeably with phonics are *sound-spelling* or *spelling-sound correspondences*, *sound-letter* or *letter-sound correspondences*, or *grapho-phonemic relationships*.

How Important Is the Code?

When you know the code, you can quickly decode (i.e., sound out any new word you encounter). Although I do not speak Spanish fluently, I do know the Spanish code (a very predictable and regular one) so that I can correctly pronounce the Spanish surnames of my friends as well as the names of streets and subdivisions where I live. During your reading thus far, you may have encountered some unfamiliar words—words that slowed down or even interrupted your reading because you weren't certain of their pronunciations. You no doubt used one or more of the following strategies to help you in your decoding:

- Analyzing and blending together the individual phonemes
- Noticing and blending together familiar spelling patterns involving more than one letter
- Making analogies to other words that you already know (Ehri, 1998)

During a first encounter with any new word, skilled readers phonologically recode the phonetic structure of the word into memory, as well as the movements of their mouth, lips, and tongue during its pronunciation, so that when the word is encountered again, they can accurately retrieve the sounds and read the word more rapidly than was possible the first time. Each time you have encountered the word *phonological* in this book, for example, you have identified it a little more quickly than you did the first time (unless of course you knew the word when you began reading). Before long, your identification of *phonological* will be fluent and accurate, matching your skill with words you already know.

Although many educators (and most major publishers) have concluded (or conceded) that phonics *should* be taught, the proliferation of phonics programs and the variety of approaches available on the market are confusing, even to a relatively knowledgeable educator. Once you have decided to teach phonics, what kind should it be? Two large-scale studies and several reviews of the research on beginning reading instruction offer additional insights.

Research and Phonics Instruction

I would advise anyone who has wondered about the research relative to phonics instruction to read it for themselves—not just to take someone else's word for what a study might say. I recommend two studies for your consideration: The First-Grade Studies (Bond & Dykstra, 1967) and The Houston Study (Foorman, Fletcher, Francis, Schatschneider, et al., 1998). Both studies appeared in peer-reviewed journals (a panel of experts selected by an editor reviewed and critiqued the studies without knowing the authors' names). Although both of these studies are quasiexperimental in nature—the assignment of students to teachers and the assignment of teachers to curricula were not made randomly (Cook & Campbell, 1979)—their findings, considered along with such comprehensive reviews of the research as Adams (1990), Chall (1967/1983), the National Reading Panel (2000), and the National Research Council (Snow et al., 1998), should leave no doubts in your mind about the critical role that phonics plays in beginning reading instruction. Explicit, systematic, supportive phonics instruction, taught as a stand-alone instructional component *but* within the context of a print-rich classroom environment with a significant literature base, is an absolutely essential (although certainly not sufficient) piece of the reading puzzle—particularly for at-risk students.

The First-Grade Studies (Bond & Dykstra, 1967), sponsored by the U.S. Office of Education, was the largest research project of its kind to that date. Twenty-seven individual projects, scattered across the country in different types of schools and with a variety of student populations, asked these questions:

- Which of the many approaches to initial reading instruction produces superior reading and spelling achievement at the end of first grade?
- Is there any program uniquely effective or ineffective for pupils with high or low readiness for reading?

The different projects compared basal readers, initial teaching alphabet, various phonics methods (both synthetic and analytic), linguistic methods, individualized methods, and language experience methods. The findings are voluminous (79 pages), but for purposes of this discussion, I will summarize the findings that are related to phonics instruction.

The First-Grade Studies found that

> the beginning reading programs that contained stronger, more systematic phonics components produced statistically significant higher end-of-first grade reading achievement than those that had weaker phonics programs—i.e., those in basal readers of the early 1960's that focused largely on reading for meaning through a whole word approach. The First-Grade Studies further found very high correlations between first-grade reading achievement and knowledge of letter names and phonemic elements—higher than IQ and vocabulary knowledge. (Chall, 1999, p. 8)

More than 30 years later, another study posed the question that all of us who have worked with large numbers of students who are poor, limited-English-proficient, and reading disabled are asking: *What instructional methods are most effective for preventing reading failure in at-risk children?* (Foorman, Fletcher, Francis, Schatschneider, et al., 1998).

The second major research study to which we can look for direction regarding phonics instruction is the Houston Study. Foorman, Fletcher, Francis, Schatschneider, et al. (1998) examined how well a variety of instructional methods worked with a group of 285 Title I students that may be similar to the students in your classroom or school. Between 3 to 8 Title I students were distributed in 65 regular education classrooms with non-Title-I students; all of the members of each class received the same instruction. The non-Title-I students were not included in the study, at the school district's request. The ethnic composition of the students overall was 60% African American, 20% Hispanic, and 20% White. More than half of the sample was boys (61%).

The study compared three different instructional methods as well as a control group. You will likely find all of these instructional methods (or some combination or permutation thereof) in your own school or district. The three instructional methods plus the control methodology were implemented during a 90-minute daily language arts period over the course of one school year. The four methods were designated as follows: (a) the control group known as implicit code-standard or IC-S, (b) the direct code group known as DC, (c) the embedded code group, EC, and (d) the implicit code group, IC. To ensure consistency across classrooms, teachers using the three experimental methods were trained to use one of those methods by the researchers and their staff. Experimental teachers received 1 week of summer inservice (30 hours) followed by retraining and demonstration lessons 1 month into the school year. The control group teachers were trained and supervised by district personnel.

The three experimental methods were implemented within the context of a "literature-rich environment in the classroom" (Foorman, Fletcher, Francis, Schatschneider, et al., 1998, p. 39). The DC method consisted of direct instruction in letter-sound correspondences practiced in decodable text; a balance of phonemic awareness with phonics (with blending as the key strategy), and

ARE YOU CONFUSING YOUR STUDENTS?

Sometimes, in our efforts to leave no stone unturned in meeting the needs of struggling readers, we end up confusing them and hence do not facilitate but rather inhibit their literacy development. Are you guilty of any of these confusing capers?

Do you ask a tutor or remedial teacher to work with your students and then fail to monitor what is being done? If you are teaching students to blend sounds together to decode words, make sure that the tutor isn't off in a corner somewhere encouraging your students to use context clues to guess at what a word might be. Classroom instruction and tutorial sessions must focus on teaching the same strategies and use the same methodologies.

Do you mix up teaching approaches or philosophies? If you are tempted to use a Word Wall, as suggested by Patricia Cunningham (1995), consider that you may be confusing your struggling readers. Typically, Word Walls are organized alphabetically, with high-frequency words listed under a letter of the alphabet (e.g., the words *orange, of, on, out, once, open,* and *off* listed under the letter *o*). Louisa Moats (1998) wryly observes, "What can a child conclude who is shown that words starting with the letter *o* begin with as many as six different sounds including the /w/ in *one* and *once*?" (p. 45). That he or she will never figure out how to read! Select only common words that you have already taught to your students to post on your Word Wall. When practicing the words with your students, use strategies that discourage guessing.

Do you use predictable texts or "leveled books" that encourage students to use context to figure out new words rather than their decoding strategies? Students at risk of reading failure need to develop consistent sounding-out strategies *before* they are taught to use context. This means that their early reading experiences should involve as little guessing as possible. If students are required to sound out words in one setting and encouraged to guess in another, they will become confused and may not learn a systematic strategy at all. Predictable books can definitely be used by higher-performing students, but give only decodable texts to students who are still learning how to decode and are practicing independent reading. Former first-grade teacher, Francine Johnston, concluded after a study of how the reading of predictable text facilitates word learning that

> predictable text may be problematic in terms of word learning. It offers considerable support from context, making it easy to read, but it may not encourage careful processing of the print. In addition, the words used to write predictable text may not be the words children find easiest to learn. (p. 674)

Do you encourage your students to do more silent reading than oral reading for practice? The goal of all reading instruction is that children will be able to read text silently for comprehension. To reach that goal, however, children who are at risk of reading failure need considerable practice orally reading passages and receiving prescriptive feedback from their teachers. Although oral passage reading may not be the *ultimate* goal of reading instruction, it is a very important intermediate step to the end of becoming a successful reader.

Do you use Round Robin oral reading? Round Robin reading is "the outmoded practice of calling on students to read orally one after the other" (Harris & Hodges, 1995, p. 222). In this kind of reading, the difficulty of the text is not controlled. Round Robin reading can often result in students who are embarrassed by stumbling over text that is too difficult or students who are bored and reading ahead silently on their own. See Chapter 4 for a variety of ways to structure oral reading.

Do you ignore the errors that students make during guided reading? If you feel guilty about giving your students corrective feedback, don't! Don't believe for a minute the popular notion that if "miscues preserve the essential meaning of the text, or if they fail to fit with the following context but are subsequently corrected by the reader, then [you have] little or no reason for concern" (Weaver, 1988, p. 325).

literature activities using *Collections for Young Scholars* (Open Court Reading, 1995). Instruction in the code was delivered as a stand-alone component apart from any literature activities. Although both literature-based and code activities were a part of the total instructional package in the DC method, they were not intermingled.

The EC method emphasized phonemic awareness and spelling patterns found in predictable books. Teachers used a common list of sequenced spelling patterns and a guide prepared by teachers that listed library books that contained those spelling patterns. Whole-class activities included shared writing, shared reading, choral or echo reading, and guided reading.

The IC method, the one implemented in the district generally, was used both as an experimental method and a control method. The major difference between the experimental group (IC) and the control group (IC-S) was the standardized training process used for the IC group teachers. The 19 teachers in the IC classrooms worked with a doctoral-level teacher-trainer who espoused the whole-language methodology. Together, they refined and defined a specific whole-language philosophy. Their stated instructional emphasis was "learning to foster competence rather than on learning to perform a skill" (Foorman, Fletcher, Francis, Schatschneider, et al., 1998, p. 40). In the IC-S classrooms, teachers continued delivering instruction as they had in the past, using district guidelines.

Although the IC and EC methods may appear similar, there was a major difference. The EC teachers directly taught students an analogy strategy for decoding words using a systematic list of spelling phonological patterns. The IC teachers drew their examples for teaching about sounds from shared and guided reading activities. In the IC classrooms, "the opportunity to learn the alphabetic code was incidental to the act of making meaning from print" (Foorman, Fletcher, Francis, Schatschneider, et al., 1998, p. 40). In addition to classroom instruction, all Title I students received tutorial instruction in small groups (3–4 students) for 30 minutes each day using the same instructional method being used in their classrooms.

Here are the major findings that educators must consider with regard to how and when to teach phonics:

- Children who were directly instructed in the alphabetic principle improved in word-reading skill at a significantly faster rate than children indirectly instructed in the alphabetic principle through exposure to literature. Nearly half of the students in the IC (46%) and EC (44%) groups exhibited *no demonstrable growth* in word reading, compared with only 15% of students in the DC group who failed to make progress.
- Students in the DC group who had lower phonological awareness skills at the beginning of the study showed *more growth in word-reading skills* than children with low phonological awareness skills in the other instructional groups.
- The end-of-year achievement scores for students in the DC group approached the national average on decoding (43rd percentile) and

passage comprehension (45th percentile), compared with the IC group (29th and 35th percentiles, respectively) and the EC group (27th and 33rd percentiles, respectively) (Foorman, Fletcher, Francis, Schatschneider, et al., 1998).

The Great Debate in the 21st Century

In the 21st century's version of The Great Debate, the Houston Study has not been without its detractors. Taylor, Anderson, Au, and Raphael (2000) were highly critical of the fact that the reading abilities of the students in the study were tested using words and nonwords to demonstrate their mastery of sound-spelling correspondences rather than connected text and sight words. They assert that Foorman and her colleagues focused unduly on instruction in word-level processing as the key to successful beginning reading and were concerned with only one aspect of literacy learning. Foorman, Fletcher, Francis, and Schatschneider (2000) responded thus:

We do not assume that training children to read words and pseudowords will enable them to read cohesive text. What we do claim is that children who are unable to read words and pseudowords will not be able to read text at age level. (p. 31)

Taylor et al. (2000) do a major disservice to practitioners everywhere by relegating the alphabetic principle to a secondary role in the acquisition of literacy. Principals and teachers who have seen dramatic increases in literacy attainment in low-performing schools have used precisely the kind of direct code instruction found to be most effective in the Foorman study (Antrim, 2001; Carter, 1999; Dobberteen, 2001; King & Torgesen, 2000; Kollars, 1999; McEwan, 1998a, 2001a). These instructional leaders know that without a *foundation of phonics*, the majority of their students would still be falling through the cracks. Successful teachers and principals also know, however, that phonics is only one piece of the reading puzzle. Without ongoing instruction in cognitive strategies, the continual development of language skills, the deepening of knowledge through solid content-area instruction, voluminous reading in all types of text, and daily opportunities to talk and write about what is read using the conventions of spoken and written language, any gains realized in kindergarten and first grade will disappear by the upper grades. Conversely, without a phonics foundation, students won't even have the option of becoming literate (Foorman et al., 2000).

Jeanne Chall (1999), commenting in *Reading Research Quarterly* on phonics research and its impact on instructional practices, had this to say about the reluctance of many researchers and reading experts to give unequivocal pro-phonics advice to practitioners: "How much research evidence is needed to turn our research findings into recommendations for practice? How many confirmations of the First-Grade Studies do we need before we put its findings to use?" (p. 10).

SPELLING

English spelling is an indirect and complex rendering of speech, and there is often no direct, one-to-one correspondence between letters and speech sounds in English orthography. Not only are sound-symbol correspondences varied and complex, but also spelling represents meaningful segments and often contains information about a word's language of origin. (Moats, 1995, p. 2)

Spelling isn't very popular in classrooms and schools these days. With the emphasis on invented spelling in primary classrooms, the popularity of journal writing that is largely unread by teachers in upper-grade classrooms, and the emphasis on prolific self-expression without regard for the conventions of spelling and grammar, instruction in spelling is often so implicit and embedded that it is hard to find. Where spelling instruction *is* found, it is likely to be taught from poorly designed curricula by inadequately trained teachers (Graham & Miller, 1979). This, despite the fact that spelling is one of the most well-researched topics in language arts (Allred, 1977).

Unfortunately, spelling is one of those skills that everybody but educators seems to think is important. One's ability to spell is usually associated with educational attainment, accuracy, and neatness, whereas poor spelling is a sure sign of illiteracy to many (Personke & Yee, 1971). For example, school board members in my district refused to hire candidates who made spelling errors on their handwritten applications. My fellow administrators and I learned the hard way that if an application contained errors and we wanted to hire that candidate, we had better ask the applicant to correct the spelling before it was presented to the Board of Education. Spelling seems like a relatively straightforward skill, but in reality, it encompasses a variety of skills: "the ability to recognize, recall, reproduce, or obtain orally or in written form the correct sequence of letters in words" (Graham & Miller, 1979, p. 76).

If you are wondering what spelling has to do with reading instruction, be assured there is a *strong* connection. Researchers agree that reading and spelling are interdependent (Ehri, 1991) and that knowledge of one or the other can be of mutual benefit. However, both students and teachers can easily become confused about the basic differences between reading and spelling instruction (Cronnell, 1978). Reading is a decoding process that moves from symbol to sound, and spelling is an encoding process that maps from sound to symbols.

When Should Formal Spelling Instruction Begin?

Although invented spelling allows children to write prolifically in kindergarten and first grade, Treiman (1993) recommends that "[children] should learn as soon as possible that every word has a conventional spelling . . . and that even if they do not yet know a word's conventional spelling, they will learn it when they get older" (p. 290). She also points out that phonological training will have a beneficial impact on spelling. Foorman (1995) suggests that direct instruction in spelling begin by midyear first grade rather than later for two reasons: (a) those students at risk of falling through the cracks will have the most difficult time with spelling, and (b) the teacher cannot assume that the knowledge gained from reading will automatically transfer to spelling without direct instruction (p. 382).

Too frequently, educators assume that spelling will develop naturally as students do more reading and writing. However, just as those students who do not have phonological skills will not develop them without direct instruction, students who are poor spellers as beginning readers will not likely grow into good spellers with a casual and incidental exposure to words. Effective spelling instruction must be focused and contain far more repetition for at-risk students than one would use with good spellers.

What Does Good Spelling Instruction Look Like?

- It is teacher directed and offers systematic practice with controlled amounts of new information.
- It is multisensory (i.e., students say, write, *and* visualize words).
- It is organized and sequential. The scope and sequence follows a natural word order that corresponds to phonological development as well as to the sounds and words being learned during reading instruction.
- It uses the test-study-test method in which teachers first determine what students know and then expect them to learn the words they don't already know.
- It emphasizes high-frequency words that are used in writing and doesn't waste instructional time on low-frequency words that students will seldom need to use in their writing.
- It begins by teaching phonemic strategies (i.e., teaching words in the primary grades that have predictable sound to spelling correspondences, such as *man, stand, and hit*), moves to teaching morphemic strategies for words made up of prefixes, suffixes, and bases (e.g., *disjoined, unreliable,* and *worried*), and then teaches words that must be taught as wholes because they are neither phonemic nor morphemic (e.g., restaurant, Wednesday, was, enough).

PITFALLS TO AVOID IN THE TEACHING OF BEGINNING READING

Watch out for the following pitfalls in teaching beginning reading that can easily undermine your efforts to *teach them all to read:* (a) the *predictable book* pitfall, (b) the *getting impatient* pitfall, (c) the *spinning plate* pitfall, (d) the *I can or I should do it all* pitfall, and (e) the *discovery zone* pitfall.

The *Predictable Book* Pitfall

Do not use predictable books to build fluency. Predictable books encourage memorization. Memorization of large amounts of text discourages attention to accurate word identification. Although some assume that word learning happens as children read and reread text (Bridge, Winograd, & Haley, 1983), this interpretation is not well supported. Individual word learning may actually be negatively affected by predictable text as students give less attention to orthography and more to the rhyme and rhythm of the text. Heed the warning of Marilyn Adams (1990) if you contemplate using predictable books for repeated reading or reading practice by at-risk readers: "Where context is strong enough to allow quick and confident identification of the unfamiliar word, there is little incentive to pore over its spelling. And without studying the word's spelling, there is no opportunity for increasing its visual familiarity" (p. 217).

The *Getting Impatient* Pitfall

There is always the temptation, particularly when faced with a variety of children at multiple points along the reading continuum, to hurry along those students who are falling behind, mistakenly believing that they will eventually catch up and catch on if they are immersed in engaging literature. When students face more and increasingly more difficult words, they will rapidly grow frustrated and may even stop trying. This is not to say, however, that there should not be a definite time and place in every instructional day for working with challenging text to develop knowledge, vocabulary, and cognitive strategies. That time, however, is *not* during independent reading.

The *Spinning Plate* Pitfall

Putting together the reading puzzle is somewhat like being in charge of the spinning-plate act in the circus. You have no doubt seen the frantic clown who barely gets his last plate spinning on the pole before the first plate he sent whirling smashes to the ground. If you want to keep your act together in beginning reading instruction, keep all of the plates spinning.

The *I Can or I Should Do It All* Pitfall

This pitfall mistakenly assumes that teachers can continue to add instructional components, interdisciplinary instructional units, and clever activities to the language arts block without ever taking anything away. I recently received an e-mail from a primary-grade teacher, who for the first time in her career had experienced the euphoria that comes when every student is reading by the end of the school year. Then, she reported the dismaying news that the board of education had recently adopted a new reading program and would be changing the curriculum.

"How can I continue to do what I was doing and also add this new program?" she asked, fully expecting me to have an answer for her.

"You can't," I replied. "You will either have to drop components of your research-based and highly successful program that just produced the best results you have ever experienced *or* change what you are doing.

Which plan of action would you recommend that she take?

The *Discovery Zone* Pitfall

The last pitfall that educators often fall into is the discovery zone pitfall. The widespread belief that creativity is the essence of effective teaching seduces many an excellent teacher off task. "This attitude is misdirected and can have ultimately disastrous consequences" (Heward & Dardig, 2001, p. 44). When teachers are tempted to make creativity and discovery their ultimate goal, the time for "real" reading will disappear. Beware of thinking that school should entertain the teacher or the student. Instruction should be designed so that students will learn to read. Schmoker (2001) refers to the time that is devoted to activities that have little relationship to acquiring the ability to read as "the crayola curriculum" and recommends that educators take a hard look at what's *really* happening during reading instruction.

SUMMARIZING CHAPTER 3

Although much research has been done to identify the causes of reading difficulties and to describe the interventions that work, there is much that we still do not know about exactly what works for whom and under what circumstances. That fact, however, should not prevent us from immediately using what we do know works in our classrooms and schools: *phonological awareness instruction, a comprehensive phonics program,* and *research-based spelling instruction.* We cannot wait until we have all of the answers. Too many students will fall through the cracks in the meantime.

LOOKING AHEAD

In Chapter 4, we will address the development, assessment, and remediation of fluency—the ability to identify words rapidly and accurately. Once students can phonemically decode, they must practice, practice, and then practice even more, to develop fluency.

4

Fluency

The Forgotten Piece of the Reading Puzzle

Repetitio est mater studiorum (*Repetition is the mother of studies*).

—Latin Proverb

Anyone who has been in the presence of a child or young adult unable to read an appropriate-level passage with the words executed accurately, effortlessly, and instantly, one after another with unwavering prosody understands why reading fluency is elusive and bewitching.

—Kame'enui and Simmons, 2001, p. 203

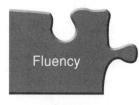

I fully expected that my son Patrick would come home from kindergarten early in the fall of 1977 and announce that he had learned to read that day. After all, his older sister by 2 years had done just that. Because Patrick had enjoyed virtually identical literacy experiences, it seemed a foregone conclusion to me that he would become a fluent reader at exactly the same time as his sister had. He did not, however. Oh, he satisfied all of the kindergarten expectations, according to his teacher, but he couldn't pick up just any book and read it when he was promoted to first grade. Nor did he demonstrate fluency at the end of first grade. Oh, Patrick was well grounded in phonics and could read simple decodable books with no difficulty, but he hadn't achieved automaticity in his reading.

Although his second-grade teacher, Patty Taylor, looked like a mild-mannered suburban school teacher, she stepped into her closet every morning before school, slipped out of her teacher togs, and turned into Wonder Woman. Of course, the principal and parents never witnessed this transformation, but my son wrote an essay in high school describing how she magically endowed him with the power to become an honors student. You see, Patrick read 1,087 books in second grade. That was a noteworthy achievement for him, but what was even more remarkable is that Mrs. Taylor motivated him to do it. She marveled at the simple reports that he wrote, listened with wide-eyed fascination as he summarized the stories for her, and then recorded every book on a chart for all to see. Wonder Woman, to be sure! She even pinned a construction paper star to his T-shirt every time he read another 10 books.

When Patrick was ready for a new book, Mrs. Taylor was there to recommend one, slightly more difficult than the previous title but not so hard as to discourage a sensitive second grader. Gradually, the books that Patrick read became more challenging, and by the end of second grade, he was reading chapter books by E. B. White, Beverly Cleary, and Laura Ingalls Wilder with ease and enjoyment. Patrick had his nose in a book almost every waking moment during second grade. His transition from a novice to a skillful reader took place almost imperceptibly, but it was no less miraculous than his sister's pronouncement that she had learned to read at school on one day in October.

Fluency (the subject of this chapter) and reading a lot (the subject of Chapter 6) are inextricably linked to one another in the reading puzzle. Students will not gain the fluency they need to become literate without reading a lot, but students whose oral reading is slow and inaccurate because of inaccurate word identification skills or speed deficiencies are unlikely to read enough voluntarily to become fluent readers. Many students fall through the cracks at precisely this point on the literacy continuum. Even those students who know how to phonemically decode can fall through the cracks if the books they choose or are given to read do not support their current reading levels. What can teachers do to ensure that all students become fluent readers? I will suggest some ways just ahead to accomplish that goal.

WHAT IS FLUENCY?

Fluency, "rate and accuracy in oral reading" (Hasbrouk & Tindal, 1992; Shinn, Good, Knutson, Tilly, & Collins, 1992) is frequently the forgotten piece of the reading puzzle. Although Anderson suggested in 1981 that fluency training was the missing ingredient in classroom reading instruction and Allington reminded us in 1983 that oral reading fluency was a neglected reading goal for both good *and* poor readers, fluency has never generated the popular books, workshops, and cultlike followings that have arisen around word walls, running records, and literature-based instruction.

In 1985, when I was looking for every possible means to bring a sizable percentage of my student body out of the bottom quartile in reading achievement,

I came upon this statement in *Becoming a Nation of Readers*: "Poor readers who engage in repeated reading show marked improvement in speed, accuracy, and expression during oral reading of new selections and more important, improvement in comprehension during silent reading" (National Academy of Education, 1985, p. 54). Repeated reading sounded like just what we needed. We subsequently put together a program for our lowest students using a group of volunteers to listen to students read and then assess their oral reading fluency. When exactly did fluency fall out of favor? Or has it always existed just below the instructional radar screen for teachers of beginning reading?

As low profile as reading fluency may seem to be, it is highly correlated (.80) with the ability to comprehend what is read (Fuchs, Fuchs, Hops, & Jenkins, 2001; Fuchs, Fuchs, & Maxwell, 1988). In fact, measures of oral reading fluency have been found to be *more* highly correlated with reading comprehension scores than were measures of silent reading rate in a sample of children whose reading skills varied across a broad range (Jenkins, Fuchs, Espin, van den Broek, & Deno, 2000). As students develop fluency in their oral reading, their comprehension scores will also improve (Calfee & Piontkowski, 1981). No wonder Anderson (1981) and Allington (1983) put so much stock in fluency. *Fluent oral readers* (given similar knowledge of the vocabulary and concepts in the text) are better able to understand what they read than are their dysfluent peers.

The National Research Council concluded, "Adequate progress in learning to read English (or any alphabetic language) beyond the initial level depends on *sufficient practice in reading to achieve fluency* [italics added] with different texts" (Snow et al., 1998, p. 223). The report also recommends that

> Because the ability to obtain meaning from print depends so strongly on the development of word recognition accuracy and reading fluency, both should be regularly assessed in the classroom, permitting *timely and effective instructional response* [italics added] when difficulty or delay is apparent. (p. 7)

FLUENCY PROBLEMS: THEIR CAUSES AND "CURES"

Lest you conclude that fluency problems are relatively rare—a concern for special education or remedial reading teachers to handle—consider the results of a large study of fluency achievement in the United States (Pinnell et al., 1995). Conducted as part of the National Assessment of Educational Progress, the study examined the fluency of a national sample of fourth-grade students. It found that 44% of students tested were dysfluent, even when reading grade-level stories that the students had already read under supportive testing conditions. Until you actually assess the oral reading fluency of your students, whatever their grade level, you will not know what part of their comprehension difficulties are actually the result of slow and inaccurate reading.

The Causes of Fluency Problems

Words . . . are the raw data of text. (Adams, 1998, p. 73)

Fluency difficulties are directly attributable to the inability of readers to identify words quickly and accurately (Lyon, 1995; Torgesen, Rashotte, & Alexander, 2001; Wise, Ring, & Olson, 1999). During the past two decades, research has provided educators with overwhelming evidence of the critical role that phonological awareness skills play in learning how to accurately identify words (Wagner, Torgesen, & Rashotte, 1994). Dysfluent or reading-disabled students are almost always phonologically deficient.

They may also have another problem, however. There has recently been a great deal of hypothesizing about a second deficit that affects many students' abilities to read fluently: visual naming speed, sometimes referred to as RAN or rapid automatic naming (Bowers, 1995; Bowers, Golden, Kennedy, & Young, 1994; Bowers & Wolf, 1993; Wolf, 1991, 2001). Some researchers have included visual naming speed under the broad umbrella of phonological awareness skills (Wagner et al., 1994; Wagner et al., 1997), whereas others have argued for what is called a "double deficit" hypothesis (Wolf & Bowers, 1999). There is evidence to suggest three types of disabled readers: (a) students with phonological processing difficulties, (b) students with naming-speed deficits, and (c) students with both phonological *and* speed problems (i.e., double deficits; Wolf, 1991). Any of these deficits can interfere with oral reading fluency.

Neurobiologists are further hypothesizing that the ability to name things quickly, RAN, may actually be a combination of many skills, among them a fast recognition reaction time to visual letters, words, or phrases (i.e., automaticity) as well as the anticipatory processing of those same stimuli (Wood, Flowers, & Grigorenko, 2001, p. 236). Researchers have found, for example, that readers will often stumble on a word they *know* if it is followed in the text by a word they do not know. Or conversely, readers will have no difficulty with that word if it is followed by a familiar word. This *anticipatory fluency* is thought by some to be as important to the act of comprehension as the actual recognition and identification of words in the text.

Still others (Stein, 2001; Stein & Talcott, 1999; Stein & Walsh, 1997) are calling for renewed attention to the role of vision in learning to read, hypothesizing that reading depends not only on the quality of the brain's processing of *auditory input* to determine the phonological structure of words but also on the brain's processing of *visual input* to acquire good orthographic skills.

The Identification, Prevention, and Remediation of Fluency Problems

The research of the past 20 years has focused intensively on *phonological awareness* and its critical importance in learning to read and has provided educators with a variety of options for the identification, prevention, and remediation of phonological awareness deficiencies (Torgesen & Mathes, 2000). The ideal scenario for students at risk for fluency problems (a child with either phonological awareness deficiencies, speed problems, or both of these deficits) would be for them to be enrolled in a classroom, school, or district where the identification and prevention of reading difficulties in kindergarten is a priority, where once a student has been identified, a systematic and explicit program of instruction begins (e.g., Adams et al., 1998; Lindamood & Lindamood, 1998; Torgesen & Bryant, 1993). This ideal setting for at-risk readers would provide training in terms of speeding up reaction times as well as phonological awareness instruction developed and delivered in consultation with the speech pathologist, special educators, and reading specialists. Students with naming-speed deficits (whether alone or in combination with phonological awareness deficiencies) are frequently misclassified as normal readers or provided with interventions that only address phonological problems (Manis & Freedman, 2001).

Essential to the prevention of fluency problems is the early identification and regular monitoring of any phonological or speed problems. Kame'enui, Simmons, Good, and Harn (2001) describe a comprehensive program using the dynamic indicators of basic early literacy (DIBELS; Kaminski & Good, 1996). The DIBELS probes differ from most phonological tests in that they include a speed (fluency) component along with the usual measures of letter naming, onset recognition, phonemic segmentation, and nonsense word recognition. For example, on the Letter Naming Fluency portion of the assessment, students are asked to name as many letters from a sheet of randomly ordered letters as they can in one minute (Kaminski & Good, 1996).

> ### MUST-READ BOOKS ABOUT READING FLUENCY
>
> Allington, R. L. (2001). *What Really Matters for Struggling Readers: Designing Research-Based Programs.* New York: Longman.
>
> Opitz, M. F., & Rasinski, T. V. (1998). *Goodbye Round Robin: 25 Effective Oral Reading Strategies.* Portsmouth, NH: Heinemann.
>
> Wolf, M. A. (Ed.). (2001). *Dyslexia, Fluency, and the Brain.* Timonium, MD: York.

The intervention options for students with a double deficit (phonological awareness deficits and speed difficulties) or just a speed deficit must feature specialized teaching designed to automatize students' skills (Fawcett & Nicolson, 2001; Kame'enui et al., 2001; Levy, 2001; Lovett, Steinbach, & Frijters, 2000; Torgesen, Rashotte, & Alexander, 2001; Wolf, Miller, & Donnelly, 2000). One such program, RAVE-O, (Segal & Wolf, 1993; Wolf & Segal, 1992) was designed as a small-group, intensive pull-out program for second and third graders to be used in conjunction with a phonological awareness training program. The first aspect of RAVE-O emphasizes repeated reading, as described later in the chapter. The second program component focuses on the development of increased processing speed or automaticity in vision-related processes, such as left-right scanning, letter recognition, orthographic pattern recognition, and faster initial and final phoneme and rime identification. RAVE-O uses a metacognitive approach to word retrieval similar to the Word Detectives program developed by Gaskins (1998a) for the Benchmark School and tested and refined over a 10-year period.

A second program that holds promise for helping students with more efficient visual processing is *Seeing Stars: Symbol Imagery for Sight Words and Spelling* (Bell, 1997). *Seeing Stars* focuses on the development of symbol imagery beginning with the visualization of individual letters and eventually dealing with contextual reading and spelling. Teachers work with students to image letters in words and apply that imagery to phonetic processing, sight words, spelling, and reading fluency. When word identification and reading fluency have not improved at the same rate as word attack skills, this program can often provide the missing piece in the learning-to-read puzzle.

Whether the underlying cause of impaired fluency is a phonological awareness deficit, a rapid-naming-speed problem, or a combination of both, students who are not identified immediately in preschool and kindergarten and who do not get the types and amounts of early instruction they need are certain to have problems with accurate and efficient word identification and hence with fluency. Fluency problems never fix themselves; they only get worse. Regrettably, even when the word accuracy and text comprehension skills of upper-grade readers with fluency problems are remediated, their fluency problems persist (Torgesen, Rashotte, et al., 2001). And even more disheartening—while their fluent peers are becoming voracious readers who read increasing quantities of text and acquire prodigious quantities of vocabulary and knowledge, dysfluent students fall farther and farther behind (Stanovich, 1986).

ASSESSING ORAL READING FLUENCY

Any plan to improve students' reading fluency must be grounded in regular and objective assessment. Whenever I give workshops that include the topic of reading fluency—how to measure, develop, and remediate it—educators have lots of questions. I have anticipated some of yours and provide answers to them just ahead.

Why Measure Oral Reading Fluency?

There is no other classroom assessment that is as simple, quick, and sensitive to the smallest incremental changes in reading ability as a measure of oral reading fluency. If students improve by at least one to two words weekly in the number of "words correct per minute" they can read, teachers can be certain progress is being made in fluency and usually also in comprehension (given good listening comprehension skills). On the other hand, if a child's oral reading fluency remains unchanged, even after several weeks of intense instruction and practice, that child needs further diagnostic tests to determine what kind of additional instruction may be needed. Measures of oral reading fluency have powerful predictive value in identifying students who need help or, conversely, in confirming that students are making progress in their abilities to read. For example, Good, Simmons, and Kame'enui (2001) found that 96% of the students who met or exceeded a third-grade oral reading fluency benchmark also met or exceeded expectations on the Oregon Statewide Assessment, a high-stakes outcome measure. Keep in mind that a test of oral reading fluency measures progress or lack thereof. It cannot explain *why* a child is not making progress.

How Is Oral Reading Fluency Measured?

Oral reading fluency is measured by asking a student to orally read an appropriate passage about 250 words in length. Estimates of a text's grade level can be ascertained by using one of the following: (a) a readability formula (Chall & Dale, 1995), (b) classroom materials that have been graded by a publisher, or (c) a standardized measure of oral reading fluency (e.g., the *Multilevel Academic Skills Inventory*; Howell, Zucker, & Morehead, 1994) that contains several testing selections for each grade level. If you are using passages from your own curriculum materials, select those that have minimal dialogue and no unusual names or words. If students are reading well below their actual grade level, select text that is at their independent reading level.

Prepare two copies of the passage—one for the student and one for the examiner. On the examiner's copy, indicate the number of words in each line. Use a stopwatch to time the student's reading. When 1 minute has passed, make a double slash mark after the last word read and stop the student. Different tests use different scoring methods, but generally, omissions, insertions, and self-corrections are *not* counted as errors. Substitutions and incorrectly identified words *are* counted as errors. The score that counts is the *number of words read correctly in 1 minute*. Subtract the errors and substitutions from the total number of words to determine the number of words read correctly.

A supplement to measuring oral reading fluency through *passage reading* should also include the periodic assessment of the accuracy and speed of a student's *word identification* skills (for both actual and nonsense words). The TOWRE (Test of Word-Reading Efficiency; Torgesen, Wagner, & Rashotte, 1999), although similar to the word-reading subtests of major test batteries (e.g., Woodcock Reading Mastery Tests-Revised, Woodcock, 1987; or the Wide Range Achievement Test-Third Edition, Wilkinson, 1995), measures an additional component that is critical to fluency—speed of identification.

What Is an Acceptable Level of Oral Reading Fluency?

Oral reading fluency is a combination of accuracy *and* rate. The fluency score is reported as *words correct per minute*. To consider either accuracy or rate by itself is a meaningless exercise. For example, students who makes no errors but read very slowly have as little likelihood of comprehending what they read as students who read very quickly but guess at and misidentify many words. According to Hasbrouk and Tindal's (1992) norms, second-grade students scoring at the 75th percentile read 82 words correct per minute in the fall of the school year, whereas those same students, read 124 words correct per minute in the spring. In the fifth grade, students at the 75th percentile read 126 words correct per minute in the fall and 151 words correct per minute in the spring. Note that even in the upper grades, students who are progressing in reading continue to increase the number of words correct per minute that they score. Although different authors and tests suggest varying target rates for students in grades one through six, based in part on differences in the difficulty of passages used and the variety of administration procedures, a score of 40 to 44 words correct per minute or less in the fall of second grade definitely flags a student who is at risk of reading failure (Davidson, 2000). The minimum acceptable oral reading fluency rate for instructional purposes in grade-appropriate texts suggested by Lovitt and Hansen (1976) is 80 words per minute with two or fewer errors.

Is There a Ceiling for Oral Reading Fluency?

Reading fluency rates continue to be an excellent indicator of reading proficiency, including comprehension abilities, through sixth grade. Once a student has reached an oral reading fluency rate of 140 correct words per minute, however, the question of rate is moot. Faster at this point is not better. When students are able to read very rapidly as well as accurately, they focus their attention on improving expressiveness, voice projection, and clarity of speech in their oral reading.

What Is the Difference Between a Test of Oral Reading Fluency and a Running Record?

A running record is a record of errors or miscues that readers make as they are reading. Marie Clay (1985) developed running records as a way for teachers to assess their students' reading behaviors. Some teachers take running records on students as part of measuring oral reading fluency; however, a running record per se *does not* measure *reading speed*. Although running records are excellent for determining the problems of individual students or identifying the strategies they are using to identify words, they do not provide the *objective* measure of reading progress that is provided by the oral reading fluency measure. To measure fluency, compute the number of *correct words per minute*.

TARGET RATES FOR READING FLUENCY IN WORDS CORRECT PER MINUTE

Grade	January	May
1	52	71
2	73	82
3	107	115
4	115	118
5	129	134
6[a]	120	131

SOURCE: Adapted from Marston and Magnusson (1988).

a. The lower scores at the sixth-grade level compared to the fifth-grade level are attributed to the increased difficulty in sixth-grade material.

HOW TO DEVELOP READING FLUENCY

Fluency development for the majority of students first means making certain they have acquired the appropriate phonemic decoding skills and then giving them continuous opportunities to practice those skills through reading a lot in text at their independent reading level: (a) orally and repeatedly with peers and parents, (b) along with their teachers in guided reading sessions, and (c) on their own in smaller amounts of silent reading that gradually increase in length of time as reading competence increases. The process sounds quite simple, but in reality, it takes highly effective teachers to make it happen in a classroom of 20-plus students.

In most classrooms, a few students will "take off" in reading and develop fluency readily without any special training. Encourage these students to read voraciously, and hold them accountable for what they read. Other students will quickly transition from needing to do several repeated oral readings to only one or two and then to almost exclusive silent reading. Still others will need a structured repeated-reading program that may extend throughout an entire school year, the summer, and on to the next school year. A few students will need all of the above and more.

In summary, students need to (a) learn lots of sight words well, (b) engage in repeated oral reading of connected text at appropriate independent levels, and (c) read a lot of different kinds of text in lots of different ways at both home and school.

Learn Lots of Sight Words Well

Students whose fluency difficulties are the result of a double deficit will require intensive drill and practice with the 1,000 most frequent words until they become rapid-fire sight words (Fry, Kress, & Fountoukidis, 2000, pp. 47–53). Sight words are those words that, although originally phonemically decoded by the reader, have been read so frequently they are now read fluently, although *not* without attention to the letters in the word. We know that practice in reading single words leads to increased fluency when those words are later found in the text (Levy, 2001; Levy, Abello, & Lysynchuk, 1997; Tan & Nicholson, 1997) and that many words can be learned through simple flash card recognition. More challenging words may need to be written several times after their introduction to draw attention to their spellings. There are many enjoyable games that can be played with flash cards as long as the games are efficient and provide lots of repetitions of the word per session. Isolated word practice permits the teacher, parent, or tutor to build in more word repetitions per unit of time than can be achieved with repeated readings. Students with a double deficit are particularly vulnerable to dysfluent text reading, and they need intensive and systematic help with both the visual *and* the auditory aspects of word recognition (Levy, 2001).

Engage in Repeated Oral Reading of Connected Text

Students have achieved fluency in the reading of a word when they can identify it automatically in less than 1 second. How many "sounding-outs" of a word does it take to reach that kind of speed? The answer is different for each student. Some students may need only three of four readings to store a word solidly in their long-term memory for automatic retrieval. They will not need to read the same text repeatedly. Urge these students to read more books and increasingly more challenging books (both fiction and nonfiction)—taking care to monitor their fluency at regular intervals. Other students may need upwards of 10 to 15 repetitions of a word to master it. They will benefit from repeated oral readings of familiar text. The students who are *most* at risk of reading failure may need up to 30 repetitions of a word before it becomes automatic. These students must orally reread text that is at their independent levels many times to gain the fluency they need to become literate. You will find a variety of ways to structure repeated readings just ahead. Also worth investigating are two programs to develop fluency: *Great Leaps* (Mercer & Campbell, 2001) and *Read Naturally* (Hasbrouck, Ihnot & Rogers, 1999; Hasbrouck, Ihnot & Woldbeck, 1997; Ihnot, 1995, 2001).

The National Reading Panel (2000) chose to investigate fluency as part of its comprehensive review of reading research and concluded that "repeated reading and other procedures that have students reading passages orally multiple times while receiving guidance or feedback from peers, parents, or teachers are effective in improving a variety of reading skills" (sec. 3, p. 20). The Panel went on to explain that "these procedures are not particularly difficult to use; nor do they require lots of special equipment or materials" (sec. 3, p. 20).

Could it be that something as important as fluency can be developed or remediated by a practice as inexpensive and old-fashioned as repeated reading? Absolutely. After all, repeated reading was a staple of 17th-century American and European reading instruction. Hornbooks, the catechism, and Biblical text were reread orally by older students as their younger peers followed along until they could chime in (Samuels, 1979, p. 408). Educators have much to learn about the power of repetition, not only from the past but also from contemporary expert musicians and sports figures. These gifted performers have always appreciated the value of repetition to develop fluency and automaticity. Musicians know that if they want to free their working memories to focus on their interpretation of a Mozart sonata or a Bach invention, their fingers need to move automatically and fluently over the keyboard. Basketball and football players know that it is only when diagrammed plays are well rehearsed and even overlearned that they can be executed flawlessly. Practice does indeed make perfect.

HOW TO CHOOSE TEXT FOR REPEATED ORAL READING

Choose a selection of about 50 to 100 words that is on the students' *independent* reading level, (the highest level at which students can read without assistance, with few errors in word recognition, and with good comprehension and recall). All too frequently, students are given text to read which is at their *frustration* level. At this level, students' reading skills break down, their fluency disappears, errors in word recognition are numerous, comprehension is faulty, recall is sketchy, and signs of emotional tension and discomfort become evident (Harris & Sipay, 1985).

Time students' reading of the sample and note the number of correct words and the number of errors. If students take more than 2 minutes to read a passage or make more than 5 errors, the passage is too difficult. If students can read a passage at 85 words per minute with two or fewer errors, then the passage is too easy. Choose a more difficult one.

If a passage is deemed suitable for repeated reading practice, then go over any errors that were made. Ask students to repeatedly read the chosen passage until they are confident in their reading, (they can read more quickly and fluently then they could at the beginning of their practice). The practice can take several forms, including reading orally to oneself, listening to an audiotape while reading along and then reading orally without the tape, or reading the selection orally to an adult or peer. Always take note of the correct words per minute. Teachers, aides, volunteers, or older students themselves can graph their progress over time on a chart. The goal is that students will improve their fluency in reading challenging material to at least 85 words correct per minute before moving on to a new passage (Gunning, 1998, p. 202).

WHAT DOES REAL READING LOOK LIKE?

Real reading is taking place when students are identifying words independently, either by means of phonemic decoding or through the rapid identification of a sight word. Although the following literacy activities are beneficial for students in the pre-reading stage, they do not count as real reading in the classroom because they do not provide the kind of reading practice that builds fluency: (a) rereading and memorizing predictable big books; (b) listening to adults read stories aloud to them; (c) writing predictable books as a class, based on predictable books that have been read aloud; (d) looking at pictures in books; (e) drawing pictures about stories that have been read aloud to them; (f) dramatizing books; (g) sharing student-authored books; and (h) creating language experience charts. To become fluent readers, students *must read a lot on their own.* They must personally process the text, practice unfamiliar words until they are stored in memory, and reread the same text repeatedly and orally to improve fluency. Each student will move through the stages from slowly sounding out and blending words to fluent silent reading on a slightly different timetable, but there are far too many students who will never achieve fluent reading because they do not do nearly enough real reading.

The theoretical rationale for repeated reading emerged from the theory of automatic information processing in reading (LaBerge & Samuels, 1974; Samuels, 1976). The distinguishing attribute of fluent readers, according to this theory, is their automaticity. Skilled readers recognize words so effortlessly *and* so quickly, their working memories are available for the real purpose of reading—constructing meaning from the text (Kiss & Savage, 1977).

For students who are at risk of falling through the cracks, fluency development is extraordinarily important. Unfortunately, students who need the *most* reading practice actually don't get very much of it during an average school day, compared to their more accomplished peers (Allington, 1977). Children in low reading groups read as few as 16 words in a week, while their "linguistically rich" classmates in higher reading groups read as many as 1,933 words per week (Allington, 1984). Teachers in the primary grades *cannot* assume that fluency will develop for all or even most of their students in the absence of a structured and well-monitored program that includes not only repeated oral reading but also reading a lot in a variety of other ways.

Read a Lot of Different Kinds of Text in Lots of Different Ways at Both Home and School

Dysfluent students need other kinds of reading experiences in addition to their twice-daily dosage of repeated oral reading (one taken before lunch at school and a second taken before bedtime at home). They also need daily experiences in the oral reading of new and interesting text at a somewhat challenging instructional level. During this guided reading period, errors should be judiciously corrected (not every error, but the ones for which some productive lesson can be learned). Keep track of difficult words, and add some of them to the sight word learning list, but first priority must go to developing automaticity with the 1,000-most-frequent-words list. Last, even the most dysfluent students need 10 to 15 minutes of daily practice reading text silently. Children must read as much as they can fit into their waking hours during early elementary school to build a solid foundation of fluency, vocabulary, and knowledge. And they must do far more "real" reading in their classrooms than they currently do. See the sidebar on p. 58 on real reading.

Just reading at school is *never* enough, however. Students *must* read voraciously, voluminously, and voluntarily outside of school as well (Shefelbine, 1999). Teachers and principals must communicate early and often to parents regarding the importance of engaging in ample amounts of repeated oral reading at home just as soon as a child acquires beginning decoding skills. Educators and parents need to support each other's efforts in this endeavor. Parents are often held hostage by big-screen TV's, computers, and interactive computer games. They must have the courage to disconnect these mind-numbing appliances that are often used as baby-sitters and make themselves available to listen to their children read aloud to them, to read aloud to their children, and to sit side by side in the same room, each reading independently. Parents often have other priorities for their children that crowd out time for reading, such as sports, music, and religious activities, but educators must relentlessly advance the cause of literacy through their words, actions, and writings (McEwan, 1999). We cannot depend solely on presidential spouses or basketball stars to get the message out. We must be relentless champions for reading a lot.

HOW MANY BOOKS SHOULD A BEGINNING READER READ?

This question sounds a little like a tongue twister if you say it very fast six times, but it is a serious question, and the answer you give may make the difference between nurturing fluent readers or fostering failure in your classroom, school, or district. Unless students are provided with a *sufficient* supply of *decodable books* in which to practice their word identification skills, they will not have the opportunity to become fluent readers. The following guidelines were adapted from the California Department of Education's (2001) Criteria for 2002 Language Arts Adoption.

Sufficient predecodable and decodable texts must be provided at the early stages of reading instruction to allow students to develop automaticity and fluency. Those materials designated by the publisher as decodable must have at least 75% (85% in the state of Texas) of the words composed solely of previously taught sound-spelling correspondences and from 15% to 20% of the words compose of previously taught high-frequency words and story words. High-frequency words introduced in predecodable and decodable texts should be taken from a list of the most commonly used words in English, prioritized by their utility. *Sufficient* is defined as follows:

Kindergarten

- At least 15 predecodable books (i.e., small books used to teach simple, beginning, high frequency words usually coupled with rebus)
- Approximately 20 decodable books, integrated with the sequence of instruction

First Grade

- Two decodable books per sound-spelling correspondence totaling a minimum of 8000 words of decodable text over the course of the school year with the ability to reproduce copies of the texts for students to take home (California Department of Education, 2001)

If you are looking for additional decodable readers to supplement your current reading program, Resource A contains a comprehensive list of published phonics readers.

A DOZEN PLUS WAYS TO DO
REPEATED ORAL READING

There are many ways to structure repeated oral reading in your classroom. Do not assume that older students or even more proficient students will not benefit from repeated oral reading of text.

The Neurological Impress Method

The neurological impress method (NIM) was originally used after World War II to teach brain-damaged adults to read again and was first described in 1969 by Heckelmann. To implement NIM, the tutor sits slightly behind the student and reads aloud into the student's ear. Some practitioners of NIM recommend sitting nearest the ear that corresponds to the hand with which the student writes or eats. The tutor and student share a book, with the tutor holding one corner of the book and the student holding the opposite one. The tutor and the student read with one voice, so to speak, with the tutor's speed slightly exceeding the student's normal rate so that the student is forced to pay attention to whole words and sentences to keep up with the tutor. The tutor tracks words by running a forefinger under them while reading. After several *joint* oral readings of the text, the student then begins to lead the reading while the tutor guides the student's finger smoothly under the words as they are read. The tracking responsibility is also gradually given over to the student after repeated readings of the same text. When a specific passage can be read at the selected target rate (usually 85 correct words per minute), a new, slightly more difficult passage should be selected. NIM is also referred to as *duet reading* (Heckelman, 1969).

Cross-Age Reading

Older readers who may be reluctant to engage in enough repeated oral readings of text at their instructional level to reach an 85-words-per-minute goal will usually jump at the chance to read aloud to younger students. In preparation for their read-aloud sessions, older readers must first engage in several repeated readings of their books without an audience and then read them aloud to as many listeners as they can find. Provide older readers with accountability forms on which the parents or teachers of younger students can sign off after the read-alouds are completed. Debrief with older readers following each set of read-aloud sessions regarding how their reading fluency improved between the first read-aloud and the last (Labbo & Teale, 1990).

Taped Reading

In this version of repeated oral reading, students read short passages (at their independent reading level) aloud once or twice and then record the passage via a tape recorder. The tapes are then replayed, and students follow along with the text and monitor their oral reading. Students then record the passage again and listen for improvement. Students continue to read, record, and monitor their recording as often as needed to reach their goals.

Paired Reading With a Parent, Older Student, Sibling, or Tutor

This technique involves a family member, volunteer, or older student pairing with a dysfluent reader. Listening to repeated oral readings of text is a perfect assignment for senior or parent volunteers. Use the guidelines given earlier for choosing the text to be repeatedly read, or investigate commercially available programs, such as *Read Naturally* (Ihnot, 2001) or *Great Leaps* (Mercer & Campbell, 2001). Tutors and readers can first read the text aloud together (shared reading). When students feel confident about reading on their own, they can then read the passage orally several times. Paired-reading contracts in which older siblings or parents agree to do repeated readings with students are a powerful way to make sure that students with fluency problems get adequate oral reading practice at home.

Paired Reading With a Peer

Paired reading with a peer is a variation of repeated reading in which peer partners who are on or about the same reading level each read a short passage aloud three to five times and then evaluate both their own and their partners' reading. The paired students take turns reading orally and keeping a record of the errors and time elapsed for their partner's reading (Koskinen & Blum, 1986).

Echo Reading

A parent, tutor, older student, or teacher orally reads the first line of the text, and the student then reads the same line, modeling the tutor's example. The tutor and the student read in echo fashion for the entire passage, gradually increasing the amount of text that either the tutor or the student reads at one time. The tutor should gradually increase the reading speed to push the student to identify words more quickly. Students can also do echo reading with peers who are more accomplished readers.

Do You Read Me?

This is just another name for assisted repeated reading in which students read orally, along with a commercial or volunteer-made tape that corresponds to a selected passage or book. Some schools set up an area in the media center for what they call *automatic reading* where students read along with a tape several times daily until they can read the story smoothly by themselves. Closely monitor the first few readings, however. Some commercially prepared tapes are read aloud at speeds that are too fast for dysfluent readers. The preparation of tapes using slightly slower readers may prove to be what is needed (Dowhower, 1989).

Choral Reading

Choral reading is the simultaneous oral reading of text by a small group or class of students. The text must be displayed on an overhead projector or everyone must have their own copy. Choral reading is an excellent way to give dysfluent students experience with more challenging text without the risk of embarrassment. Choose a poem or famous speech and read it repeatedly with the class over several days until the fluency, expression, and diction are near perfect. Then invite a guest to hear students perform before choosing another selection to prepare for performance (Miccinati, 1985).

Readers' Theatre

This method of repeated reading enables students to participate in the reading of a play without the props, scenery, and endless rehearsals. Students do not memorize lines or wear costumes. They just repeatedly read their parts orally in preparation for the "performance." Play tapes of old radio shows to show students how powerful text can be when read fluently and with appropriate expression (Opitz & Rasinski, 1998).

Take It Home

Form partnerships with parents as early as possible in the school year. Invite them to school for a repeated-reading training session in which teachers demonstrate how to do repeated reading and how to measure oral reading fluency. Share research with parents that demonstrates how powerful repeated reading is and ask them to contract with teachers to listen to their child do 10 to 15 minutes of repeated reading three to five times per week combined with reading aloud more challenging text to their children. Many teachers have seen their students realize enormous growth in oral reading fluency when they enlist parents as their partners in achieving this goal (Topping, 1987).

Fluency Development Lesson

Fluency development lesson is a combination of reading aloud, choral reading, listening to students read, and reading performance and is implemented over an extended period. Students first listen to the teacher read a poem or other text to the class. They then read the text chorally, pair up and practice reading the text with a classmate, and then perform for an interested audience (Rasinski, Padak, Linke, & Sturdevant, 1994).

Keeping Track

This method of repeated reading involves having students graph their own oral reading fluency scores over a period of time. As older students become familiar with the process, they can work with a partner to do the timing and error counting. When students assess and monitor their own fluency, they are

---

THE CASE OF THE HIGHLY MOTIVATED DYSFLUENT READER

It's not often that reading specialist, Jan Price, works one-on-one with students any-more. Her current job description now includes consultative work and staff develop-ment on top of teaching classes all day. So she was surprised when a fourth grader knocked on her office door at recess time asking for help. "He had sort of a hang dog look," she says, "and I couldn't refuse to see him." It was March, and Jason told Jan he was worried about his reading. He didn't have a label, and he hadn't been referred, but he knew where he stood. "I felt so sorry for him that I squeezed him in between all of my other commitments that day," Jan related. She checked on his status before the appoint-ment and discovered that in October, Jason's oral reading fluency was abysmally low—27 words per minute (85 words correct per minute is the minimum for comprehending text). Now, it was March, and although his fluency had improved somewhat, it was still very low (50 words per minute).

Jan was intrigued by a student who was motivated enough to seek her out, and she couldn't refuse his plea for help. She talked at length with Jason about exactly what he would have to do, explained that it would take a lot of oral reading to improve his fluency, but that he could definitely get better before June. She suggested that he set a goal and agreed to give him passages to read at home and to test him every other day. Then, she asked him what his goal would be. After reviewing Jan's chart for district standards, Jason boldly ventured a goal of 118 words per minute by June. Jan was a bit dubious about what she perceived to be a highly unrealistic goal, but Jason was resolute. It was 118 words per minute, and that was that.

During the warm spring months when other students were enjoying the lengthening evening hours out of doors, Jason was inside doing a lot of repeated oral reading. In the beginning, Jan provided Jason with short passages on which to practice. He stopped by without fail every other day to be tested and to have his new rate posted on a graph that Jan hung on her office wall. He decided his progress would be even faster if he started reading book chapters aloud repeatedly and began stopping by the library to find things to read. The increase in his oral reading fluency was gradual, but it moved steadily upward. Jason's mother contacted his teacher; she couldn't believe the change in her son. He was bringing home books to read every afternoon and reading voraciously every evening. She had never seen him so motivated to read and wondered what was behind this frenzy of reading activity. Jan explained Jason's goal and how committed he was to reaching it. His mother got in the act, offering her support and encouragement every day. By June, Jason was reading over 130 correct words per minute. His oral reading rate shot off the charts. Jason not only exceeded the "impossible" goal he set for himself but, in the process, also discovered the pleasure and enjoyment that comes from reading.

---

highly motivated to work harder for increased fluency. Take time to read about The Case of the Highly Motivated Dysfluent Reader.

Radio Reading

In radio reading, students independently practice selected portions of the text ahead of time by reading them orally as often as needed to develop expres-sion and fluency. This type of repeated reading can be used in lieu of the teacher reading aloud to students. Small groups of students work together and prepare sections of a chapter to be read chorally. More proficient students might read parts of the chapter solo. Assign one student to be the announcer who reads the opening and closing portions of the chapter (Searfoss, 1975).

Read Around

This method of repeated reading is best used with older students. Students choose a favorite part of a story or book they particularly like; rehearse it until they read it fluently; and then read it for peers, a small group, or the entire class. Students can choose poetry, narrative text, or even the lyrics of a song they particularly like (be sure to have the lyrics preapproved by the teacher). Read Around can be a required activity or offered as an optional opportunity for students once or twice a week (Tompkins, 1998).

Teacher Modeling and Repeated Reading

Teacher modeling and repeated reading (TMRR) combines a number of features from previously mentioned variations of repeated reading. In TMRR, students first read their selected passage orally to a partner or teacher for 1 minute and determine the number of correct words per minute. Next, students read along silently while listening to an audiotape of the passage that models correct expression and phrasing. Using a 1-minute timer, students then repeatedly read the passage until able to read it at a predetermined goal rate. Last, the teacher monitors the students' final reading of the passage determining the words correct per minute, and students graph the number of words read correctly *before* practicing and words read correctly *during* the final testing (Ihnot, 1995).

SUMMARIZING CHAPTER 4

Repeated oral reading is a powerful tool to build fluency in readers of all ages. The "ability to read connected text rapidly, smoothly, effortlessly, and automatically with little conscious attention to the mechanics of reading such as decoding" (Meyer & Felton, 1999, p. 284) is not a reading skill that can be taken for granted. With the current emphasis on silent reading, many students fall through the cracks at precisely this point in developing literacy. Measuring oral reading fluency and then using repeated oral reading to develop fluency in dysfluent students is an essential piece of the reading puzzle.

LOOKING AHEAD

In Chapter 5, we will add three more pieces to our puzzle: *language, knowledge,* and *cognitive strategies.* Although we are putting the pieces of the reading puzzle together in a step-by-step fashion, do not forget that in balanced literacy instruction at every grade level, all of the pieces of the puzzle are being assembled simultaneously every day of the school year.

5

The Meaning Pieces

Language, Knowledge, and Cognitive Strategies

From third grade onward, Eliza's class is divided into math and reading groups. Eliza's reading group is called the Racecars. She likes it okay until she learns that the other reading group is called the Rockets. The Rockets read from a paperback that has The Great Books printed on its cover in gallant letters. When she asks Jared Montgomery what's inside, he tells her that his group is reading excerpts from 'the canon,' and Eliza feels too stupid to ask if that means something other than a large gun. She can't help but wonder if someone told her which books were great and which ones were just so-so, if she'd like reading more.

—Goldberg, 2000, p. 7

Comprehension, the ability to construct meaning from text, is the *sine qua non* of reading. In an annual rite of spring, millions of students across the country pour over graded reading passages, answer multiple-choice questions, and write short essays—all in the name of assessing their skills in comprehending what they read, both as individuals and collectively. Kids are sorted, teachers are evaluated, schools are ranked, and districts are labeled. As students progress through school, the passages get longer, the words become harder, the content is more challenging, and the time limits grow more stringent. The basic question never changes, however: How well do our students actually understand what they read?

Having the mechanics of decoding—being able to accurately and automatically identify words—is a necessary but insufficient skill to gain meaning, the ultimate goal of reading. The precipitous drop in reading achievement that many students experience at the upper grade levels, even though they know how to decode and are able to read primary-grade-level text fluently, should alarm all educators who are working with at-risk students. Without the meaning pieces of the reading puzzle—*language, knowledge,* and *cognitive strategies*—even those students who know how to read will continue to fall through the cracks in large numbers.

During the workshops I give on cognitive-strategy instruction, I display five different one-page reading samples on the overhead projector and give the participants a few minutes to look over each sample. Then, I ask them which one they would like to use for a comprehension test to determine their upcoming salary. They laugh nervously, not sure how serious I am, but they always select the two samples that contain the easiest and most familiar (to them) reading material. If the participants know anything about history or read a lot of nonfiction, they invariably choose the sample from *D-Day: The Climactic Battle of World War II* by Stephen Ambrose (1994). Those who teach literature or enjoy reading fiction usually opt for the excerpt from *Treasure Island* by Robert Louis Stevenson (1911). The other text samples are drawn from the disciplines of philosophy, economics, and linguistics. Even the most skilled readers in the workshop aren't eager to read these samples; they are packed with unfamiliar vocabulary and foreign concepts.

The participants breathe a sigh of relief when they realize I am just kidding about the comprehension test. Their relief turns to anxiety, however, when they realize that the next activity does involve reading one of the samples that no one chose—a philosophy text. Many of these fluent readers are initially paralyzed by the incomprehensibility of the text. They immediately realize they will need far more than fluent word identification skills to navigate *this* reading assignment.

First, they need to figure out the meanings of a number of unfamiliar words and phrases. Second, they need to access knowledge from several different domains—Latin, fairy tales, Biblical literature, law, as well as a smattering of French and English history. But even extensive vocabulary and domain knowledge do not provide all that the readers need to construct meaning from the passage. Even those who have extensive vocabularies and a depth of background knowledge experience frustration with the text because it is "inconsiderate" and dense. At this point, the participants need to draw on their knowledge of the critical cognitive strategies.

The strategic readers stand out in their respective cooperative groups. They reread, ask questions, think-aloud, and are highly motivated to "get it." They use a variety of strategies to construct meaning from the text and are confident in their abilities to understand. Perfetti, Marron, and Foltz (1996) point out that a reader's willingness to expend effort at deep comprehension is critical to gaining meaning from challenging text (p. 159). Skilled readers demonstrate a desire and motivation to work at comprehension. Unskilled readers waste time and distract their colleagues with complaints about the assignment. Some of them lack what Perfetti calls "good habits of intellect"—the willingness to be active, engaged readers.

I include this exercise in the workshop for several reasons, not the least of which is to show teachers that if they are unwilling or unable to use cognitive strategies in their own reading and study, they will be unable to model and teach them to their students. This exercise also reveals the critical role that language abilities, domain knowledge, and cognitive strategies play in gaining meaning from what is read, particularly when the text is challenging.

Those of us who have worked in schools serving high percentages of at-risk students are depressingly familiar with what often happens to "linguistically poor" and "academically deprived" students once they leave the cocoon of the primary grades. If these students are not consistently, directly, and intensively provided with an academic environment that is filled with language, knowledge, and the modeling of cognitive strategies (habits of the mind), their hard-won achievement gains from the primary grades will begin to fade as they struggle to handle the demands of more difficult upper-grade texts. Low-SES students, racial and ethnic minority students, and non-native-English-speaking students are especially hard-hit by both "linguistic poverty" (Moats, 2001, p. 8) and academic deprivation.

Linguistic poverty, as defined by Moats (2001), includes partial knowledge of word meanings, confusion regarding words that sound similar but that contrast in one or two phonemes, limited knowledge of how and when words are typically used, and knowledge of only one meaning or function of a word when it has several. I have coined the term *academic deprivation* to describe the lack of opportunities that students have had to learn academic habits and skills by observing competent adults (whether parents, siblings, or teachers). Students need a wide range of opportunities to serve cognitive apprenticeships in both reading and writing (Schoenbach, Greenleaf, Cziko, & Hurwitz, 1999) through observing the behaviors and listening to the thinking aloud of skilled practitioners. Only then will they acquire the strategies and have the confidence to tackle difficult reading assignments.

There is also a third way in which students at risk of falling through the cracks are impoverished—in the area that E. D. Hirsch (1989) calls *cultural literacy*—knowledge about subjects such as mythology, geography, history, medicine, science, folk and fairy tales, poetry, and the arts. Without this kind of domain-specific knowledge, students will find understanding more challenging texts to be very difficult.

If students have learned to read, can read fluently, and then fail to acquire the language, knowledge, and cognitive strategies necessary to read for personal and academic gain, the results are particularly tragic. Unfortunately, few classroom teachers view themselves as linguistic and cognitive specialists, nor do they always have the instructional expertise to develop language skills, enrich domain knowledge in a variety of disciplines, and facilitate the acquisition of a tool kit of cognitive strategies. However, unless educators at every grade level and in every content area are able to assemble these pieces of the reading puzzle, the students they worked so hard to keep from falling through the cracks in first and second grade will disappear into an academic Bermuda Triangle—this time, for good.

LANGUAGE

Language, the first of the three meaning pieces of the reading puzzle, is multifaceted and for purposes of our discussion will be defined as (a) the meanings of words (lexicon), (b) how words are put together in utterances to convey a message (semantics and syntax), and (c) how discourse, or conversational interaction of various kinds, is carried out (Menyuk, 1999, p. 2). Menyuk also includes another aspect of language in her definition—the speech-sound system (phonology) —but I have covered that one already in Chapter 3.

I originally chose the word *vocabulary* to label this piece of the puzzle, but I was frustrated by the limitations of focusing solely on the meanings of words. *Language* involves a much broader set of understandings and skills. Putting the *language* piece of the puzzle in place in classrooms, schools, and districts involves the following five steps:

1. Helping students understand how language works (i.e., teaching the conventions of grammar in speech and writing in age-appropriate ways)

2. Providing continuous and excellent conversational, reading, and writing models for students to emulate

3. Continually expanding students' vocabulary through reading aloud, using new words during instruction and in conversation with students, directly teaching the meanings of new words, and exposing students to a wide variety of challenging texts

4. Developing a knowledge base of word parts and foreign language cognates to which students can turn to figure out or remember the meanings of unfamiliar words

5. Showing students the myriad ways in which language is constructed in texts—understanding story grammar in narrative texts or how a discussion of cause and effect would be presented in a piece of expository text

To reach these five instructional goals in preschool and early elementary school, students need consistent, intensive, and systematic language development. Then, teachers in Grades 4 through 12 must be language developers in the context of their various academic disciplines. To teach students who are at risk of falling through the cracks means being a *language teacher* in addition to being a *science*, *history*, or *math* teacher. Every discipline from physics to physical education has a distinctive vocabulary and way of communicating. These languages must be directly taught to students as if they were learning foreign languages.

Language Development in the Primary Grades

One of the biggest hurdles that educators face in *teaching them ALL to read* has to do with the huge differences in language development that exist between various subpopulations of students. White and Watts (1973) were among the earliest researchers to contrast the home environments of advantaged and disadvantaged children, noting the marked differences in the amount of conversation directed to children in one environment as compared to the other. When parents or day care providers seriously engage in dialogue with language-learning preschoolers, children develop language more rapidly. On the other hand, lack of dialogue delays language development.

In a later study of language in the home, Wells (1985) found a significant correlation between the total amount of talking adults do with children and the quality and gains in their language over time. In *Meaningful Differences in the Everyday Experiences of Young American Children*, Hart and Risley (1995) present the most comprehensive picture to date of the gap that exists in language experiences between advantaged and disadvantaged children:

> To illustrate the differences in the amount of children's language experience using numbers, rather than just *more* and *less*, we can derive an estimate based simply on words heard per hour. The longitudinal data showed that in the everyday interactions at home, the average (rounded) number of words children heard per hour was 2,150 in the professional families, 1,250 in working-class families, and 620 in welfare families. . . . Given the consistency we saw in the data, we might venture to extrapolate to the first 3 years of life. By age 3 the children in professional families would have heard more than 30 million words, the children in working class families 20 million words, and the children in welfare families, 10 million. (p. 131)

By the end of first grade, the word knowledge differences between linguistically rich and linguistically poor students amount to about 15,000 words. Linguistically rich first graders know the meanings of approximately 20,000 words, whereas their linguistically poor peers know the meanings of only about 5,000 words. Although we can teach most linguistically poor students how to read using best instructional practices, and although we can enable them to read and understand primary text with strong instructional support, the durability of their achievements is suspect (Chall, Jacobs, & Baldwin, 1990; Moats, 2001) unless we provide ongoing language development.

In a highly informative snapshot of how language development differs as a function of SES and ethnicity, Shirley Brice Heath (1983) describes how parents in a lower-socioeconomic-class African American community (Trackton) emphasized nonverbal communication much more than did their counterparts in Roadville (a lower-socioeconomic-class white community) and Gateway (a middle-socioeconomic-class white community). Although the children of Trackton gained the literacy skills they needed to survive in their own community, they were far less likely to gain the verbal skills needed to be successful in reading and in the academic world of school. Louisa Moats (2001) reminds educators that

> Early instruction in phoneme awareness is only the first layer of the direct language teaching necessary for children at risk. From the time they enter preschool, students must experience language stimulation all day long if they are to compensate for their incoming linguistic differences. Teachers must immerse them in the rich language of books. Children need to rehearse the rules of discourse, such as staying on topic, taking turns, and giving enough information so the listener understands. Children must learn how to speak in discussion, to question, paraphrase, retell and summarize. Teachers must teach directly the form, meaning, and use of words, phrases, sentences and texts. (p. 9)

Language development is inextricably linked to reading success (Biemiller, 1999), and educators must intentionally develop language skills, both oral and written, in preschool and early elementary students. Research reveals that we should

- Read *challenging* stories aloud to students multiple times, explaining the meanings of up to three new words before each reading (Feitelson, Kita, & Goldstein, 1986; Senechal, 1997).
- Confine discussions and explanations about a story to before and after reading it aloud. Before oral reading, however, make predictions about the story, explain new vocabulary, and activate prior knowledge. After the story, provide opportunities for child-initiated talk, for instance, asking students for their questions about or reactions to the story (Dickinson & Smith, 1994).
- Directly teach the form, meaning, and usage of frequently used words and phrases while continually developing comprehensive meanings of words for students who have only partial or inaccurate word meanings. Continually clarify confusion regarding words that sound similar but that contrast with one or two phonemes.

Language Development in Upper Elementary, Middle, and High School

The importance of vocabulary is daily demonstrated in schools and out. In the classroom, the achieving students possess the most adequate vocabularies. Because of the verbal nature of most classroom activities, knowledge of words and ability to use language are essential to success in these activities. After schooling has ended, adequacy of vocabulary is almost equally essential for achievement in vocations and in society. (Petty, Herold, & Stoll, 1967, p. 7)

In spite of an almost universal recognition that knowing the meanings of lots of words is essential to understanding text, upper-grade teachers don't teach very much vocabulary, and what little they do teach is often poorly presented (Blachowicz, 1987). Having a literate vocabulary has even become cause for criticism, as I recently discovered. An educator who reviewed one of my manuscripts took me to task; she didn't like the number of "big" words I used and specifically pointed out the ones she didn't know—all without a hint of embarrassment.

> **MUST-READ BOOKS ABOUT LANGUAGE**
>
> Biemiller, A. (1999). *Language and Reading Success*. Cambridge, MA: Brookline.
>
> Menyuk, P. (1999). *Reading and Linguistic Development*. Cambridge, MA: Brookline.
>
> Stahl, S. A. (1999). *Vocabulary Development*. Cambridge, MA: Brookline.
>
> Stotsky, S. (1999). *Losing Our Language: How Multicultural Classroom Instruction Is Undermining Our Children's Ability to Read, Write, and Reason*. New York: Free Press.

There are three basic ways for students to learn new words: (a) by being read to, (b) by reading themselves, or (c) from direct instruction in word meanings. There is no doubt about the benefits of reading aloud to young children (and even older ones) with regard to their acquisition of vocabulary (Dickinson & Smith, 1994; Robbins & Ehri, 1994). Once students can read on their own, however, their vocabularies will expand exponentially if they voraciously read more challenging and well-written materials independently (Stanovich & Cunningham, 1993). In fact, there is ample evidence to support the notion that learning vocabulary incidentally through reading is absolutely essential. There are far too many words that must be learned to teach them all directly in the classroom (Sternberg, 1987). One author claims that by the middle grades, if students are to make grade-level progress (i.e., learning 3,000 to 5,000 new words per year), they should be reading more than 1.1 million words a year of outside-school reading (25 to 35 books or the equivalent) and about 1.7 million words in school texts (Honig, 1996, p. 103). Are your students reading 2.8 million words yearly?

If students are to acquire the word meanings they need to read with understanding, they must not only read a lot, they must also learn how to become independent word learners. Carr & Wixon (1986) suggest that students must be taught how to (a) acquire word meanings (from context, structural analysis, and activating prior knowledge), (b) monitor their own understanding of new vocabulary (be ready to look up words they don't know), and (d) gain the capacity to change or modify strategies for understanding in the event of a comprehension failure.

Vocabulary Instruction: What We Can Learn From Research

Vocabulary instruction is one of the most well-investigated topics in reading instruction. Here are three recommended best practices: (a) give students *both* definitional *and* contextual information about new words, (b) ensure that students perform some type of cognitive operation with any new words that are introduced, and (c) talk about new words constantly.

Definitions Are Not Enough

Simply giving students definitions of new words is not enough to improve their comprehension when they encounter those words in future reading (Stahl & Fairbanks, 1986). However, if students are provided with *both* definitional and contextual information about a new word, comprehension improves significantly. Contextual information includes giving students several sentences that illustrate the word being used in different contexts, creating a short story or scenario in which the word plays a role, or acting out the word or drawing a picture for younger students.

Brain-Based Vocabulary Acquisition

Students (and adults) remember new information more readily when they perform some type of cognitive operation on that information (e.g., rehearsing responses in anticipation of answering questions about a word; connecting the word and its meaning to prior learning or experiences; personally paraphrasing the definition of the word; or coming up with antonyms, synonyms, examples, and nonexamples of the word; Craik & Tulving, 1975).

Play With Words

Engage students in lively class discussions to determine what experiences they have had with a new word. Freewheeling vocabulary discussions are particularly helpful for linguistically poor students who have partial or totally inaccurate definitions of words or who have confused the word with another similar-sounding word (e.g., jail and gel). Share your students' excitement on discovering an unknown word. Stir their curiosities, and motivate them to find out what new words mean. Help them collect new words in vocabulary journals and then record other hearings and sightings of these words.

A surefire way to ensure that students remember key vocabulary is to build in some action during your lesson. Pantomime, draw pictures, do dictionary drills, or play word detective (give points to students who can report sightings or hearings of the word in the real world). Choose a word of the week, and give students points for using it in their writing or speaking throughout the week. Buy an inexpensive trophy, and award it each week to the student who is able to use the week's word(s) most creatively or frequently. The whole idea behind having fun with words is to make sure that students process, notice, think about, and use new words.

KNOWLEDGE

Knowledge

People who don't know anything about the Holocaust and anti-Semitism also don't know very much about a host of other topics that they might encounter in political, social, and cultural texts. They are at risk for failing in comprehension for a wide range of texts dealing with the ordinary discourse of educated persons. Furthermore, their difficulties in knowledge will associate with difficulties in lexical processing and working-memory constraints. (Perfetti et al., 1996, p. 147)

Perhaps you have heard the rather tired argument about knowledge being irrelevant. We have all been stuffed with statistics about the exponential rate at which knowledge is growing and how impossible it is to contain it all in any one brain, much less the brain of a child who may not be developmentally ready to handle the cognitive demands. The idea that knowledge is somehow suspect has been around for over a century (Cubberly, 1909; Hall, 1900). It enjoyed a healthy revival in the 1960s (Holt, 1964; Neil, 1960) and is still going strong, albeit presently cloaked in the antistandards and antitesting movements (Kohn, 1999). Contemporary educators who downplay the role of knowledge in schooling usually point out that they can't possibly teach children everything there is to know, so a far better use of instructional time is to teach students ways to access and acquire information on their own. The persons who pontificate about the futility of cluttering kids' minds with facts are unable to tell you *when* children will actually become literate—knowing about art, literature, politics, science, history, religion, philosophy, or geography. Then again, perhaps it really *isn't* important in their grand scheme of things for students to know about the Holocaust, the countries that fought in World War II, the continents of the world, the books of the Bible, the Civil War, DNA, Shakespeare, Greek mythology, or the chemical elements.

Pat Oliphant (as quoted in Morissey, 1985), the political cartoonist who lampoons just about everything and everybody in his offbeat drawings, lamented the demise of the educated reader.

The problem is that as education becomes more and more of a mess in this country and people learn less and less about the arts and history, the possibility of using those sorts of metaphors [familiar artistic and literacy icons] is disappearing. It will get to a stage where eventually you won't be able to use the classics at all, or allusions to historical events. (p. B3)

Diane Ravitch (2000) recently took up the cause of knowledge in her book, *Left Back: A Century of Battles Over School Reform:*

Schools must do far more than teach children "how to learn" and "how to look things up"; they must teach them what knowledge has most value, how to use that knowledge, how to organize what they know, how to understand the relationship between past and present, how to tell the difference between accurate information and propaganda, and how to turn information into understanding. (p. 17)

The major problem with the denigration of knowledge per se is that knowledge is thought by most laypersons to be a byproduct of education, *and* the lack of knowledge is often a major contributor to poor reading comprehension

(Perfetti et al., 1996). Some researchers have argued for a concept of comprehension that is unaffected by the reader's domain knowledge (Perfetti, 1989), but it is difficult to make a case that sports illiteracy will not affect one's ability to enjoy an article in *Sports Illustrated* or that ignorance regarding the vocabulary of science won't affect one's understanding of an article in *Scientific American*.

To those who have subscribed to the notion that emphasizing knowledge in classrooms is merely rote learning and that "learning to learn" is a more worthy goal, E. D. Hirsch, Jr. (2001a, pp. 3–4) suggests four principles: (a) The ability to learn something new about a specific discipline or domain or knowledge is highly dependent on what is already known about that subject, (b) The general ability to learn is highly correlated with general knowledge, (c) The best way to learn a subject is to learn about its general principles and concepts as well as to investigate specific and diverse examples of those principles and concepts, and (d) Broad general knowledge is the best way to access deep knowledge.

I heartily concur with Hirsch (1989), who wrote in his preface to *A First Dictionary of Cultural Literacy*,

> Our schools' emphasis on skills rather than knowledge has . . . had the unintended effect of injuring disadvantaged students more than advantaged ones. Since more so-called skills are really based on specific knowledge, those who have already received literate knowledge from their homes are better able to understand what teachers and textbooks are saying and are therefore better able to learn new things than are children from nonliterate backgrounds. Consequently when schools emphasize skills over knowledge, they consistently widen the gap between the haves and have-nots instead of narrowing it. (p. xi)

More recently, Hirsch (2001b) spoke to the difficulty educators face in sustaining the early reading gains that disadvantaged students make as a result of intensive intervention and prevention programs. He suggested a way to narrow the ever-widening achievement gap that exists between the academically richest and poorest students: *teach knowledge*. Advantaged children have been acquiring knowledge in natural and implicit ways for 5 years before they enter kindergarten. Disadvantaged children are already so far behind when they enter school they can ill afford to wait for "natural and implicit" acquisition to occur. Hirsch recommends that if educators want students to learn fast, they must be explicit and break down each domain to be learned into manageable elements that can be mastered.

MUST-READ BOOKS ABOUT KNOWLEDGE

Bloom, A. (1987). *The Closing of the American Mind*. New York: Simon & Schuster.

Hirsch, E. D., Jr. (1996). *The Schools We Need and Why We Don't Have Them*. New York: Doubleday.

Ravitch, D. (2000). *Left Back: A Century of Battles Over School Reform*. New York: Simon & Schuster.

COGNITIVE STRATEGIES

Cognitive
Strategies

The best way to pursue meaning is through the conscious, controlled use of strategies. (Duffy, 1993, p. 223)

Cognitive strategies, the third "meaning" piece of the literacy puzzle, are mental tools, tricks, or shortcuts to gaining meaning, understanding, and knowledge. Duffy et al. (1987) call them "plans [that] readers use flexibly and adaptively depending on the situation" (p. 415). Cognitive strategies are also defined as "behaviors and thoughts that a learner engages in during learning that are intended to influence the learner's encoding process" (Weinstein & Mayer, 1986, p. 315). Such behaviors could include actions—note taking, constructing a graphic organizer, previewing the text, looking back to check on an answer, writing a summary, retelling a story—or thinking out loud, rehearsing the steps or the ideas that are unclear or need to be remembered. The thoughts referred to might include processes such as activating prior knowledge, monitoring comprehension, or inferring meaning.

Strategies have the power to enhance and enlarge the scope of learning by making it more efficient. Strategic students learn and remember more in shorter periods of time with far less frustration. They are able to tackle assignments with a higher level of organizational skill, and more important, they can face challenging assignments with confidence. Figure 5.1 pictures my choices for the essential cognitive strategies, based on research and my own personal experiences as a strategic reader and prolific writer. Each of the strategies is multifaceted; using them involves multiple thoughts and behaviors that depend on the reader's purpose for reading as well as the degree of success the reader has in constructing meaning from the text. They can all be modeled for and taught to students from kindergarten through high school.

Brain-Based Reading

I have coined the term *brain-based reading* to describe what skilled readers do when they use the four essential cognitive strategies that are pictured in Figure 5.1. Brain-based reading is characterized by involvement and intentional action on the part of the reader. It is the exact opposite of the kind of reading the teachers in my workshops laughingly tell me that their students often do: "brain-dead" reading. This is reading in which students simply stare at the page hoping for a cognitive miracle. Educators are also hoping for cognitive miracles, but they won't happen unless teachers regularly model and directly teach cognitive strategies.

Pearson and Fielding (1991) describe what happens during brain-based reading:

Students understand and remember ideas better when they have to transform those ideas from one form to another. Apparently it is in this transformation process that the *author's* ideas become [the] *reader's*

Figure 5.1 The Essential Cognitive Strategies

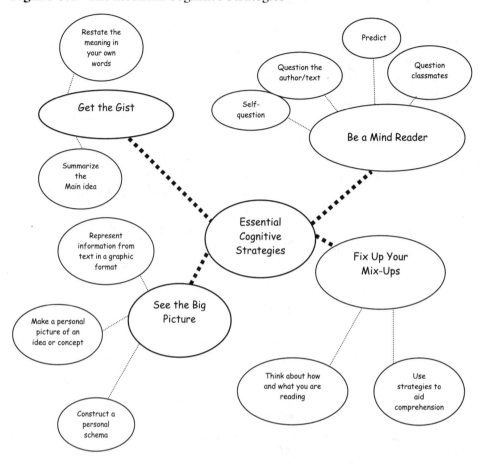

ideas, rendering them more memorable. Examined from the teacher's
perspective, what this means is that teachers have many options to
choose from when they try to engage students more actively in their
own comprehension: summarizing; monitoring . . . engaging visual
representation, and requiring students to ask their own questions all
seem to generate learning. (Pearson & Fielding, 1991, p. 847)

Developing Strategic Teachers

There is one huge hurdle to implementing a cognitive strategies program in
your classroom, school, or district, however. "Becoming an effective . . . strategies instruction teacher takes several years" (Brown et al., 1996, p. 20).
Training and developing strategic teachers requires a not inconsiderable
investment of human and monetary resources. Teaching cognitive strategies
is a vastly different undertaking from teaching "skills" as we did in the 60s
and 70s. Skills are "procedures readers over-learn through repetition so that
speed and accuracy are assured every time the response is called for" (Duffy &

Roehler, 1987, p. 415), whereas strategies, on the other hand, tap higher-order thinking skills in response to the demands of unique reading tasks. Strategies are used situationally. Teaching students how and when to use cognitive strategies is a vastly different enterprise than drilling students on a discrete skill or serving up a smorgasbord of content and expecting students to help themselves.

To develop strategic teachers takes a devotion to professional development that is seldom seen in most school districts. Duffy (1993) points out that "helping teachers [become good strategy teachers] will require a significant change in how teacher educators and staff developers work with teachers and what they count as important about learning to be a teacher" (pp. 244–245). The process will take far more than a day or two of casual staff development because most teachers did not experience this kind of instruction as students themselves. Irene Gaskins, the founder and director of The Benchmark School (Gaskins & Elliott, 1991), advises that it takes teachers at least 3 years to become strategic teachers (I. Gaskins, personal communication, July 5, 2000).

Collins, Brown, and Holum (1991) observed that the practice of strategic reading is not at all obvious in most classrooms where "the processes of thinking are often invisible to both the students and the teacher" (p. 6). That may have more to do with the difficulty of becoming a strategic teacher than with any difficulty students might have learning how to comprehend if only they were well taught. Teaching comprehension is hard work. It is much easier to *talk* about the importance of comprehension or to *test* comprehension than it is to actually *teach* it. In a year-long series of observations in 10 fourth- and fifth-grade classrooms, Pressley et al. (1995) found a disturbing lack of comprehension instruction, despite over two decades of research on how to do it and the benefits that students derive from it (p. 198). Pressley further notes that "we are living in a country with a lot of assessment of comprehension and not enough instruction" (M. Pressley, personal communication, September 8, 2001).

You are no doubt painfully aware of similar deficiencies in your own classroom, school, or district. Oh, there may be a smattering of study skills lessons or a frenzy of test preparation activities just prior to the administration of the state assessments or a standardized test. Students typically read a few brief selections, answer some questions, get a low score, receive a lecture about the importance of "thinking" about what they are reading, a reminder to "concentrate harder" the next time, and then the cycle begins again the next day. To break out of this mind-numbing waste of instructional time, teachers need sufficient and well-developed training in how to teach cognitive strategies on a daily basis, opportunities to practice using the strategies in their own reading and thinking, ample amounts of coaching and follow-up in their classrooms, and administrative expectations that the strategies will be taught.

The typical approach to strategy instruction in most schools is haphazard. Someone, typically an administrator or the reading teacher, becomes aware of the power of cognitive strategies to improve reading achievement and convenes a committee to design a staff development program. The strategies chosen for implementation are often selected at random, based on the preferences of the teacher who will be doing the training. They may or may not be bundled as a multiple-strategy instruction program. Teachers may not see the relevance of a particular strategy to their teaching or understand the importance of modeling strategies to students and emphasizing the motivational aspects of effective strategy instruction. Furthermore, implementation schedules are often too ambitious, leaving teachers undertrained and overwhelmed.

The National Reading Panel (2000) warned that

> in spite of heavy emphasis on modeling and metacognitive instruction, even very good teachers may have trouble implementing, and may even omit, crucial aspects of strategic reasoning. The research suggests that, when partially implemented, students of strategic teachers will still improve. But it is not easy for teachers to develop readers' conceptions about what it means to be strategic. It takes time, coaching, and careful monitoring to help both teachers and students to be successful. (sec. 4, p. 49)

The Essential Strategies

> *Every book has a skeleton hidden between its covers. Your job as an analytical reader is to find it. A book comes to you with flesh on its bare bones and clothes over its flesh. It is all dressed up. You do not have to undress it or tear the flesh off its limbs to get at the firm structure that underlies the soft surface. But you must read the book with X-ray eyes, for it is an essential part of your apprehension of any book to grasp its structure.* (Adler & Van Doren, 1972, p. 75)

The essential cognitive strategies that skilled strategic readers are known to employ (monitoring, questioning, organizing and summarizing) were displayed in Figure 5.1. You may also be familiar with a variety of so-called name brand comprehension strategies that have been designed by teachers, reading educators, and staff developers. They are frequently the topics of articles in popular journals (Jones, Pierce, & Hunter, 1988/1998), workshops (Farr, 1998), and countless books (Harvey & Goudvis, 2000; Johns & Lenski, 1997; Keene & Zimmermann, 1997). These name brand varieties are given catchy titles like "click or clunk" in which, after reading a portion of text, students ask themselves if what they have read *clicks* (they understand it) or *clunks* (they need to use a fix-up strategy (Weaver, 1994, p. 157). Another cleverly named strategy is "trash and treasure," in which students decide what portions of the text are irrelevant and redundant and "trash" them along with determining which portions of the text contain important main ideas and details—the treasure. Questions are described as "thick [large and global questions] or thin [incidental clarifying questions]" (Harvey & Goudvis, 2000, p. 90). Another Harvey and Goudvis brand name strategy is their Post-it-note approach to reading. They recommend that students code their thinking and write reactions and questions regarding their reading on varying sizes of Post-it notes that they then stick on the pages of their texts to keep them actively engaged while reading.

Name brand strategies are usually taught in 1-day "hit and run" workshops for teachers. This approach presents three major problems: (a) The strategies are often taught with little or no connection to teachers' disciplines or curriculum, (b) a single strategy is taught as a stand-alone strategy rather than as part of a well-conceived multiple-strategy school model, and (c) teachers are led to believe that teaching cognitive strategies to students is just another pleasurable activity, rather than a rigorous, lengthy, and ongoing process—one that requires a major commitment of time and intellectual energy by both teachers and students. I grow frustrated with my own inability to change this approach. School districts are looking for quick fixes and are unwilling to invest the time and energy that excellent cognitive-strategy instruction demands. My vision for model strategy instruction includes an extensive strategic reading across the curriculum program but using *only* the following core strategies with their related permutations and combinations: (a) questioning, (b) summarizing, (c) organizing, and (d) monitoring.

To make these strategies more memorable for both you and your students, I have given them my own name brand labels: (a) *Be a Mind-Reader* (questioning), (b) *Get the Gist* (summarizing), (c) *See the Big Picture* (organizing), and (d) *Fix Up Your Mix-Ups* (monitoring). Following are brief descriptions of these four essential cognitive strategies; a comprehensive lesson plan for each of them can be found in Resource B. The plans are generic and must be adapted to specific grade levels or disciplines.

> ### MUST-READ BOOKS ABOUT STRATEGY INSTRUCTION
>
> Gaskins, I. W., & Elliot, T. T. (1991). *Implementing Cognitive Strategy Instruction Across the School: The Benchmark Manual for Teachers.* Cambridge, MA: Brookline.
>
> Ong, F., & Breneman, B. (Eds.). (2000). *Strategic Teaching and Learning: Standards-Based Instruction to Promote Content Literacy in Grades Four Through Twelve.* Sacramento, CA: California Department of Education.
>
> Pressley, M., et al. (1995). *Cognitive Strategy Instruction That Really Improves Children's Academic Performance.* Cambridge, MA: Brookline.
>
> Wood, E., Woloshyn, V. E., & Willoughby, T. (1995). *Cognitive Strategy Instruction for Middle and High Schools.* Cambridge, MA: Brookline.

Be a Mind Reader: The Questioning Strategy

Asking questions is a big part of what teachers do constantly. But has it ever occurred to you that the wrong people are asking most of the questions in today's classrooms? The students are the ones who should be *asking* the questions and then turning around and *answering* them as well as replying to the questions of their classmates. One of my favorite questioning strategies when I was a student myself involved predicting what questions my teachers would ask on a quiz, midterm, or final exam and then making sure I knew the answers. The last time I used this strategy was in preparation for my doctoral comprehensives when I correctly identified three out of the four essay questions that were in my envelope when I opened it. I always gave myself a silent cheer before writing an exam when I had second-guessed the teacher correctly. Although I called it second-guessing, in reality, it was a savvy questioning strategy in which I personally identified what I thought were the most important ideas and concepts (based on lectures, readings, and any clues I could glean from the teacher during the semester) and then made sure that I processed, manipulated, and internalized both the *teacher's* and the *textbook's* ideas into my own schema through graphically organizing and summarizing the material. In essence, I became a mind reader—first getting into the psyches of my teachers and the minds of the textbooks' authors—and then posing the questions to which they had already provided the answers.

This kind of processing (rehearsal, review, comparing, contrasting, and making connections) strengthens students' knowledge networks and increases the likelihood that their newly acquired knowledge will actually be stored in long-term memory. The questioning (and answering) cognitive strategy is an essential one for students at every grade level, even primary-grade students. Pressley notes, "With respect to comprehension strategies, second graders have no trouble learning them *if* they are exposed to them. The problem is that second graders are almost never exposed to comprehension strategies" (M. Pressley, personal communication, September 9, 2001). Students at every grade level must be shown how to use cognitive strategies through modeling; coached to proficiency through guided practice; and then expected to routinely explain, elaborate, or defend their positions or answers before, during, and after their reading. When students are expected from the earliest grades to articulate explanations, they are forced and become accustomed to evaluating, integrating, and elaborating knowledge in new ways.

Get the Gist: The Summarization Strategy

The second essential cognitive strategy is summarization—getting the gist of what is read. One of the most difficult assignments for students, whether in kindergarten or college, is writing or orally giving summaries of what they have read. That is, unless they have seen the summarization strategy modeled numerous times by their teachers, been carefully taught the various aspects of the strategy, and then had an opportunity to practice it in cooperative groups under the watchful eye of their teacher—all before being expected to summarize on their own (Brown & Day, 1983; Brown, Day, & Jones, 1983). Researchers have found that summarization instruction improves students' recall of what they read compared to students who are taught using traditional reading comprehension instruction (Armbruster, Anderson, & Ostertag, 1987; Berkowitz, 1986; Taylor & Beach, 1984). Summarization training is a powerful intervention, with "many variations of the technique improving long-term memory of text" (Pressley et al., 1995, p. 62).

There are some students for whom the skill of summarization is extraordinarily difficult, well beyond what it should be for the average or even slightly below average reader. Bell (1991a, 1991b) calls this problem "underdeveloped concept imagery," or the inability to visualize concepts. These students often process only parts of the language they hear and read rather than getting the gestalt or big picture. Bell's program, called *Visualizing and Verbalizing for Language Comprehension and Thinking*, is designed to meet the needs of students who can read words accurately but cannot comprehend content. If words seemingly go in one ear and out the other, a student is probably having difficulty creating an imaged gestalt—a whole. *Visualizing and Verbalizing*, when taught in a clinical setting, has been shown to stimulate concept imagery and improve language comprehension, reasoning for critical thinking, and expressive language skills.

See the Big Picture: The Organizing Strategy

Organizing, the third essential cognitive strategy, involves constructing graphic or visual representations that "help the learner to comprehend, summarize, and synthesize complex ideas in ways that, in many instances, surpass verbal statements" (Jones, Pierce, & Hunter, 1988/1989, p. 21). By the time students enter high school, they should be able to construct a variety of graphic organizers to use in understanding and remembering what they read, as well as for the purpose of organizing their thoughts in preparation for writing (e.g., flow charts, Venn diagrams, webs, concept maps, time lines, cycles, and continuums). Johns and Lenski (1997) provide templates of multiple graphic organizers that may be reproduced for educational purposes. The National Reading Panel (2000) found that

> Teaching students to use a systematic, visual graphic to organize the ideas that they are reading about develops the ability of the students to remember what they read and may transfer in general to better comprehension and achievement in social studies and science content areas. (sec. 4, p. 75)

Fix Up Your Mix-Ups: The Monitoring Strategy

Monitoring, the final strategy, involves two related and often seemingly simultaneous abilities: (a) being able to think about how and what one is reading while engaged in the act of reading, for purposes of determining if one is comprehending the text, and (b) being able to use a wide variety of strategies to aid in comprehension, if needed. Monitoring actually begins before the reader reads any text and continues long after the skilled reader has finished reading. Monitoring one's comprehension is like knowing when you are lost on the freeway or in the forest and being both willing and able to use a fix-up strategy to find your way back. Some misguided souls wander needlessly, refusing to admit that they are lost. And many readers won't admit or are seemingly unaware that they don't understand what they are reading, either. They need systematic instruction in all of the substrategies found in Resource B, Figure B.3: Fix-Up Your Mix-Ups: The Comprehension Monitoring Checklist.

A Model for Multiple-Strategy Instruction

> *Despite a significant body of research in the 1980s suggesting the effectiveness of strategy instruction, especially for lower-achieving readers, strategy instruction has not been implemented in many American classrooms.* (Dole, 2000, p. 62)

Cognitive-strategy instruction as a field of study and research has become increasingly more sophisticated during the past 20 years. Researchers, intrigued with the success of single strategies to improve comprehension, have gone on to combine several strategies to produce even more powerful results (Palincsar & Brown, 1984). Rosenshine, Meister, and Chapman (1996) assert that "students at all skill levels would benefit from being taught these strategies [summarizing, organizing, questioning, and monitoring]" (p. 201).

The biggest challenge for administrators and staff developers with regard to strategy instruction is that being strategic is much more than knowing a few or even a great many individual strategies. Strategy use is not a paint-by-the-numbers activity. "When faced with a comprehension problem, strategic readers coordinate and shift strategies as appropriate. They constantly alter, adjust, modify, and test until they construct meaning and the problem is solved" (National Reading Panel, 2000, sec. 4, p. 47). What is needed is a model that (a) allows for the ambiguity and messiness that occurs during real reading, (b) helps teachers deal with constant decision making and unanticipated actions and reactions, (c) encourages teachers to become strategic readers themselves in the each-one-teach-one tradition, and (d) allows time for teachers to become expert (Gaskins & Elliot, 1991; Pressley et al., 1995).

SUMMARIZING CHAPTER 5

The "meaning" pieces of the reading puzzle—*language, knowledge,* and *cognitive strategies*—provide the tools that will enable students to read challenging text with understanding and enjoyment. To neglect systematic and direct language, knowledge, and strategy instruction at any level of schooling is to put even more students at risk of falling through the cracks. Catch them before they fall. Teach them what they need to know to construct meaning from text. Teach them how to read to learn.

LOOKING AHEAD

Chapter 6 will enable you to put one more piece of the reading puzzle in place: *reading a lot.* To become literate, students must devour books. The goal for all students is that they will become voracious, voluminous, and most especially, voluntary readers.

6

Putting It All Together

Reading a Lot

The great gift is the passion for reading. It is cheap. It consoles, it distracts, it excites. It gives you knowledge of the world and experience of a wide kind. It is a moral illumination.

—Hardwick as quoted in Gilbar, 1990, p. 24

Reading a lot

Reading isn't a very popular pastime these days. In fact, the percentage of Americans who read regularly is at an all-time low, according to a recent Gallup poll (Weeks, 2001). Only 7% of Americans read more than one book per week, and 59% said they had read fewer than 10 books in the previous year. Although the pollsters did not query individuals about why they are avoiding the printed page, figuring out their reasons isn't that difficult. Some people would *like* to read and *do* read whenever they have the opportunity (e.g., at the beach or on vacation), but they just don't have the time to read in a recreational sense. They are far too busy (or so they think).

Then there's another group—those who are capable of reading if it is required in the course of their daily lives or at work but who don't particularly like to read. They may prefer doing things that are more active and hands-on, or they may never have been introduced to books that were compelling enough to get them hooked on reading. Then, there is the final group of nonreaders— the folks who fell through the cracks when they were in school. When *they* are confronted with a reading task, they get sweaty palms and heart palpitations. They may have entertained thoughts from time to time of getting a degree or more advanced job training, but the idea of having to read and take tests stops them cold.

DOES SILENT READING A LOT IMPROVE FLUENCY AND COMPREHENSION?

KINDERGARTEN CHECKOUT

Get your students into the reading habit on the very first day of their school careers. Every preschool and kindergarten student should have the opportunity to check out a book from the school library every day and take it home for a bedtime read aloud. Children can actually train their parents to read aloud to them every evening if the kindergarten teacher will encourage and keep track of each child's outside-of-school reading (e.g., a chart in which he or she places a star for every book read aloud).

I am one of those individuals who firmly believe that the answer to the problem not only of low reading achievement but also of personal satisfaction, career advancement, world peace, global warming, and inflation is reading a lot. Well, maybe reading a lot won't solve *all* of those problems, but surely it has to play a role in reversing declining reading achievement or even in making it go up.

Between 1983 and 1991, when the students in my K-6 elementary school increased the amount of time they spent reading, our library's circulation figures *and* our school's standardized test scores went up in tandem almost every year for 8 years. Of course, I cannot say with certainty what percentage of our achievement gains was due to increased voluntary reading by our students and what percentage was attributable to any or all of the other instructional interventions that we employed:

- More time spent on reading instruction
- More direct instruction by teachers
- More cooperative learning during both reading and writing instruction
- A reading homework plan for each grade level
- Increased professional development in cognitive-strategy instruction and schoolwide implementation of cognitive-strategy instruction
- Higher expectations and accountability for students, teachers, *and* parents
- Increased opportunities for teachers to meet with one another to make joint plans, discuss the progress of at-risk students, and work on curriculum alignment
- Increased participation by staff members in decision-making
- Regular RIF (Reading Is Fundamental) special events and book giveaways
- After-school tutoring programs, summer school, and school-business partnership enrichment programs

I must, however, give *some* of the credit to reading a lot, because it was a major emphasis every year.

Therefore, I was more than a little distressed when I received my copy of the National Reading Panel's report in the summer of 2000 and read their conclusion that educators really had no solid experimental research to demonstrate that when we motivate students to do more silent reading, their abilities to read more fluently as well as to better understand what they read will improve. In fact, the panel's search for experimental studies to verify our long-standing belief in the efficacy of a daily period of sustained silent reading turned up only slightly more than a dozen studies, none of which enabled the panel to conclude that schools should adopt programs to encourage more reading. The panel reported that

> Despite widespread acceptance of the idea that schools can successfully encourage students to read more and that these increases in reading practice will be translated into better fluency and higher reading achievement, there is not adequate evidence to sustain this claim. (National Reading Panel, 2000, sec. 3, p. 28)

I am far from ready to recommend that teachers and principals *stop* motivating students to read more just because we don't have exactly the right kind of research available yet. But the panel's report did compel me to go looking for any additional evidence I could find regarding the benefits of reading a lot, experimental or not. I found a great deal. Figure 6.1 summarizes the impact of reading a lot, both on the reading abilities and the reading achievement of students.

LET'S BRING BACK INDIVIDUALIZED READING!

Individualized reading classes in middle and high schools have been around since the 1930s and enjoyed a brief resurgence in the 1970s (Blow, 1976). Perhaps the time has come to reinvent this wheel or at least polish it up a bit in the new millennium—not just for secondary schools but also for the elementary level. Individualized reading classes are clearly an option for more advanced elementary school readers at any grade level, even kindergarten. The media specialist in my elementary school held after-school reading clubs, designed individualized reading programs for groups of gifted K-2 students, and offered all students the opportunity to become a Newbery Reader by reading a certain number of the award-winning books and discussing them with her by appointment.

Individualized classes or groups offers several advantages: (a) the time students need to read without other content pressures, (b) opportunities to talk about books with peers and a teacher, (c) accountability for what is read, and (d) choice. Individualized reading classes in the past focused primarily on reading literature, and that is certainly one option. However, individualized reading programs could also be structured as an independent study for credit in which a student and teacher might develop a reading list based on a topic (e.g., genetics, the Civil War), a genre (e.g., science fiction), an author (e.g., Charles Dickens), or a specific individual (e.g., Charles Lindbergh or Hillary Clinton) and meet periodically to talk about what has been read.

The individualized reading class or independent study is not remedial in nature nor does it teach specific strategies. Its sole purpose is to give students opportunity (and credit) during the school day to read more widely than they would have time for otherwise.

Figure 6.1 The Research on Reading a Lot

Type of Research	*Research Findings*
Differences in the amount of reading done by high- and low-achieving students	Higher-achieving students do more reading in school than their lower achieving counterparts (Allington, 1977, 1980, 1983, 1984; Allington & McGill-Franzen, 1989).
	Higher-achieving students read more outside of school (Anderson, Wilson, & Fielding, 1988; Nagy & Anderson, 1984). Anderson and his colleagues found that students achieving at the 90th percentile read 40 minutes per day, which amounted to well over 2 million words per year, while students achieving at the 50th percentile read only 12.9 minutes per day for a total of 601,000 words per year, and students achieving at the 10th percentile read a scant 1.6 minutes per day for an appallingly low 51,000 words per year.
Correlational research showing a relationship between amount of reading both in and out of school and reading achievement	The most persuasive, contemporary, and extensive correlational study showing a relationship between reading a lot and achievement is the 1998 National Assessment of Educational Progress. At all grades (4, 8, and 12), students who reported reading more pages daily in school and for homework had higher average scale scores than students who reported reading fewer pages daily (Donahue et al., 1999).
Acquisition of second languages through reading a lot	Reading a lot makes a huge impact on the acquisition of a second language when the learners are beyond the beginning reading level. There is a wide body of literature that makes one wonder why we aren't more proactive about motivating our ESL students to read a lot in English (Pilgreen & Krashen, 1993). Language and literacy development around the world has been stimulated by reading a lot: United States (Krashen, 1993), England (Hafiz & Tudor, 1989), Japan (Mason & Krashen, 1997), the Fiji Islands (Elley & Mangubhai, 1983), South Africa (Elley, 1999); Sri Lanka (Elley, 1999), Ireland (Greaney & Clarke, 1973), Singapore (Elley, 1991), and Hong Kong (Tsang, 1996).
Relationship of academic learning time and student achievement	When students are actually engaged in learning tasks with a high level of success, their achievement goes up (Berliner, 1981; Fisher & Berliner, 1985). A logical conclusion one can draw from this literature is that time spent reading at a high level of success will result in reading achievement.

WHY CAN'T WE JUST DROP EVERYTHING AND READ?

When I . . . discovered libraries, it was like having Christmas every day.
(Fritz as quoted in Gilbar, 1990, p. 154).

We all enjoy the romantic notion of eager readers curled up on a cozy couch in a classroom corner or tucked away in an ancient bathtub piled high with pillows. But don't get too entranced by this vision of reading for enjoyment. To answer the question of why we can't just turn kids loose to read, I reflected on my own personal reading habits. I am a voracious and voluminous reader. I love to read. I do a great deal of sustained silent reading every single day. No one needs to tell *me* to drop everything and read. If I were a student today, I would be in hot pursuit of every prize that was being offered. However, I must confess that some of what I do read nearly every day is absolutely worthless in terms of raising my reading achievement—mysteries, psychological thrillers, and courtroom dramas. Many students are stuffing themselves with the same kind of junk that I read to fall asleep at night or to stave off boredom on airplanes. *The Babysitters Club* (Martin, 1996), *Give Yourself Goosebumps* (Stine, 1998), *The Fear Street Sagas* (Stine, 1996), *Sweet Valley High* (Pascal, 1995, 2001), and other types of formulaic fiction are just a sampling of the current crop of "junk reading."

Although these books are wonderful for engaging reluctant readers and developing the language skills of ESL (English as a second language) students, and they certainly don't do other kids any harm, skilled readers acquire very little new vocabulary or knowledge when they are overdosing on the predictable. I seldom, if ever, have to use a cognitive strategy or look up an unfamiliar word in the dictionary while I am reading Grisham or Grafton.

On the other hand, a great deal of my reading does qualify as brain-based. During these reading experiences, I am forced to wrestle with new ideas, master unfamiliar vocabulary, graphically organize complex concepts, and then summarize both in my mind and on paper what I have read. In some cases, I must synthesize, evaluate, and create to prepare a manuscript for publication. I am constantly processing, rehearsing, and connecting what I have read to what I already know.

Cognitive scientists call what I am doing *constructing meaning*. However, don't make the mistake of thinking that when I am "constructing," meaning, I am making up my own version of a given author's intent. Sometimes, I do construct in the original sense, blending my thinking and ideas with what another author

I GOT CAUGHT READING

Catch kids reading, and ask them to orally summarize the main idea of their book thus far. Give out stickers, homework passes, chances for a free book drawing, or an opportunity to join a group of students for a special event, such as a bowling or swimming party or picnic to those students who are tuned in to and can talk about what they are reading.

has said to come up with a new idea. Often, however, I am simply trying to understand and make sense of what the author intends to convey to me in the most literal sense that I can.

Reading to learn is far different from the daily reading to enjoy that I do. No one is assessing my understanding or holding me accountable for paraphrasing or summarizing the novels that I read. On the other hand, when I engage in brain-based reading for my work as a consultant and author, I am in what Jeanne Chall (as quoted in Curtis & Longo, 1999) calls "the construction and reconstruction stage of reading: able to use reading for personal and professional needs in such a way that prior knowledge gets synthesized and analyzed" (p. 10).

For reading to result in increased learning and achievement, students must be engaged in brain-based reading. Steven Stahl (1999b) in a commentary on the current deemphasis on *reading to learn*, which has been supplanted by the whole-language movement's *reading-to-enjoy* thrust, makes this observation: "Whole language instruction stresses the personal response of individuals to quality literature, as opposed to their recall or comprehension of the stories" (p. 18). "Talking around the text" without ever actually "talking about the text" with any degree of understanding has become the instructional norm (McMahon, 1992). We need a balance of both kinds of reading. The literate person needs to be able to read for enjoyment as well as read to learn.

> ## RECESS IS FOR READING
>
> Recess isn't just for jumping rope or climbing monkey bars. It can also be for reading. Erect reading benches on the playground. On lovely spring (or fall) days, encourage students to take books outside and read during lunch recess. Some eager readers will even choose to read on frosty winter mornings. More power to them!

To read to learn, students *must* be tuned in, on task, and strategically involved. Their heads must be in the text, not in the clouds. They must be reading in what I call *the zone*, the intersection or overlapping of (a) reading a lot, (b) reading at an appropriate or somewhat challenging level of difficulty, and (c) reading with accountability. See Figure 6.2.

SCHOOLWIDE READING IN THE ZONE

As I reflected on what schoolwide reading in the zone might look like, I recalled our experiences with the Battle of the Books program when I was an elementary school principal. For 5 years, the Battle of the Books program brought the fourth through sixth grades at Lincoln School into a reading zone (Cook & Page, 1994). The building virtually hummed with excitement over books.

The program, which ran from October to March of each school year, involved the strategic reading of large quantities of challenging, well-written, and varied text; reciprocal teaching and cooperative learning; group and individual accountability; and healthy team competition. All of this was in addition to what students gained from their regular reading class. Although the faculty did not conduct any formal research during the years we participated in the project, during 5 of the 8 years we focused on raising reading achievement, Battle of the Books was specifically responsible for the engagement, empowerment, and achievement of a sizable number of our most reluctant readers.

Figure 6.2 Reading in the Zone

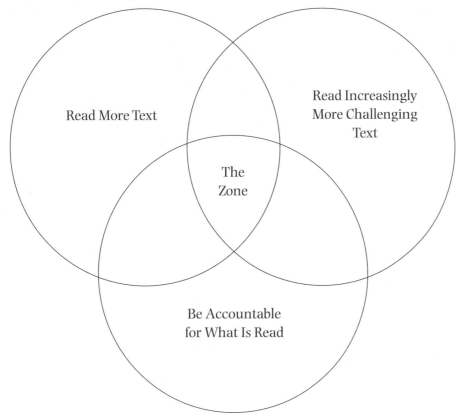

Every student participated in a cooperative team made up of five students with varying reading abilities. This was not a voluntary or negotiable activity. It was part of each student's reading grade. Each team was jointly responsible for reading a list of 40 books chosen by our town's youth services librarian. The books ranged in reading level from third to ninth grade. Students reached consensus in their teams regarding which books would be read by each team member, with eight books being the *minimum* number to be read by an individual. Some team members chose to read all 40 books, but each student was accountable for reading his or her assigned eight books and knowing them inside out. Team competitions were organized at the building level to prepare for the library-sponsored competition, and students made up questions for other teams to answer. Teams met during lunch and after school to talk about the books they had read and to anticipate what types of questions the library staff would select to stump them during the semifinal and final rounds. Our librarian ordered multiple copies of all of the titles so that no one would have to wait to read a chosen book. Teachers read some of the more challenging titles aloud in class and discussed complex themes and difficult vocabulary with students. Some teachers personally read all of the titles themselves and discussed the books with their students, not only during reading class but also at odd moments on the playground, while waiting in line for music or art classes, or before being called to the gym for an assembly. Every spare moment of the school day was spent talking about books.

As the date for the library competition to select the team that would represent our school drew near, our teams began to meet on their own initiative in the evenings and on weekends. During the initial year of competition, one of our sixth-grade teams took first place in the city. One of the team members had only attended our school since fourth grade and could scarcely read a word when she enrolled—a student who had definitely fallen through the cracks. She learned to read almost overnight, it seemed, under the tutelage of our special education teacher and became one of our most avid readers.

Although our school was the acknowledged underdog, we soundly defeated all of the other teams from the private and more privileged schools in our district. What was responsible for our stellar showing? Our students were engaged in reading for a purpose. They were focused on gaining meaning from what they read as opposed to putting in time. After our first-year success, students were motivated to read with even more intensity and focus in successive years. We managed to capture two more titles during a 5-year period, until other schools discovered our secret strategy—brain-based reading.

HOW MUCH *SHOULD* STUDENTS READ?

> *"Why don't you go and do something?" my mother would say.*
> *"I am doing something. I'm reading."*
> *"It isn't healthy just lying there with your nose in a book," she would say, just as she said to my father.*
> *Thus harassed, I would find places to read where I couldn't be found—in the attic, in the woods, and at night under the bedclothes with a flashlight.*
> (MacNeil as quoted in Gilbar, 1990, p. 142)

Although most educators will agree that students should read more, there is really no agreed-on standard for exactly *how much* they should be reading—either at the elementary or secondary levels. Many educators think in terms of words, pages, or books (Honig, 1996, p. 103), but Allington (2001) recommends, and I concur, that reading volume should be measured in *time*. To expect a beginning or slower reader to read the same number of pages or books as a more skilled reader can easily lead to frustration and discouragement for less-voluminous readers. Time was the variable we always used in our reading incentive programs. Because every student has the same amount of it available in the day, each one should be reading for the same amount of time. Actually,

---

SUMMER READING CLUB

Encourage summer reading by forming the Principal's Postcard Club. Students are required to read 20 books over the summer and send a postcard to the principal for each book that they read. The card must contain the title, author, and a sentence or two about the book. When school resumes in the fall, the members of this elite club (and membership is open to any student who will read) are treated to lunch by a local restaurant.

to catch up, struggling readers should be spending even more time reading than their peers who are reading fluently. Allington (2001) asserts that the volume of daily *in-school* reading that most elementary school children experience is far below an optimum level and suggests that students should be doing an absolutely mind-boggling 90 minutes of *actual* reading *in school* every day. Try that one on for size in your classroom, school, or district.

This 90 minutes would include any and all kinds of reading during the school day—content area reading, reading done during reading instruction, silent reading, voluntary reading, assigned reading for which the student is held accountable, oral reading, repeated reading, guided reading, and buddy reading. Allington (2001) further recommends that teachers at each grade level jointly develop reading volume standards that are zealously adhered to by *every* staff member.

I would also recommend that *out-of-school* reading volume standards be established. We developed reading homework standards and expected every student to read for a certain period of time nightly (or weekly, depending on the grade level). This reading could include a read-aloud by an adult or older sibling to a student, listening to a commercially taped read-aloud, reading aloud by the student to an adult or sibling, repeated oral reading, or silent reading.

> **BOOKS FOR BREAKFAST**
>
> Provide read-alouds during the serving of breakfast. The readers can be students of any age, teachers, or members of the community. Be sure to use a microphone so that everyone can hear. Schedule one read-aloud per week in the beginning. Prepare a sheet of read-aloud guidelines, and suggest that students rehearse in their own classrooms (asking for constructive feedback from their classmates) before reading aloud to a larger audience.

To summarize, the total amount of reading a lot that students do should ideally be composed of three kinds of reading: (a) guided and supervised reading in the zone during the school day (up to 90 minutes); (b) a staff agreed-on daily reading homework period in which students read anything they like but are held accountable for what they read in some minimal way (e.g., reading log, journal, or parent signature in homework book); and (c) *voluntary* (over and above what is required at school *or* for homework), *voracious* (enthusiastic and excited), and *voluminous* (lots and lots of books) *reading* outside of school that is facilitated and motivated by ongoing and meaningful incentives (Cameron & Pierce, 1994). Expecting students to do this much reading may sound unrealistic or even impossible, but you will never know until you actually set forth the requirements and then expect your students and parents to drop everything and read *at home*!

THE IMPORTANCE OF READING CHALLENGING, WELL-WRITTEN, AND VARIED TEXT

"Reading books is good, Reading good books is better." (Powell as quoted in Gilbar, 1990, p. 55).

It's not enough for students just to read. They must read challenging, well-written, and varied text.

Challenging Text

I recently received a question from the parent of an eighth grader who wondered about the advisability of her daughter spending 6 weeks of Language Arts class on the novel *Who Put That Hair in My Toothbrush?* (Spinelli, 1994). I obtained a copy of this young adult novel by Newbery-award-winning author, Jerry Spinelli, (1990, *Maniac Magee*) to check it out for myself. The plot is an appealing one to adolescents with its offbeat humor and theme of sibling rivalry. The only problem is the unsuitability of this book for a long-term, in-depth classroom study.

I applied a readability formula to the text (Chall & Dale, 1995) and discovered that reading levels in the book ranged from a low of first grade (based on a passage containing 16 sentences and no unfamiliar words) to a high of fourth grade. The eighth-grade students who spent over 6 weeks of instructional time "reading" this book didn't learn one new word that they should not have mastered by fourth grade or earlier, nor were they exposed to any worthy themes or new information that might result in increased reading achievement in the future.

Sandra Stotsky's (1999) thought-provoking and somewhat controversial book, *Losing Our Language*, examines the erosion of academic expectations in reading over the past century. She points out that the incident of the eighth-grade class reading fourth-grade text is not a recent phenomenon but part of a steady decline over the course of the 20th century. She wonders "how much lower academic expectations can fall without significant breakdowns in thinking and communication at higher levels of education, in the workforce, and in public life" (p. 3).

Stotsky (1999) offers samples of reading texts from four different eras: the turn of the century, the 1950s, the 1970s, and late 1990s for comparison. The decline of vocabulary and syntax is startling. She also points out a more recent trend: multiculturalism. In an effort to serve up a smorgasbord of literature from other cultures, publishers are spicing up English texts with dozens of foreign words. French, Japanese, Spanish, and even invented Native American phrases dot the pages of current reading books. This linguistic polyglot does little to increase the English-language vocabulary of students in general and totally befuddles ESL students who are trying to learn English. Do you know what *your* students are reading during reading class?

Well-Written Text

In the course of my career as a librarian and media specialist, I've fought for the right to have all kinds of books on the shelves of my libraries. I don't believe

---

THE FULL-SERVICE LIBRARY

Open your school library early in the morning or during the evenings and summers for supervised reading and homework help. Offer computer classes to parents and students. Make sure the library is ready to serve students on the very first day of school and has an open-for-business policy all day, every day thereafter. Students should be able to come to the library at any time to check out books.

KEEPING TRACK

Give each student a personalized reading journal in second grade. Require students to record the titles, authors, and a two-sentence summary of every book they read from that moment forward. Teachers can use the journal to monitor the quantity and quality of their students' reading, and as they grow older, students will enjoy looking back at the titles and authors that consumed their interest in early elementary school.

in censorship, but lately, I've become more than a little distressed by some of the realistic fiction that's making the rounds. Students seem to be reading a lot of what Ann Tobias (as quoted in Duin, 1999), a book agent based in Arlington, VA, calls "the 4D books: death, divorce, drugs, or dismemberment." Educators lament the violence, hatred, and mayhem in our schools and society. We are quick to point fingers of blame at television, video games, films, and even parents as probable sources of the problem, but I never hear anyone blaming the books we are giving our students to read. Perhaps we should take a closer look at what's being recommended.

Consider the title, *Making Up Megaboy* (Walter, 1998), a story about a 13-year-old boy who walks into an inner-city grocery and kills its elderly Korean owner. The cast of narrators (a newspaper reporter, a policeman, the social worker, a teacher, and his friends) can't figure out why he did it. The boy remains silent, just drawing sketches of his imaginary superhero, Megaboy. Or take a look at *I Was a Teen-age Fairy* (Block, 1998). It features the topic of pedophilia as the centerpiece for the story of a teen-age model who is lured into the world of drugs, sex, and alcohol.

Even the list of nominees for the prestigious Rebecca Caudill Award, selected by Illinois students in Grades 4 through 8, is top-heavy with tough, gritty stories that would depress even the most upbeat, optimistic adults, to say nothing of impressionable young people. Many of the nominees over the past 3 years portray a world that is evil, ugly, and cruel, like Katherine Paterson's (1996) *Jip: His Story*, about which a reviewer in *The New York Times Book Review* stated, "Poverty, child abuse, slavery, racism, rape, insanity and death may not be what you expect to find in a novel for young readers" (Jewett, 2000).

Many recent young adult books are just plain confusing and ill conceived, such as *View From Saturday* by E. L. Konigsburg (1996). One teacher who posted a review on amazon.com put it this way:

> This was by far the worst book I have ever had the misfortune of reading. The author owes me the money and time I spent on this worthless pursuit. . . . Once again, the Newbery Medal choice [this book received the medal in 1997] boggles the imagination. The Newbery has become a way to tell us teachers what books not to bring into the classroom. (amazon.com, 2000)

Where are the biographies of famous and not-so-famous men and women who have made the world better? Isn't anybody writing stories of discovery, invention, selflessness, and learning? Aren't there any positive family relationships left in the world? I believe that students should have lots of choices from which to select their *voluntary* recreational reading. I also believe, however, that

THE READING BUS

Reduce discipline problems on the bus like one rural bus driver in rural Missouri did—encourage students to read while they are riding. Some students may experience motion sickness, of course, so reading cannot be required, but every student with his or her nose in a book is one less student distracting the driver.

BOOK REVIEWS

Encourage students and even teachers to write brief review for their favorite books and present them to students during the lunch hour. The advertisers can come solo or in an ensemble to "sell" their recommendations. Make sure to have a microphone available.

teachers should use their precious instructional time to focus on books that are challenging, are well-written, and have meaningful and enduring themes.

Varied Text

SPEND A DAY WITH AN AUTHOR

Invite an author to spend the day at your school. Encourage teachers to read the author's works aloud. Ask him or her to visit classrooms to talk about the writing process and then have an autograph session in conjunction with your annual book fair. I have done this on many occasions myself and find that students of all ages read far more thoughtfully when they know the author is expecting them to ask good questions and be critical, in a positive sense, of what they have read.

AN INCENTIVE TO READ

Set a goal for a total number of collective minutes to be read by the entire school community. Include students, teachers, parents, classified staff, and volunteers. Post a thermometer or other type of measure to keep track of the growing number. Choose what you believe is a wildly impossible amount of time and then watch it happen.

Not only must students read ample amounts of challenging text, they must read both expository and narrative texts. The early childhood emphasis on picture books and fairy tales plus the literature-based instruction that has dominated the reading diets of many early elementary students has not prepared most upper-grade, middle, and high school students for reading expository text. They can deal with plots, settings, and characters. But they are baffled by comparing and contrasting, cause and effect, or a sequence of historical events. With the advent of the Readers' Workshop (Atwell, 1998) and literature-based instruction (Peterson & Eeds, 1990), nonfiction has fallen on hard times.

ACT, the nation's largest provider of tests for college-bound students, periodically surveys middle-school, high school, and college teachers regarding the types of skills thought to be needed by students to succeed in college as well as the type of reading that should consume the majority of students' reading time. Teachers across the levels were in agreement about the skills needed for success in college, with drawing conclusions and making inferences from the text rated as the top two skills. They differed, however, on the most important type of reading needed for college success.

Middle- and high school teachers ranked prose fiction as the most important type of reading, ahead of text from the social sciences, humanities, and sciences. College teachers, on the other hand, ranked social science reading as being most important, with the humanities second and prose fiction third (ACT, 2000, p. 10). "There should be greater use of multiple texts in reading instruction, and most especially, the texts studied should not only be narrative, but also expository" (Kibby, 1993, p. 48). Don't forsake expository text totally in favor of fiction, particularly fiction with watered-down vocabulary and simple syntax (e.g., *Who Put That Hair in My Toothbrush?*).

THE IMPORTANCE OF ACCOUNTABILITY

Pervasive reading—reading in every subject, in every physical space, reading just about anything, just about all the time—is the key to reading success. A book is a piece of technology best used by the individual, not by the group.

Try to liberate readers from the group, and capture the intimate pleasures of reading, as often as possible. (Peter Temes, Director of the Great Books Foundation, personal communication, April, 2000).

The mother of a fourth grader contacted me not long ago to bemoan the fact that her son had not read a book from cover to cover in at least 2 years. She decried the current trend of project-based book reports in which students do not write in response to what they have read but, rather, make dioramas, mobiles, posters, and radio commercials. Her son's typical response to a book report assignment is to build a volcano. "He's been making these volcanoes since second grade, and they get bigger and more spectacular in their eruptions every year," his mother reported. "The only problem is that he never reads the books about volcanoes. He only builds them."

Project-based book reports are all the rage in middle and high schools as well. My high school granddaughter assured me that she *had* indeed read the book for which she was developing a slick brochure using a desktop publishing program. But she went on to share that most of her friends didn't bother to do so—they got all the information they needed for the assignment from the back cover copy and the blurb on the inside of the front cover.

If students of any age are to gain academic and personal benefits from the reading they do, they must be held accountable in meaningful and important ways. In response to their reading a lot, students must cognitively process what they read, talk about their reading with teachers and peers, and frequently write in response to what they have read. Teachers must hold their students accountable for reading books with understanding. There must be a balance between student-selected and teacher-directed reading, and less able readers must receive the instructional support they need to improve their reading skills.

The recent trend toward computer-based motivational reading programs, such as *Accelerated Reader* (Advantage Learning Systems, 2001) and *Reading Counts* (Scholastic, 2001a), has left the mistaken impression with some teachers that they no longer need to be concerned about either what or how well their students are reading because the computer will handle that. In reality, answering a few, relatively easy factual questions about a book that may or may not be at an appropriate level of difficulty is not the kind of accountability that reading in the zone demands. Meaningful accountability demands the flexing of cognitive muscles. Teachers must also be aware that students, eager to earn points and prizes, are often expending more energy beating the computer's scoring system than in reading books. There are dozens of ways to encourage students' creativity, personal response, and interpretation while still ensuring accountability. Figure 6.3 displays just a few of them.

THE ROMANCE OF READING

You can't give someone a cold if you don't have a cold, and it's tough to give someone a love of reading if you don't have it yourself. Jim Trelease (2001), author of *The Read-Aloud Handbook.*

Figure 6.3 Ways to Hold Students Accountable for Their Reading

Type	*Description*
Portfolios	A portfolio is "a collection of student work, connected to what has been read and studied, that reveals student progress. It might include items such as personal responses to reading assignments; self-assessments, teacher observations, attitude and interest surveys; writing samples (both complete and in progress); evidence that the student reads for enjoyment and information; and summaries" (Educational Research Service, 1998, p. 5). It might also include a list of books read by the student; a summary of several books read during the school year; a listing of books read categorized by genre to illustrate the breadth of reading during a school year; a description of a favorite book, a list of books read at home, or a list read at school; a brief description of the five latest books read; or a list or descriptions of favorite authors. Portfolios can be adapted to any grade level from second grade through high school.
Reading journals	Reading journals contain daily written responses to what has been read during a silent reading period or for an assignment. There are many ways to approach journal writing in response to reading, depending on the grade level or the type of text (narrative or expository). For a comprehensive description of a variety of reading journals and how to use them, see Ong and Breneman (2000).
Reading logs	Learning logs serve as a running record of students' perceptions of how and what they are learning. The paper is divided into three columns: "What I Did," "How I Worked and Learned," and "What I Learned." (Alvermann & Phelps, 1998).
Every-pupil response activities	After reading a portion of text, either in class or for a homework assignment, every student completes a brief written response to the text. Students then participate in a discussion with a partner. The writing assignment might include a brief explanation of a specific situation, problem, or question as a way of assessing their understanding of the concepts about which they were reading. These self-assessments are collected sporadically and never graded. The goal is to reach consensus with their partners regarding the question that was posed, by supporting their responses with text evidence and good reasoning as well as by considering the evidence and rationale presented by their partners (Gaskins et al., 1994, pp. 559–560).

Raising reading achievement was the last thing on my mind when I worked so vigorously as a teacher and media specialist at putting kids and books together. At that point in my career, I just wanted the students with whom I worked to enjoy the benefits of reading, both personal and professional, that I enjoyed. In fact, that was my reason for becoming a media specialist in the first place: to instill a love of books and develop the habits of reading in every student. I believed that there was no one I could not convince of the benefits of reading. Some individuals were harder to sell than others, however.

Fran,[1] an experienced upper-grade teacher, told me that she didn't have time to read silently at the same time as her students. "Too many papers to grade and lessons to plan," she explained.

I pushed, cajoled, and even intimated that she might lose her prime-time library slot if she didn't at least *pretend* to read during SSR (sustained silent reading). Under duress, she finally confessed the reason for her reluctance. "I hate to read," she said.

I was dumbfounded. How could she be a teacher and not love to read? She told me that she had just never found anything that she enjoyed. Without thinking, I challenged her. "What if I could find you something to read that you *would* enjoy? Would you read then?"

She was skeptical, but I'd backed her into a corner. I knew immediately what Fran needed—romance. I picked up a couple of romance novels at the local bookstore. They were what I call "bodice-ripping romances," for reasons you can no doubt deduce without further explanation. I also bought a quilted paperback book cover. Fran's hormonally charged students didn't need to be distracted during silent reading. Soon, Fran was reading, not only during silent reading in her classroom but during her planning period, lunch break, and any other spare minutes she could find. I suspected there were even days that Fran cancelled math and scheduled silent reading. That's what happens when someone discovers the delights of reading.

> ## MUST-READ BOOKS ABOUT READING A LOT
>
> Allington, R. (2001). *What Really Matters for Struggling Readers*. New York: Longman.
>
> Pilgreen, J. (2000). *The SSR Handbook: How to Organize and Manage a Sustained Silent Reading Program*. Portsmouth, NH: Boyton/Cook.
>
> Quindlen, A. (1998). *How Reading Changed My Life*. New York: Ballantine.

Convincing students to read who haven't yet discovered anything they want to read is a lot like motivating Fran. Reluctant readers need some romance, adventure, horror, or mystery in their lives. Whether you call them series books, junk reading, or beach reading, the genre of books that contains predictable plots, easy vocabulary, and continuing characters is often the foot in the door that educators need to engage reluctant readers. I heavily relied on such junk books to sell students on the idea that reading was a wonderful way to forget one's troubles. I do appreciate the concerns voiced by Egoff (1972) when she laments the time that students waste reading junk. But if I had given Fran a Joyce Carol Oates or Barbara Kingsolver novel, I know what her response would have been. Reluctant readers don't want to work too hard at their reading—at least not in the beginning. Fran needed something far more predictable and much less challenging. Once we have students (and their teachers) actually *reading a lot*, then we can wean them from the mind-numbing mediocrity of the

HOW TO PUT THE STUDENT AND THE BOOK TOGETHER

My biggest challenge as a media specialist was helping reluctant readers find the right book. First of all, it had to be interesting and appealing to the reader. Then, it had to be on the right reading level—not too babyish, or the student would be embarrassed and refuse to read the book, but not too hard, or the student couldn't read the book. Now, there's an answer to leveling books with almost pinpoint accuracy: the Lexile Framework (MetaMetrics, 1998). It is a tool that makes it possible to place readers and text on the same scale and eliminate the guesswork from helping readers choose books.

The difference between a reader's Lexile as measured by the Scholastic Reading Inventory (Scholastic, 2001b) and the Lexile of a specific book can be used to forecast the degree of understanding a reader will experience with that text. The Lexile Framework was developed under the auspices of the National Institute of Health and Human Development and includes a software program called the *Lexile Analyzer* that measures the difficulty of text using vocabulary. When a reader has the same Lexile measure as a text, the reader should be able to read that text with 75% comprehension. When the reader's measure exceeds the Lexile of a book, comprehension goes up to 90%, and the reader experiences total control and automaticity. The Lexile Framework has the potential for reducing the risk of frustrating readers and turning them off with text that is too difficult. "In reality, there are no poor readers—only mistargeted readers who are being challenged inappropriately" (Stenner, 1996).

Sweet Valley High (Pascal, 1995, 2001) or Choose Your Own Adventure (Packard, 1998) series and introduce them to more challenging and well-written fiction. Oh, by the way, Fran came to me when her romance novel was nearly finished and admitted that she was sorry to see the book end. I knew the feeling all too well.

"Would you like another one just like it?" I asked.

"You mean there are more?"

"Not to worry," I assured her. "Harlequin releases 50 new romance titles every week. You can have romance wherever or whenever you want it—in the Middle Ages, outer space, or in your own hometown." I've lost track of Fran but hope her reading tastes have matured.

Identifying and nurturing the context variables that genuinely motivate students to become engaged readers rather than students who merely pretend to read is undeniably a challenge. These variables include (a) teachers who love to read and are excited about recommending books to their students, (b) the skills to read with confidence and success, (c) an ample supply of books on every level but especially books for reluctant readers at lower reading levels, (d) opportunities for directed and focused silent reading during the school day, (e) the promotion of books and reading by every classroom teacher, and (f) superior library and media services.

SUMMARIZING CHAPTER 6

Hopefully, I have sold you on the benefits of reading a lot, despite the report of the National Reading Panel (2000). Let me caution you, however, about simply blocking out 20 minutes daily in your plan book or school schedule to drop everything and read, as one of the high schools in my area recently did. It will do little or nothing to raise the literacy levels of individual students or raise scores on your state or standardized assessments. To accomplish that, you will have to be far more focused and intentional in your efforts: (a) Find the students in your classroom, school, or district who don't know how to read, and teach them to read; (b) search out the dysfluent readers, and develop a fluency-building program for them immediately; (c) identify the students who need language and knowledge development and begin to systematically teach them the critical vocabulary and information they need to deal with the text at their grade level; (d) locate the huge numbers of students who are reading but don't get it, and integrate the four essential cognitive strategies into all curricular areas. Literacy involves putting all of the pieces of the puzzle in place—not just organizing a reading-incentive program.

LOOKING AHEAD

In Chapter 7, you will have the opportunity to look at a photo album. These aren't pictures of my vacation but, rather, before-and-after snapshots of schools and classrooms where individuals have discovered the exhilaration of *teaching them ALL to read.*

NOTE

1. Fran is not the real name of the teacher with whom I worked. A pseudonym has been used to protect her privacy.

7

Snapshots of Success

Classrooms and Schools That Work

There are many individuals who *know* a great deal about reading instruction—the academics in the field. They conduct research and publish for a living. I am grateful for these folks (at least, most of them) who are devoting their lives to solving the mysteries of reading so that we who labor down in the trenches can be more effective. However, there does come a time when words no longer suffice; *action* is what is needed. If you are a teacher or principal, you do not have time to hypothesize about reading instruction. You have classrooms of children who are falling through the cracks. If you are a central-office administrator, the pressures are no less intense. The taxpayers, parents, and the board of education don't want references and research. They want results!

I remember with some amusement a conversation about raising reading achievement that I had with an eminent reading professor when I was a brand-new principal. Faced with standardized test scores that were hovering at the 20th percentile overall in my K-6 elementary school, I naively assumed that a reading academic of stature and renown would be able to help me. Although his daily consulting fee was triple what I had in my staff development budget, I wasn't shy. I asked him what kinds of things he would do if we hired him to help us raise literacy levels at Lincoln School. He told me without a hint of embarrassment that he didn't know. "I've never worked with a school as low as yours," he said. "But, we'll figure it out as we go." Obviously, it is easier to write about reading instruction than it is to actually catch the kids who are falling through the cracks in reading.

To do that, educators must undeniably understand the critical attributes of the eight pieces of the reading puzzle we have discussed thus far: (a) phonological awareness, (b) phonics, (c) spelling, (d) fluency, (e) language, (f) knowledge, (g) cognitive strategies, and (h) reading a lot. But that is not enough. The reading professor with whom I chatted back in the fall of 1983 knew enough about reading to write several best-selling volumes. However, he was missing the most important piece of the puzzle—how to take what he knew intellectually and make it operational in a challenging school environment. He had no idea how to create a pervasive and persuasive reading culture.

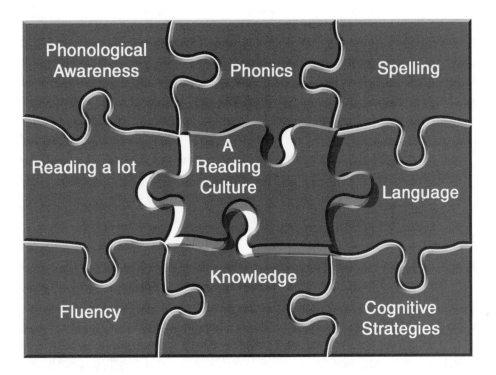

TWELVE TRAITS OF A PERVASIVE AND PERSUASIVE READING CULTURE

To teach them all to read, the attention of every individual who works in, attends, or sends children to a school must be focused on literacy. This is the defining quality of a *pervasive* reading culture. In addition, any newcomers to the school community will immediately be made aware of the commitment of all of the stakeholders to literacy for every student and soon find that they have been enlisted in the cause as well. That is what a *persuasive* reading culture is like. Pervasive and persuasive reading cultures are characterized by the following 12 traits:

- Strong instructional leadership by both administrators and teacher leaders to include shared decision making regarding vital curricular and instructional issues

- High expectations and accountability for students, teachers, and parents—a sense of academic press that is shared by the entire school community
- A relentless commitment to results driven by meaningful and measurable short- and long-term goals
- A research-based curriculum
- A well-designed instructional delivery system that offers "coordinated and differentiated instructional interventions for the full range of learners" (Coyne, Kame'enui, & Simmons, 2001, p. 69)
- Comprehensive assessment of student progress that includes early identification and frequent monitoring of students at risk of reading failure
- The scrupulous use of allocated instructional time and the creative marshalling of extracurricular instructional time (e.g., vacations, before and after school)
- The integration and coordination of special services (e.g., special education, Title I, remedial reading, and speech)
- Constant communication and coordination between and among teachers regarding curriculum and instruction
- Ongoing and meaningful staff development
- The support of parents and the community for literacy
- The availability and allocation of adequate resources

SOME BEFORE-AND-AFTER SNAPSHOTS

There are classrooms and schools by the score across the country in which hundreds of thousands of students fall through the cracks every year. Their teachers and principals are hardworking, well-meaning, and caring individuals, but they are missing a key piece of the reading puzzle. In the pages ahead, you will meet some educators from around the country who know precisely what is missing from these classrooms and schools. They have "been there and done that." They have experienced the frustration that comes from well-intentioned but ineffective efforts. The difference is that these individuals no longer feel powerless. They are doing something about the problem—something that works! They are *teaching them all to read!* Take a look at the before-and-after snapshots of their schools and classrooms.

The Before-and-After Snapshots of La Mesa Dale Elementary School, La Mesa Dale, California

Kathie Dobberteen is the principal of La Mesa Dale Elementary School in the San Diego area. Following is her description of La Mesa Dale *before* she and her staff worked together to assemble all of the pieces of the reading puzzle.

Seven years ago, La Mesa Dale was a typical elementary school staffed by caring teachers who worked in a self-contained environment; they were committed to doing their best for students in their classrooms.

Collegiality was not a priority, and although camaraderie existed, the staff worked independently to meet the challenges of educating their students who came primarily from low-income homes. Reading, although an important aspect of the educational process, was not a focus. It was treated with a remedial flavor—putting Band-Aids on small groups of children who were experiencing difficulties. The staff at La Mesa Dale lacked a common vision and felt no sense of personal accountability for the achievement of their students. The school was ruled by the belief that the low socioeconomic status of our students meant we would have correspondingly low achievement. Although we sensed that change was needed, we initially grasped at anything that was new. First, we focused on multicultural education, hoping to build acceptance and tolerance among our culturally diverse population. Then, we emphasized conflict resolution to encourage respect, self-reliance, and student ownership of what took place at school. None of these programs had any impact on student achievement, however.

Then, the winds of change began to blow. Kathie Dobberteen caught a vision of what could happen in a school when educators changed their beliefs and values. Teachers began to think and work and plan and dream *together* instead of separately. They discovered that "the wizard was within them" and that if they collectively focused on a goal, they were unstoppable. They have never looked back.

The "after" snapshots of La Mesa Dale School are inspiring. The first one shows the fifth-grade graduating class of 2001—a group of exuberant pre-adolescents who can't wait to get to middle school. Ninety-four percent of them are reading above grade level, and a third of them are reading at eighth- and ninth-grade levels. In their youthful naivete, they are oblivious to their amazing achievements. Their parents and teachers, however, are all too aware of what could have happened to them. They might well have fallen through the cracks, but instead, they learned to read and write.

The next photo in the album shows the staff and principal of La Mesa Dale. They are surrounded by the plaques, certificates, and awards they have collected during the past 3 years in recognition of their accomplishments with students —a Title I Distinguished School, a California Distinguished School, and a Change Award from the Chase Manhattan Bank and Fordham University. You can tell that some of them are a bit uncomfortable with all of this recognition. They would feel more at ease back in their classrooms doing what they have done daily for the past 5 years—quietly teaching them all to read.

The last picture in the La Mesa Dale album was shot from the roof of the school and shows a sea of smiling faces. Every student is wearing the school colors and grinning broadly to celebrate the fact that 90% of the student body at this Title I school was reading at or above grade level in the spring of 2001 (up from 42% in 1996). What took place during those 5 years to bring about such a dramatic improvement? All of the pieces of the reading puzzle were assembled, including the all-important piece in the center of the puzzle—a pervasive and persuasive reading culture.

The Before-and-After Snapshot of Hartsfield Elementary School, Tallahassee, Florida

More than 3,000 miles across the country, in Tallahassee, Florida, the educators at the Hartsfield Elementary School were having similar experiences to their counterparts in California. Their "before" snapshot shows a demoralized staff on film. Accustomed to teaching above-average students from advantaged homes, they were ill prepared for the increasing instructional demands in their rapidly changing neighborhood. Their overall attitude was one of providing the content and watching the students who were able, learn, while the rest continued to fall further behind academically. There was no sense of ownership by the regular classroom teachers of the achievement of their students and no coordination of the content or instruction within or across grade levels. In 1994, nearly a third of Hartsfield's first graders scored in the bottom quartile on an end-of-year reading test. The students who needed the most instruction actually received the least. At-risk learners were constantly on the move throughout the school, going from pullout program to pullout program and finding a multitude of ways to waste their time as they went. They felt accountable to no one.

The picture changed dramatically under the strong instructional leadership of Ray King. During 5 years of intense culture building that included an ever-increasing sense of ownership and accountability for all students, the replacement of over half of the staff with new hires over a 4-year period, a realignment of the curriculum and instructional delivery system, and a relentless search at the end of every school year for additional ways to tighten the safety net and notch up everyone's performance (students, teachers, administrators, and parents), the assessment picture became much brighter and more focused.

In 1999, fewer than 4% of first graders at Hartsfield scored in the bottom quartile on an end-of-year reading assessment. In second grade, the percentage of students below the 25th percentile dipped to less than 2%. During that same year, Hartsfield Elementary School, with a 60% free- and reduced-lunch population, produced the highest scores in their district on the state writing assessment—the sixth-best narrative writing scores in the state of Florida. Literacy was no longer just a vision or a mission for Hartsfield. It was a reality.

The Before-and-After Snapshot of Project PRIDE, Rockford, Illinois

In Rockford, about 75 miles northwest of Chicago, there are dozens of schools and hundreds of teachers struggling with the challenges of meeting the needs of low-SES and racial or ethnic minority students, as well as countless numbers of limited-English-proficient students from a variety of countries and cultures. It is an ideal setting in which to demonstrate the power of early identification and the direct teaching of literacy skills, the focus of Project PRIDE, developed by Bill Bursuck and Dennis Munk, professors at Northern Illinois University. The Rockford district is still recovering from the deleterious effects of a desegregation lawsuit that went on for more than a decade, resources are limited, and the challenges are enormous. But the teachers in the trenches keep trudging along, doing what all well-intentioned and caring teachers do— the best they know how for the kids in their classrooms.

Kindergarten teacher Paula Larson has been trudging for 9 years, from whole-language to Success for All and everything in between. However, none of these approaches gave her the kind of satisfaction and instructional success she experienced during the first year of using the Project PRIDE model. "I've often felt left out of the mix by all of the staff development and different programs I've been through," she explained.

> Kindergarten almost seemed like an add-on sometimes. No matter what program I used or what I did, though, the results were inevitably the same. None of my students went on to first grade with the skills they needed to read, much less reading.

That is, until the 2000–2001 school year. For the first time in her career, all of Paula's students, 100% of them on free lunch and a sizable percentage of them also limited English proficient, knew at least 20 sounds and were able to orally blend those sounds to make spoken words by the end of the year. But even more exhilarating to Paula was the fact that eight of her students, nearly one third of her all-day kindergarten class were reading! Paula credits the instructional strategies provided by the Project PRIDE training and coaching with making all the difference in the world. "I was so floored with my results," she said, " that I was telling anyone who would listen."

Reading achievement overall is well under the 50th percentile in the three schools served by Project PRIDE (Preventing and Remediating Reading Problems through Early Identification and Direct Teaching of Early Literacy Skills), a Model Demonstration Project for Children with Disabilities funded through the Office of Special Education Programs (H324T990024-01). PRIDE is a multitiered model for grades K-3 that offers extra support for students at the first sign of reading difficulty. See Resource C for a comprehensive description.

Bill, Dennis, and Mary Damer, their on-site coordinator and coach, are using every strategy in their toolkits to help the teachers of Rockford catch those students who are most likely to fall through the cracks *before* they begin to spiral downward. The PRIDE team began training kindergarten classroom and Title I teachers as well as paraprofessionals during the summer of 2000, and the program components were put into place with incoming kindergarten students that fall. In the fall of 2001, the program added a second cohort of kindergarten students, trained the first-grade teachers, and put program components into place in the first-grade classrooms.

Project PRIDE has four main goals: (a) to provide teachers with the skills and assessments to identify at-risk readers, (b) to show teachers how to adapt their current curriculum and reading series to provide the necessary early intervention, (c) to teach teachers how to use instructional strategies that are known to be effective with students at risk of reading failure, and (d) to show administrators and teachers how to design support systems for those students who need more intensive help.

Paula says, "Using the PRIDE model has changed everything and changed nothing." What she means by this cryptic remark is that she is teaching the same content she has always taught in kindergarten and is even using the same reading series (Harcourt). The difference is in the *how* of teaching the content and the ways in which she is interacting with her students. "I still teach the literature component of the program and I still teach the sounds," she explains. "But now I am using instructional strategies that virtually ensure success for every child—the I Do It, We Do It, You Do It lesson sequence; signaling, advance organizers, unison responding, and especially the repetition and review."

Paula made the following revelatory statement regarding what had always troubled her about her teaching in the past: "I'm not tricking my children anymore," she explained, "by making them feel successful when they really aren't. Now my students don't feel the stress of failure anymore—just the thrill of success!" And the successes of their kindergarten year (2000–2001) definitely carried over to first grade, even after a long summer break when at-risk students traditionally lose ground.

Dottie Lindblade, an experienced educator turned paraprofessional, teaches several Project PRIDE kindergarten booster groups (an additional instructional session that reinforces regular classroom instruction) and is also working with a group of first-grade PRIDE graduates. "It's amazing what these kids have retained over the summer," Dottie reported. "They are still sounding out and blending with accuracy. Even the lowest students have kept a handle on the majority of their sounds and can sound out words."

Sheri Hayes, a Title I teacher, believes the secret lies in the intensive, regular practice sessions and the small-group structure. "At-risk students don't necessarily need something different to be successful," she said. "They just need a lot more of it, and they need it in a small-group setting."

Mary Damer, Project PRIDE's trainer, coach, and all-around encourager, has an extensive background in teaching and administration in the public schools and is full of accolades for the teachers' success with students. She reports that without Sheri's focused teaching using the PRIDE model, coupled with her "won't give up" attitude, two of her most challenging students (one, limited English proficient and the other, ADHD), would definitely be bound for special education. At this point in first grade, however, they are upward bound.

A former math teacher, principal Marcia Strothoff is especially thrilled by the arrival of Project PRIDE in her building. She confesses that she didn't know much about reading instruction when she took the job. "What I do understand is data," she explains. "I am a data-driven person." And the achievement data in her school were depressing when she arrived—at the 38th percentile in reading. Eighty percent of her students are on free lunch, and the school is located in a culturally diverse neighborhood. Far too many of her students were falling through the cracks, and she had no idea what to do about it. "I called central office looking for anything they could give me," she said. What they gave her was Project PRIDE.

The project was assigned to her building and the pretest and end-of-year posttest data from her two kindergarten classes made Marcia decide that this was a program she wanted to keep. She immediately set about crunching numbers to figure out how she could keep the critical coaching component of the program in place after the 4-year demonstration program ends. "I wrote a grant, got it, and I've hired a teacher who is closely working with the PRIDE coach to learn the ropes," she explained. " I want this initiative to sustain itself."

There are a number of "after" snapshots in the Rockford photo album. The first one shows a group of smiling and proud teachers. They feel a renewed sense of efficacy as a result of their ability to make a difference in the lives of students, most of whom would have fallen through the cracks without their effective teaching. Picture number two is of an energized building principal who finally sees hope for sending her students on to middle school with the ability to read. The next photo is a group shot showing more than 300 five- and six-year-olds happily waving books at the camera—books they can read. The folks in the last picture look a little weary but very satisfied. They are the Project PRIDE designers, Bill Bursuck and Dennis Munk, along with their indefatigable coach, Mary Damer. They weathered the frustration, indifference, and downright hostility that anyone who is trying to create a pervasive and persuasive reading culture encounters, and they survived to move their program up to the next grade level!

The Before-and-After Snapshots of Nettie Griffin, Kindergarten Teacher, Oakbrook, Illinois

Nettie Griffin came to the teaching profession in a roundabout way after a successful but unfulfilling career in marketing and advertising. Restless and looking for an outlet, she started tutoring students at a Chicago housing project and then went on to become an adult Literacy Volunteer. The intrinsic rewards of these experiences motivated her to leave a well-paying job in business and earn her MA in teaching. Her consuming passion: to teach kids to read. She was in for a big surprise. Here is her story in her own words.

I just assumed that in graduate school, I would be learning how to teach children to read. Instead, I learned about whole language, developmentally appropriate practices, and child-centered classrooms. I must confess that although it wasn't the way I had learned to read and write, it sounded like a lot of fun! In addition, I discovered that I didn't have to be tied to textbooks. I could develop my own themes and teach children to read and write using any ideas or topics I chose. I only needed to immerse students in language, and they would magically learn to read and write—just as they had learned to talk! It was all very exciting.

Phonics was never mentioned in any of my classes; nor was spelling. The words *direct instruction* were equivalent to child abuse, according to my university professors. Since I was in education to help children and would never do anything to hurt them, I came to believe that structured instruction was harmful to children.

Even after I graduated, I had no idea how I was going to teach my students to read and write. But I was naive enough to believe that given the right combination of magical immersion and my personal giftedness as a teacher, they would learn! If I motivated them to love books and reading, the rest of the pieces would fall into place. When I took my first job, I began doing the most wonderful thematic units you can imagine. My students loved it. Did any of them learn to read that first year? Only one. Of course, she would no doubt have learned no matter how I taught! None of my students learned to read during my second year of teaching, either. I reassured myself that it was OK. My college professors and the whole-language gurus told me that these children were not developmentally ready to read. "Childhood is a journey after all," they told me.

I even hosted a workshop for the parents of my students to let them know that their children *would* learn to read and write just as they had learned to speak. I told them that workbooks were bad, flashcards were evil, and direct instruction was destructive. I advised them, "Don't push your children. They will learn to read. It may not happen until second or third grade," but, according to my college professors, "they would bloom when they were ready."

Yet during all of those years, in the back of my mind, I knew that something was wrong. Why weren't any of my students ever developmentally ready? Why weren't they learning to read? After all, I used developmentally appropriate practices, my room was child centered, I was facilitating rather than teaching, and my students were totally immersed in language. At the same time, I kept hearing complaints in the media from parents, upset because their children weren't learning to read. Every time I turned on the TV, someone was bashing teachers.

I began to think that perhaps I was wrong. Maybe those parents did have a point. After all, I reasoned, I learned to read and write in a teacher-centered, direct-instruction-oriented classroom, and my self-esteem was intact. My creativity didn't suffer. I learned to love to read. So with that in mind, I unsubscribed from the whole-language listserv and began to search the Internet for resources about how to teach reading. I discovered phonemic awareness and began to read the research. I left my whole-language-oriented private school and went to work in a public school. During the interview before I was hired, I was asked questions about phonemic awareness and phonics. Here was a school where I could actually teach and not merely facilitate.

Nettie's research-based program and how she assembled the pieces to teach them all to read is described in Chapter 8. Before you read ahead, however, imagine you are glancing at Nettie's "after" snapshot. If you look closely at the kindergarten group picture taken on the playground just before summer vacation, you can spy Nettie in the back row kneeling beside one of her students. Everyone is smiling broadly. The reason? They all learned to read in Nettie's kindergarten class!

SUMMARIZING CHAPTER 7

We can, whenever and wherever we choose, successfully teach all children to read. We already know more than we need to do that. Whether or not we do it must finally depend on how we feel about the fact that we haven't so far. All of the educators described in this chapter experienced a deep sense of dissatisfaction with the status quo. Too many of their students were failing to learn to read. But rather than accepting the seeming inevitability of that failure, they realized that they had the power to bring about change. And so do you!

LOOKING AHEAD

The final chapter of the book puts all of the pieces of the reading puzzle together and shows you precisely what the finished product looks like. You will find out exactly what Kathie Dobberteen, Nettie Griffin, Ray King, and the Project PRIDE team have done. There are 50 site-tested strategies (I've included some that we used in the 1980s at Lincoln Elementary School in West Chicago, Illinois), each one illustrated with specific examples that will help you to build a reading culture in your classroom, school, or district *and,* at the same time, realize your goal of teaching them ALL to read.

8

Putting the Final Piece in Place

Creating a Pervasive and Persuasive Reading Culture

There is no prescription, potion, or purchased program that can create the kind of pervasive and persuasive reading culture that refuses to let children fail. That kind of culture can only be developed over time as strong instructional leaders and highly effective teachers perceive needs and respond to them in research-based ways. There are, however, multiple strategies that successful educators across the country are using with amazing results. I have organized these strategies in categories that correspond to the 12 characteristics of a reading culture.

FIFTY SITE-TESTED STRATEGIES TO BUILD A PERVASIVE AND PERSUASIVE READING CULTURE

1.0. Develop Strong Instructional Leadership and Implement Shared Decision Making by Administrators and Teacher Leaders

An instructional leader has a sense of purpose, broad knowledge of the educational process and knows learning theory. He or she is a risk taker, has people skills, and unlimited energy. (McEwan, 1998a, p. 7)

An instructional leader has a passion for great teaching and a vision for what schools should be doing for children. He should have well thought out answers for three fundamental questions about schooling: How do children learn? How should we teach children? and How should we treat subject matter? (p. 7)

1.1. Begin Wth Principals, Not Programs

The community may provide a frame of reference for defining a school's mission, but it is the leader's vision that guides the day-to-day functioning of schools. (Weber, 1987, p. 13)

Instructional leadership is the key to building a pervasive and persuasive reading culture. If you are a central office administrator charged with improving literacy in your district, the place to begin is always with the principals. First, sit down with each one individually to talk about what is going on in their schools. Examine achievement data in both aggregated and disaggregated formats. Do not be unduly impressed by an aggregated positive achievement picture until you have determined how effectively the school is serving its at-risk students in comparison to everyone else. Examine the percentage of students in special education and remedial reading. Do those categories contain a disproportionate number of low-SES or ethnic and racial minority students? Does achievement data indicate a leveling off or a sharp drop-off after third or fourth grade? What is the current dropout rate at the high school level? Who are the students who are dropping out? What does longitudinal achievement data reveal? Are the scores moving in a positive or negative direction?

Determine what each principal's vision is for catching the kids who are falling through the cracks. Encourage them to read this book as well as one of the companion volumes that is grade-level specific—*The Principal's Guide to Raising Reading Achievement* (McEwan, 1998b) for elementary school principals or *Raising Reading Achievement in Middle and High Schools: Five Simple-to-Follow Strategies for Principals* (McEwan, 2001a). After you have met individually with the principals, gather them together as a group, and ask each one to share publicly what they are already doing that is making a difference in their schools.

Then, do a Force Field Analysis, shown in Figure E.1 found in Resource E, to identify the obstacles that are standing in the way of catching the kids who are falling through the cracks. Nurture and support outstanding principals. Remediate problem principals, and if necessary, dismiss them. It is impossible to bring about meaningful change and sustain it without strong instructional leadership. Spending money on programs without hiring strong principals to lead them is a waste of resources.

1.2. Have a Vision and a Mission Worth Working For

By each interaction, teachers and administrators confirm or erode that set of professional norms and relations on which steady improvement rests. (Bird & Little, 1985, p. 3)

The hallmark of Kathie Dobberteen's strong instructional leadership is her overriding personal mission statement: "*We will not allow the demographics of the neighborhood to determine the destiny of our children. We are willing to do whatever it takes to make sure that children will be literate.*" Kathie's staff members have responded to her articulation of this mission in both her words and actions with substantive results. When the percentage of economically disadvantaged students scoring above the 50th percentile in reading at La Mesa Dale is compared with the rest of the state (California), the percentages at La Mesa Dale are two to three times higher at every grade level than the state's averages. "*At La Mesa Dale, we are absolutely determined not to let a single student slip through the cracks.*" That is a vision worth working for.

The cornerstone of success at Hartsfield Elementary was the creation of a culture focused on increased expectations for students and teachers as well as a focus, both academic and financial, on reading and writing for all students. The school improvement plan was the blueprint, and the school budget was *completely* devoted to the goals of the plan. Ray King believes that his actions as a leader must mirror his words and that his efforts must be unyielding. His staff followed where he led—even when the going was tough.

1.3. Follow the Seven Steps to Effective Instructional Leadership

Shadow strong instructional leaders, and you will see them following these seven steps. Strong instructional leaders are intentional, focused, and consistent in their efforts to

- Establish, implement, and achieve academic standards
- Be instructional resources for their staffs
- Create a school culture and climate conducive to learning
- Communicate the vision and mission of their schools
- Set high expectations for their staffs and themselves
- Develop teacher leaders
- Develop and maintain positive relationships with students, staff, and parents

If you or someone you supervise needs guidance in becoming a strong instructional leader or would benefit from encouragement to persevere in the face of discouragement and obstacles, consult *Seven Steps to Effective Instructional Leadership* (McEwan, 1998a).

1.4. Develop Teacher Leaders

Highly effective teachers exert leadership by influencing others to change, learn, grow, expand, move forward, do things differently, become independent, take responsibility, and achieve goals. Here are some of the ways that the teachers at La Mesa Dale and Hartsfield have responded to the leadership challenge: (a) mentoring and coaching new teachers; (b) collaborating with all staff members, regardless of personal affiliation or preference; (c) learning and growing with a view to bringing new ideas to the classroom and school; (d) polishing writing and presentation skills to share knowledge with others; (e) engaging in creative problem solving and decision making with increased student learning as the goal; (f) being willing to take risks in front of peers; and (g) being willing to share ideas, opinions, and evaluative judgments confidently with the principal. (McEwan, 2001b)

1.5. *Form a Building Leadership Team to Focus on Reading Improvement*

Essential to creating a reading culture is the formation of a team of teachers and parents to write a mission statement and provide overall leadership for any improvement initiative. The building leadership team at Lincoln School met monthly for half a day. Our agenda focused exclusively on instruction and curricular issues. Here are just a few of the projects that consumed our efforts during an 8-year period: (a) developing a booklet for parents that contained the school's learning standards in language arts and mathematics that predated the development of state and local standards; (b) developing a set of academic expectations for students, teachers, and parents; (c) writing a buildingwide behavior plan; (d) establishing and overseeing the building's academic awards program; (e) disaggregating and examining achievement data to determine gaps in learning; (f) studying time-on-task data schoolwide to determine how allocated instructional time was being used; (g) planning enrichment and extracurricular programs, such as Battle of the Books, RIF reading celebration events, and the Ball Seed Company learning partnership; (h) developing a report card by which parents evaluated various aspects of our school; (i) developing a peer observation and coaching model; (j) giving yearly feedback to the principal for purposes of improving her instructional leadership; (k) setting yearly buildingwide achievement goals; and (l) planning celebrations in honor of staff achievements.

Hartsfield School's Advisory Council, composed of parents, teachers, and representatives of the parent-teacher organization, worked collaboratively on a series of belief statements and a school vision that emphasized student responsibility and achievement. This document provided the impetus as well as the foundation for a gradual change process at the school that involved, among other variables, (a) increased parent and teacher expectations for behavior and academic performance, (b) a commitment to meeting individual student needs at all levels, (c) the adoption and implementation of a research-based reading curriculum, (d) objective assessment to evaluate student progress and the effectiveness of reading programs, (e) the design and implementation of an effective instructional delivery system, (f) maximizing available instructional time, and (g) administrative monitoring of student progress and program implementation.

2.0. Hold High Expectations and Make Everyone Accountable for Achievement

2.1. *Communicate a Can-Do Attitude to Every Student*

It is one thing for educators to talk about high expectations for students. It is quite another when the students themselves can "feel" and articulate these expectations. A student at La Mesa Dale School was overheard explaining how things worked at his school to some visitors: "Our teachers won't let us fail. That's why my mom sends us here!" (There is open enrollment in the La Mesa Dale District.) It is not enough to just have high expectations for students. The students must experience them on a daily basis.

2.2. Communicate the Status of Student Performance to Students and Parents in Specific and Meaningful Ways

Kathie Dobberteen explains how this strategy is operationalized in her school:

In the past, we used a report card that was very nonspecific about student performance. Students were marked in developmental stages and parents had no ideas whether students were actually achieving at grade level. Now, students are tested and assigned to reading groups based on their reading level. For students who are not attaining standards in reading, we hold a second parent teacher conference to focus only on reading. The meetings include members of the Reading Resource Team and the reading specialist. Suggestions and techniques are shared with parents so they can become an integral part of the instructional team and we offer assistance at home that complements the instruction program at school.

2.3. Apply Ample Amounts of Academic Press

We will never know the extent to which many students, whether higher or lower achieving, *can* achieve if we do not continually raise the bar. Stahl, Pagnucco, and Suttles (1996) examined two schools that operated under very different instructional philosophies to determine which of the approaches would result in higher reading achievement. The process-oriented school, as described by the researchers, was characterized by a developmentally appropriate mind-set. The teachers were unwilling to push children; they allowed them to choose and read only those materials with which they were most comfortable, and they emphasized self-esteem rather than achievement. The result is that their students read relatively easy material.

In contrast, the traditional school stressed achievement. Teachers pushed students to read more and also to read more difficult material that was available to them in the form of a graded basal reader. The researchers observed large differences on the students' Informal Reading Inventory scores favoring the traditional school. The differences were greater than had been expected by the researchers and even came as a surprise to them because they personally favored the activities in the process school. The major difference between the two schools as noted by the investigators was in the amount and intensity of *academic press*, an instructional relentlessness that pushed students to tackle more difficult work and to reach for higher levels of achievement. Also noteworthy, and certainly a factor to be considered in the higher scores at the traditional school although it was not mentioned in the research summary, was the fact that the traditional school taught between two to three times as much phonics as the process-oriented school.

2.4. Hold Classroom Teachers Accountable for the Reading
Achievement of Their Students.

Several images comes to mind when thinking about those occasions when
the principal is in direct contact with a teacher or teachers with regard to the
instructional process: the captain with sword drawn, leading the charge; the
coach in the huddle during a timeout diagramming a play; the sales manager
giving a peptalk; the orchestra director conducting a rehearsal. (Acheson,
1985, p. 1)

Even if a student receives remedial or tutorial assistance, Kathie Dobberteen
holds the child's classroom teacher accountable for what happens to that student in terms of learning to read. She explains how she does this:

Teachers take a far greater interest in what is happening in remedial
classes when they know that they are ultimately responsible for the
reading levels of their students. It makes them consult more with the
teacher who is doing the intervention. Because we have an extensive
reading database of every students' scores, I can track how much
progress each child is making, how well the classroom as a whole is
progressing compared to other classes at that grade level, how much
progress a specific grade level is making as compared to the whole
school, and finally how much whole-school progress we are making
compared to other school years. I talk to teachers about their low
readers both formally (in a principal/teacher conference format) and
informally as I observe in classrooms.

3.0. Develop a Relentless Commitment to Results Driven by Long- and Short-Term Goals

3.1. Set Meaningful and Measurable Long-Term Goals

Set long-term goals that can be measured. For example, in the first year of
school improvement at Lincoln, our goal was to reduce the number of students
who scored in the bottom quartile on the standardized test by 15%. First,
we developed a target list—the name of every student currently scoring below
the 25th percentile in reading. Second, we gave a more comprehensive reading
test to all of the target students to determine specific areas of need. Next, I held
meetings with every teacher to talk about his or her personal target list. I
invited the reading teacher, the psychologist, and the central office administrators in charge of special education, bilingual education, and Title I. I knew that
to meet the needs of our target students, the ability to coordinate services
across special programs and find additional resources and alternative ways to
deliver services was essential. After our initial meeting, I asked the teachers
to think about what they could do on a daily basis that would notch up expectations, offer additional instructional support, and provide extra practice opportunities for these students.

We then held a second meeting to develop an individualized plan for each
student. Teachers kept the names of these students in their plan books and built

something into every lesson especially for them. Options included, but were not limited to, vocabulary development for ESL students, extra oral reading practice for a dysfluent student, peer tutoring to keep a student on-task, or a booster skill session after school or during recess. The teachers kept up the academic press all year long.

One teacher told me later that it was that list of names that kept her focused on the goal. She said, "Every time I looked at that list, I thought, 'What else can I do that will enable this student to be a more successful reader by the end of the school year?'"

3.2. Use the 30-Minute/30-Day Rapid-Results Goal-Setting Process to Keep Teachers Focused on the Constant Development and Attainment of Short-Term Goals

Long-term goals are essential, but they are not enough to keep teachers' focused over a 9-month period. The staff at La Mesa Dale Elementary School has taken goal setting to the next higher level. They have adapted Mike Schmoker's (1999) 30-minute time-efficient meeting (pp. 119–120) into a 30-minute/30-day rapid-results goal-setting process. When a goal has been met, they hold another meeting and set another goal. During a 30-minute meeting, a group of grade-level teachers can brainstorm an instructional area for focus, determine a meaningful goal and a way to measure it, and develop several strategies for producing increased student learning. See Forms E.2 and E.3 in Resource E for sample goal-setting forms. The results that the La Mesa Dale staff have achieved by focusing the collective energies of all of the teachers at a grade level on a specific instructional problem or deficit bring Carl Glickman's (1993) words to life: "The litmus test for a good school is not its innovations but rather the solid, purposeful, enduring results it . . . obtain[s] for its students" (p. 50).

4.0. Focus on the Research

4.1. Personally Read the Research

Anna Quindlen (1998) has written a wonderful book titled *How Reading Changed My Life*. Kindergarten teacher Nettie Griffin could have written the same book. When she started reading books about reading instruction, she discovered that she had been misled in graduate school. Oh, her professors were well-meaning, but they had no idea how to teach children to read. Some of the books that changed Nettie's life and ultimately the lives of her students are listed here. If too many of your students are falling through the cracks, read some of Nettie's recommendations. Reading may change your life, as well of as your students' lives, too.

Adams, M., Foorman, B. R., Lundberg, I., & Beeler, T. (1998). *Phonemic Awareness in Young Children: A Classroom Curriculum*. Baltimore: Brookes.

Burns, M. S., Griffin, P., & Snow, C. (Eds.). (1999). *Starting Out Right: A Guide to Promoting Children's Reading Success*. Washington, DC: National Academy Press. Retrieved January 5, 2002 from www.nap.edu/catalog/6014.html

Hall, S., & Moats, L. (1998). *Straight Talk About Reading*. New York: McGraw-Hill.

Institute for Multisensory Education. (1998). *Sensational Strategies for Teaching Beginning Readers*.
Retrieved January 5, 2002, from www.ortongillingham.com

McGuinness, C., & McGuinness, G. (1998). *Reading Reflex*. New York: Simon & Schuster.

O'Connor, R. E., Notari-Syverson, A., & Vadasy, P. (1997). *Ladders to Literacy: A Kindergarten Activity Book*. Baltimore: Brookes.

Savage, J. (2000). *Sound It Out! Phonics in a Balanced Reading Program*. New York: McGraw-Hill.

4.2. Conduct Action Research in Your Classroom, School, or District

Linda Thomas is a reading specialist at the Fletcher Hills School in the La Mesa-Spring Valley School District in California. Although the majority of Linda's students usually met with success when she used the three-cueing system as a word identification strategy, every year there was a small percentage who showed little or no progress with that approach. It usually took a year of frustration and failure before these at-risk students were eligible for the resource specialist's phonics program, but by then, they had already lost not only a year of instructional time but also their initial enthusiasm for learning to read.

Rather than concluding that the children were the problem, Linda remained open to the possibility that her methodology could be at fault. She decided to do some action research to determine whether another approach might work more effectively to foster decoding and comprehension among her beginning reading students, especially those at-risk of reading failure. She hypothesized, based on what she had seen happen to many of her students, that beginning readers who received instruction in phonics would decode more successfully than beginning readers who received instruction in the cueing systems.

Linda's action research, although limited in scope, certainly convinced her of the power of phonics instruction. Not only were the students who received instruction in phonics able to decode more successfully than beginning readers receiving instruction in the cueing systems, the phonics-instruction group also had better comprehension scores (Thomas, 2000).

Linda is recommending that her district emphasize phonics over the simultaneous use of the three systems in kindergarten and first grade. Although they currently have a phonics component, it is not emphasized. Her recommendation is based not just on her own action research but also on her extensive review of existing research (Adams, 1990; Chall, 1967, 1983; Iverson & Tunmer, 1993). Subsequent research by Chapman, Tunmer, and Prochnow (2001) demonstrated that students enrolled in a remedial program that did not include direct instruction in decoding skills and strategies (i.e., Reading Recovery) failed to acquire the phonological processing skills they needed to be successful readers.

4.3. Collaboratively Study the Research

Ray King and his staff used the key ideas from Marilyn Adams's (1990) classic work, *Beginning to Read: Thinking and Learning About Print*, as a focus for their study of the reading research. Dr. Joe Torgesen of Florida State University worked with the staff to help them understand what the research said about the essential components of reading instruction and what was critical in choosing an instructional approach and a curriculum. Two other excellent research summaries that could be used for this purpose are the *Executive Summary of the National Reading Panel* (National Reading Panel, 2000) and Preventing Reading Difficulties in Young Children (Snow et al., 1998).

4.4. Make Research-Based Decisions

After the Hartsfield staff reviewed the research, they established a set of criteria they believed to be important in the light of that research and then examined a variety of published reading programs. They narrowed their choices to Open Court's (1995) *Collection for Young Scholars* and the *Reading Mastery* series (SRA/McGraw-Hill, 1999). Both programs met the criteria they had established ahead of time. The Open Court curriculum offered a balance of phonemic awareness and phonics instruction (with blending as the key strategy), along with a variety of literature selections and activities. A parallel strand provided Big Books and story-sharing activities to promote oral language comprehension and love of literature in the primary grades. *Reading Mastery*, also one of the components of Project PRIDE, was used as a supplementary program for those students who needed extra help in addition to the regular reading curriculum.

5.0. Develop a Meaningful Instructional Delivery System

5.1. Provide Instructional Diversity

If we take seriously the huge differences that children bring to school in their talent and preparation for learning to read, then we must have available to them educational opportunities that are equally diverse. Instructional diversity does not mean that children with early reading difficulties need to be taught *different* skills and knowledge than average readers but rather that they require more *powerful* instruction that is *targeted* to their specific difficulties in reading. A collection of recent early-intervention studies has shown that children who fall through the cracks of early reading instruction require instruction that is more intensive, more explicit, and more supportive than what is *typically* provided in the regular classroom (Felton, 1993; Hiebert, 1994; Torgesen, Alexander, et al., 2001; Torgesen, Rashotte, et al., 2001; Vellutino et al., 2000).

Snow et al. (1998) advise that the first step toward ensuring that all children acquire effective reading skills involves installing a sound basic curriculum in kindergarten through second grade. Ray King and his staff took that advice seriously and began their improvement initiative in the primary grades.

They immediately discovered that it was not as easy as buying a new reading series, training the teachers, and watching the scores go up. They had overlooked the critical importance of instructional diversity—having the resources, both monetary and human, to *immediately* deliver effective small-group or even individual instruction to higher-risk children at the first sign of their difficulty in whole-group instruction.

Here are the occasions when a teacher who is highly skilled in delivering explicit, systematic, and supportive instruction should be waiting in the wings to teach a daily booster or tutorial session: (a) when students are falling behind their peers, (b) when students are losing confidence and interest in school, (c) when students need to be able to do something right away and are already behind the rest of the class, or (d) when students are easily confused by holistic instruction and thematic approaches (Spiegel, 1999, pp. 250-251). The Project PRIDE model is demonstrating the difference that teachers trained in using explicit and systematic instruction can make in the lives of at-risk students.

5.2. *Provide a Foundation for Success in Kindergarten*

Balanced literacy in kindergarten includes the following instructional components: (a) direct instruction in reading skills to include phonological awareness, phonics, or both as appropriate to the child's current skill level; (b) direct instruction in language development as appropriate to the child's current skill level (e.g., *Language for Learning*); (c) a literature-based activity in which classic works of children's literature are read aloud, enjoyed, explored in depth, and used as a springboard for motivating students to want to learn to read; (d) a language challenge activity in which children's literature (both narrative and expository) is read aloud and used as a springboard for language, knowledge, and cognitive-strategy development; (e) an enrichment or tutorial enhancement in which accelerated learners receive reading instruction appropriate to their grade level and at-risk learners receive a booster session of phonological awareness skills.

Check out one of Nettie Griffin's weekly newsletters to parents in Figure E.2 in Resource E. Here are some of the instructional materials that Nettie uses in her classroom:

- Torgesen, J. K., & Bryant, B. R. (1993). *Phonological Awareness Training for Reading*. Austin, TX: PRO-ED.
- An extensive collection of the classics in children's literature—close to 2,000 personal books in her room library, which she uses for literature-based instruction, for reading aloud, and for more advanced readers to read.
- An extensive collection of decodable texts in which students are able to practice their emerging independent decoding skills: (a) Phonics Clubhouse books from Scholastic, (b) the Waterford reading program's decodable books that Nettie picked up at a garage sale (they cannot be purchased apart from the Waterford Program), (c) decodable readers from Saxon phonics (Nettie thought the stories were strange, but her kids absolutely adored them), and (d) a book of reproducible decodable stories that she sends home with students (McCormick, 2000).

5.3. Provide Balanced Literacy in Grades 1–2

A balanced literacy program in first and second grades, which includes the following instructional components on a daily basis:

- At least 30 minutes of explicit, systematic, supportive instruction in a continuum of reading skills to include phonological awareness, letter identification, phonics, spelling and word-study skills designed to provide K-1 readers with three critical strategies—knowing how to say the sounds that correspond to the letters, knowing how to sequentially blend those sounds to read a word, and knowing how to spell the words
- At least 30 minutes of "real" independent reading (i.e., practice in sufficient quantities of *decodable texts* for beginning readers to achieve fluency and ample amounts of text at students' independent level for more advanced readers)
- At least 30 minutes of supportive or scaffolded reading in small groups at students' specific instructional levels, to include vocabulary, language, and cognitive-strategy instruction as well as the opportunity to individually process texts (both expository and narrative) at a more challenging level
- At least 15 to 20 minutes of literature-based instruction in either a whole-group or cooperative-group setting to motivate all students to read more and to read more challenging books
- At least 15 to 20 minutes of required *response to reading*, either orally or in writing (e.g., retelling of stories, construction of graphic organizers, or writing a short summary or personal reflection)
- At least 30 minutes daily of *tutorial or enrichment enhancement* in which rapidly advancing readers are expected to read and write at challenging levels with the goal of developing increasingly higher-level thinking skills and in which struggling readers who need extra help will have small-group, explicit, systematic, supportive instruction in areas of the curriculum that are specifically identified by assessment (e.g., phonological awareness, phonics, language development, or fluency)

One possible way to handle the curricular demands of the primary grades with regard to science and social studies instruction is to alternately use those texts as part of the language challenge activity or the whole-group or cooperative-group activity.

5.4. Teach Them All to Read to Learn

If I were an administrator today, I would expect every teacher (K-12) to integrate content and strategy instruction into every lesson plan—day after day and year after year. *But*—I would hire a full-time staff member experienced in teaching both students and teachers to model for teachers and then coach them to proficiency. My vision for model strategy instruction includes an extensive strategic reading across the curriculum program but using *only* the following core strategies with their related permutations and combinations: (a) questioning, (b) summarizing, (c) organizing, and (d) monitoring.

At Lincoln Elementary School, we established a very primitive version of this model, training teachers in the use of four strategies and implementing the program schoolwide. In spite of some success, we definitely experienced what the National Reading Panel (2000) warned about in its report.

> In spite of heavy emphasis on modeling and metacognitive instruction, even very good teachers may have trouble implementing, and may even omit, crucial aspects of strategic reasoning. The research suggests that, when partially implemented, students of strategic teachers will still improve. But it is not easy for teachers to develop readers' conceptions about what it means to be strategic. It takes time, coaching, and careful monitoring to help both teachers and students to be successful. (sec. 4, p. 49)

Be prepared to "play through the pain" of getting cognitive strategy instruction off the ground (i.e., time, frustration, lack of instant success and payoff).

5.5. *Provide* Every *Child With Whole-Group (Heterogeneous) and Small-Group (Skill-Based Homogeneous) Instruction*

This strategy highlights the importance of giving *every* child the benefits that accrue from being a part of both small-group (skill-based) and whole-group (heterogeneous) instruction. The advantages of whole-group instruction have been widely discussed and debated in recent years (Reutzel & Cooter, 1996). Reutzel (1999) asserts that

> whole-class grouping shields the individual within a community of learners from potentially harsh emotional and psychological consequences that may result from the risk associated with *solo reading* [and] reduces some of the negative effect of labeling young children as "slow," "special needs," or "disabled."

But he also points out that "whole-class grouping used exclusively clearly fails to meet the needs of individual children" (pp. 273–274).

Reutzel (1999) cites no benefits for faster learners in whole-group instruction settings, but we discovered many at Lincoln School using Slavin, Madden, Dolan, and Wasik's (1996) Cooperative Integrated Reading and Composition model, a precursor to Success for All. The best teachers know that when anyone (adult or student) is asked to explain or teach something to someone else, they definitely acquire a deeper understanding of the material. The only year in which our reading achievement initiative stalled at Lincoln occurred when we placed all of our gifted students in one classroom (to implement a new gifted model conceived at central office with no regard for the dynamics of our school). We discovered to our dismay that the reading achievement of a substantial number of students leveled off when our cooperative groups were more homogeneous in structure and included a majority of lower-achieving students. There is a large body of research showing that students (both high- and low-achieving) in cooperative groups make greater gains in achievement than students who are learning in other grouping arrangements (Johnson, Maruyama, Johnson, Nelson, & Skon, 1981; Slavin, 1988, 1991).

Consider La Mesa Dale School's answer to meeting the diverse instructional needs of their students as described by Kathie Dobberteen:

> Our enrichment/tutorial program is held for 30 minutes each day per grade level. Each grade uses this time in slightly different ways, but we have seen the most dramatic results in first grade. We assess students in their phonemic awareness and phonics skills at the beginning of the school year, and then, depending on their needs, they are assigned to one of four small tutorial groups. The remaining students participate in literature enrichment activities. We have added a reading teacher to supplement the five first grade teachers so that the tutorial groups can be smaller (i.e., 4 tutorial groups and 2 enrichment groups).
>
> The tutorial teachers use the Open Court (1995) phonemic awareness program to give returning first-graders and students new to our school another opportunity to solidly master these skills. Then teachers move on from the phonemic awareness activities to a structured phonics program that combines the lessons from our Harcourt Brace text with the decodable books from Scholastic. First-graders in the two enrichment groups are pushed to read more challenging text and develop their writing and thinking abilities. This model has resulted in unprecedented achievement levels in first grade.

5.6. Use Research-Based Instructional Strategies

Critical to the success of struggling readers who are trying to make sense of beginning reading instruction is the use of research-based instructional strategies. These strategies are essential to the success of the PRIDE model (remember Paula Larson's explanation of their importance in Chapter 7) and are described in detail in Resource C. They include (a) advance organizers; (b) unison responding; (c) the judicious use of teacher talk; (d) a perky pace; (e) increased opportunities for practice; (f) the "I do it, we do it, you do it" lesson sequence; (g) systematic error correction; (h) cumulative review; (i) example selection; and (j) motivational strategies.

5.7. Teach Less in a More Thorough and Diligent Fashion

Kame'enui and Carnine (1998) recommend that rather than trying to teach *more* in *less* time, which is a frequent instructional response to students who are having difficulty in beginning reading, that educators focus instead on the "big ideas" and "critical strategies" that are *essential* for success rather than trying to do it all. For example, use the reading puzzle for your big ideas in the primary grades. Students need phonological awareness, alphabetic understanding (phonics and spelling), automaticity with the code (fluency), and voluminous amounts of reading a lot to be successful in reading (Coyne et al., 2001). Then, use the Project PRIDE instructional strategies as your critical strategies. Mary Damer, Project PRIDE coach, recommends two books to help you learn more about these strategies: (a) Carnine, D. W., Silbert, J., & Kame'enui, E. J. (1997). *Direct Instruction Reading.* (3rd ed.). Upper Saddle River, NJ: Merrill, and (b) Kame'enui, E. J., & Carnine, D. (Eds.). (1998). *Effective Teaching Strategies That Accommodate Diverse Learners.* Upper Saddle River, NJ: Prentice-Hall.

5.8. *Form Lesson Study Groups*

There are many different models of staff development, and I have tried just about all of them. The one I would implement today, if I were to become a principal again, is one in which the school strives to become a learning community, not only for its students but also for its teachers. The most important element that is missing in our current school structure is time. In other countries (e.g., Japan), teachers are given time to plan lessons collaboratively, teach them for each other, and then gather again to talk about, fine-tune, and improve them. (Yoshida, 1999). In my "dream" school as a learning community, I would beg, borrow, and steal more time for teachers to work together.

I heartily concur with Raywid (1993), who says,

> If collaborative endeavor is necessary to school adequacy, then schools must provide it. The responsibility rests with schools not individual teachers. Further, administrators, policymakers, and public alike must accept a new conception of school time. If we are to redefine teachers' responsibilities to include collaborative sessions with colleagues—and both organizational research and teacher effectiveness research now suggest they are essential to good schools—then it is necessary to reconstrue teacher time. (p. 34)

6.0. **Develop a Comprehensive Monitoring and Assessment System**

6.1. *Develop an Assessment Mind-Set*

> Whether for a small child, a school system, or a society, continual assessment is fundamental to the learning process. Ongoing evaluation keeps us responsive to our students' immediate needs. We use assessment data constantly—to develop long-term goals as well as to inform our daily instruction.

Kathie Dobberteen's statements about assessment reflect an attitude that is essential if you want to teach them all to read. She has conveyed this attitude to her staff, and they continually use assessment information to modify curriculum and instruction, thereby responding directly to what they know with certainty that their students need—not what they *think* their students need.

6.2. *Develop an Assessment Calendar*

Most schools are required to participate in districtwide standardized testing (e.g., SAT 9) as well as statewide assessments at various grade levels. Ray King and his staff found, however, that the most effective assessments for determining the progress of their students were those that could be administered and scored in their building and then aggregated to determine overall program effectiveness. They recommend the Woodcock-Johnson Test of Reading Mastery (Woodcock, 1987) and the *TOWRE: Test of Word Reading Efficiency* (Torgesen et al., 1999). These two tests told them everything they needed to know about their students' abilities to read as well as the effectiveness of their program overall.

6.3. Use Frequent Curriculum-Based Assessments

Put curriculum-based assessment tools in the hands of all teachers. To measure phonemic awareness, use *Dynamic Indicators of Basic Early Literacy, DIBELS* (Good, 2000). To assess automatic word recognition, use the *TOWRE: Test of Word Reading Efficiency* (Torgesen et al., 1999). To test oral reading fluency, use the *Multilevel Academic Skills Inventory* (Howell et al., 1994) or adapt your own graded materials using the guidelines in Chapter 4. Schedule these assessments periodically, and use the results to inform instruction, to set short-term goals using the 30-day/30-minute rapid-results goal-setting process, or to determine the need for additional interventions.

6.4. Know Your Students

In schools where students are learning to read as well as reading to learn, administrators and teachers must know how *every* student is progressing in reading at any given time—not just the students who are having difficulties in reading. Assessments that give a global picture of students' reading achievement are not sufficient to plan instruction, enrichment, or remediation. Compile a comprehensive picture of every student. Kathie Dobberteen explains the advantages of her data-driven system that looks at the whole child:

> With accurate and complete data we can target both remediation and enrichment far more effectively. We stage all of our students so that we know their exact reading levels. Because we always have this information at our fingertips, we can form groups quickly and be assured that the instruction will be targeted to students' specific needs. For example, in first grade we use phonemic awareness and phonics assessments as well as comprehension test scores to configure our guided process reading groups and the tutorial/enrichment groups.

6.5. Hit the Ground Running With New Students

At La Mesa Dale, the reading specialist and two half-time support teachers test every new student within 2 to 3 days of his or her registration for the purposes of placing the student into the appropriate guided-process reading group. They use district assessments as well as the *Ekwall-Shanker Reading Inventory* (Shanker, Ekwall, & Ekwall, 1993). Students who are below grade level are (a) placed in the appropriate guided-process reading group, even if they have to leave their homeroom; (b) placed in one of the half-hour daily tutorial groups;

and (c) recommended for placement in an after-school reading group taught by parents, college student helpers, and student teachers (all trained by the reading specialist) for another dose of guided-process reading.

7.0. Get Time on Your Side

7.1. Eliminate Time Wasting

If you are serious about raising achievement for at-risk students, determine just how effectively the time allocated for reading instruction is being used. How much instructional time during the school year is devoted to assemblies, parties, field days, and cultural arts events? Too many special events can undermine your schools' focus and distract both students and teachers from their academic goals. How much instructional time is lost because of incessant intercom announcements, lack of classroom management, or poorly planned instruction? How many teachers are teaching their own curriculum rather than the agreed-on one? How much of the time that your students spend in the classroom are they actually engaged in learning? The research is clear: The more time students spend on learning, the more they learn. Hartsfield Elementary School eliminated pullout programs because their neediest students were spending too much time coming and going and also rearranged the daily schedule to give every teacher an uninterrupted block of reading instruction time.

7.2. Capture Extracurricular Time for Learning

The organizational structure of La Mesa Dale School reflects the belief that every child can master the California state standards if given enough time to do so. They don't depend on getting the job done completely during the school day. Here are the other options they use:

- Before-, during-, and after-school intervention programs in reading, ESL, and other academic subjects
- An Academic Summer School that provides additional time for students to learn standards through focused summer instruction
- A Spring Break Intervention Program, called Surf Camp, especially designed for below-grade-level readers to give these students an additional opportunity to solidify skills and practice reading
- An extended day program, called AM/PM, that is open from 6:00 a.m. until 6:00 p.m. to provide high-quality child care for 130 students; the AM/PM program supports the academic program through its Academic Brain Bowl that includes speech contests, Math Challenge 24, and spelling bees.
- Library hours from 7:30 a.m. until 4:00 p.m. so students can check out books, read, and study both before and after school

Hartsfield instituted a reading period before the school day even started. While students are waiting for up to 20 minutes in the morning for school to begin, they are required to bring a book and read in the cafeteria or media center. They are even able to check out books in the cafeteria. The librarian changes the assortment of available books on a weekly basis. Parents receive read-at-home packets containing a book to be read by their primary-age students (chosen for the students' specific independent reading level) along with a sign-off sheet. The students are also expected to reread the same book at school the next day in a small group to promote fluency.

7.3. Use Time Differently

In schools where the instructional needs of at-risk students are being met, existing personnel are using their time differently than they have in the past. The focus of many special educators, speech pathologists, and reading specialists has become early intervention and prevention rather than remediation. They are catching kids before they fall thereby eliminating the need for their services in the upper grades.

8.0. Create a Seamless Integration, Coordination, and Continuum of Special Services

8.1. Team Special Education and Remedial Reading Teachers to Provide Alternative Grouping Strategies in the Regular Classroom

The coordination of academic and learning support services at La Mesa Dale School begins with safety net meetings early in the fall of each school year. Each teacher brings the names of at-risk students to the student support team that includes a full-time counselor, principal, resource specialist, and speech therapist. The team discusses each child with the teacher to determine appropriate interventions. All programs are coordinated at this meeting to provide the most cohesive plan for each student. The schoolwide assessment database allows support personnel to see at a glance the programs in which students are enrolled or the services for which they are eligible. This, coupled with ongoing contact between the student support team and classroom teachers, promotes ongoing monitoring of students' academics and learning.

A number of examples illustrates how specially funded students receive services to address their needs:

- The guided-process reading groups are configured so that the resource specialist and bilingual aides work with those students who are specifically identified for these services.
- To support the teaching of phonemic awareness, specially funded students receive assistance from the speech therapist that includes time with the computer program, *Earobics* (Cognitive Concepts, 2001).
- La Mesa Dale moved from a Targeted Assistance Title I school to a schoolwide Title I school and thus was afforded greater flexibility in directing its categorical resources.
- Identified Title I students receive the assistance of three half-time reading teachers, six specially trained college students, and an on-site

reading specialist in the intensive and multilevel guided-process reading program.

8.2. Catch Them in Kindergarten, Before They Fall

Use the service of remedial reading, speech-language, bilingual, and special educators in kindergarten to test and teach students as well as to provide coaching and staff development for teachers. In the programs described in Chapter 7, teachers focus energy, resources, and intensive teaching of phonological awareness skills and phonemic decoding skills in kindergarten. They assess at the beginning of kindergarten and continue to do curriculum-based assessments regularly.

9.0. Facilitate Teacher Collaboration and Coordination

9.1. Provide Teachers With Tools to Assist in Planning for Instruction

The lesson plan format that is used for La Mesa Dale's reading groups was designed by the teachers to ensure that the California standards, which are tested on a yearly basis, are being taught consistently and intentionally. See Form E.4 in Resource E. The teachers discovered that although their students were improving in reading achievement, their writing lagged behind. They jointly agreed to make writing in response to reading a required *daily* activity for every student, and they include the kind of writing they do each day on the lesson plan.

9.2. Expect Teachers to Coordinate Instruction and Standards on a Vertical Basis

At least twice yearly, plan for teachers to meet with the grade-level teams above and below them. Possible questions to address might include these: (a) Are there any gaps in skills or knowledge that you have noticed in the students who have moved from our grade level to yours? (b) What else could we be doing to prepare our students for success at the next grade level? (c) Do we use the same language, strategies, and approaches at every grade level?

9.3. Expect Grade-Level Teams to Meet Regularly to Provide Horizontal Consistency

Five years ago at La Mesa Dale, the weekly staff meetings were used to disseminate information and discuss some schoolwide issues. Now, teachers meet in grade-level teams at least twice per month to work on short- and long-term plans, analyze samples of student work, and discuss methods for reaching standards. To eliminate administrivia from meetings entirely, issue a weekly staff bulletin. This practice will keep teachers up to date; provide a running record of meetings, activities, and decisions; and leave any planned meeting times free to focus on reading instruction.

10.0. Develop Ongoing and Meaningful Staff Development

10.1. Train New Staff Members Intensively

Principals can no longer depend on newly hired staff members to have the kind of expertise that is essential to creating a reading culture. New teachers at La Mesa Dale are hired only after a very careful selection process that starts with the district assessment of their qualifications. Once they have passed the initial screening, they are then interviewed at the school site. New teachers are provided with a formative assessment during their first 3 months of employment. An individualized induction plan is put together based on that assessment. Mentor teachers are assigned to provide support and assistance throughout their first 2 years. Each grade-level team is responsible for working with new teachers in planning and goal setting. For additional tips on hiring, mentoring, and coaching teachers, see *Ten Traits of Highly Effective Teachers: How to Hire, Mentor, and Coach Successful Teachers* (McEwan, 2001b).

10.2. Develop Effective Teachers

The highly effective teacher is an instructional virtuoso: a skilled communicator with a repertoire of essential abilities, behaviors, models, and principles that lead all students to learning. (McEwan, 2001b, p. 81)

The research is clear about which teacher behaviors are related to student learning: (a) designing lessons that are clear and meaningful, (b) providing instructional variety, (c) being oriented to time on- task and task completion, (d) engaging students in the learning process, and (e) ensuring a high rate of student success (Brophy, 1989; Brophy & Good, 1986; Dunkin & Biddle, 1974; Rosenshine, 1971; Teddlie & Stringfield, 1993; Walberg, 1986).

Strong instructional leaders know that hiring teachers is one of the most important things they do. Kathie Dobberteen describes the way that La Mesa Dale has transformed itself from having just one or two master teachers to having cultivated a staff that is the envy of other schools in the district:

> While new staff members must seem overwhelmed by the amount of activity that pervades the school site, they are nurtured and encouraged by existing staff who bring them into the fold by their positive approaches and assurance that they too will soon be in the central scheme of things. This is enhanced through our grade-level teams and our Beginning Teacher Support Program. We receive visits on a very consistent basis from teachers and administrators from other schools who would like to observe our program.

10.3. Don't Cut Corners on Preimplementation Staff Development

Provide enough inservice to make sure that everyone is familiar with teaching procedures prior to beginning a new program. Budget monies to provide summer training experiences that are extensive enough to be helpful. Project PRIDE trained its kindergarten, Title I, and special education teachers for 1 week in the summer prior to fall start-up and has offered monthly follow-up training sessions.

10.4. Provide Coaching in Classrooms

The "I do it, we do it, you do it" teaching model that works so well with students (see Resource D) is an effective one to use in staff development as well. To ensure that reading improvement initiatives and curricular changes are implemented effectively, provide coaching sessions for teachers in the early months of implementation.

10.5. Focus Staff Development on the Mission of the School

Eliminate "hit and run" staff development. Michael Fullan (1990) says, "Staff development will never have its intended effect if it is grafted on schools in the form of discrete, unconnected projects" (p. 3). Make sure that every professional development activity you sponsor, promote, endorse, or institute has a connection to the mission of your school. A case can always be made for development that improves instruction, but sending teachers to workshops that are not specifically linked to the focus in your school can often have the unintended effect of taking teachers (and their students) off task.

10.6. Train Your Own Staff-Development Cadre

I constantly encouraged my teachers to take their skills and ideas "on the road" and become teachers of teachers. I remember a discussion I had with my reading teacher, Joan Will, after a particularly dismal presentation by a staff developer from the county office. "I could do that," said Joan.

"You not only could do that. You'd be much better," I said, and immediately signed her up to present at our next inservice day. Once she had spoken so boldly, she began to get cold feet, but I walked her through the presentation and cheered her on from the front row. Today, she's a star—presenting on strategic reading all over the county and directing the reading program in the district.

When Kathie Dobberteen read Resource B (the cognitive-strategies lesson plans) before publication, she immediately sat down with a group of teachers to figure out how they could begin to use and practice teaching some of the strategies in their own classrooms in anticipation of helping the rest of the staff to get started.

10.7. Prioritize Implementation of New Programs

If other initiatives are running concurrently with a reading initiative, it could result in too little instructional time, administrative monitoring, or staff development being devoted to your top priority. Don't overload staff members with too many new things at once. Ray King prioritized his spending as well, devoting most of his budget to reading improvement.

11.0. Build the Support of Parents and Community Members for Literacy

11.1. Involve Parents in the Writing of School Goals

At La Mesa Dale, schoolwide goals are developed with the assistance of the school site council, the PTA, and surveys of the parent community. Each grade level then writes specific goals that are based on the schoolwide goals. These goals are almost always stated in meaningful and measurable ways. They are posted on the bulletin board outside the Parent Center. The staff's feelings about these goals are captured in the heading on the board, "We've come so far . . . but we're not satisfied yet."

11.2. Make Parents and Community Members Part of Your Team

Families and community members are viewed as critical members of the school team at La Mesa Dale. Staff members want parents to be comfortable visiting and working in their school and to that end have established an on-site Parent Volunteer Center, where parents can be found working and planning throughout the school day and into the afternoon. During a recent school year, volunteers at La Mesa Dale (parents, community members, men and women from the U.S.S. Dubuque, and senior citizens who volunteer in the Kids and Seniors Together program) logged over 11,000 hours. The school provides regular parent education on a variety of issues in both English and Spanish. Many activities are provided and well attended that encourage children to broaden and enrich their lives before and after school.

The school leadership team realized that with their transient student population, many children were never able to bond with grandparents or older adults, so in collaboration with the La Mesa Recreation Department, they started an innovative program called Kids and Seniors Together. At-risk children and senior citizens are brought together after school every day for 2 hours in a 12-week session. Activities include homework, reading, crafts, and games.

11.3. Get the Word Out Regarding Reading Instruction in the Classrooms

Each week, Nettie Griffin sends home an attractive one-page newsletter informing parents about the happenings of the week as well as upcoming events. She always includes important information about reading instruction to educate parents about topics such as phonemic awareness. See Figure E.2 in Resource E for a sample of Nettie's weekly newsletters.

11.4. Get the Word Out Regarding Gains in Achievement

Kathie Dobberteen doesn't believe in keeping secrets. When her staff achieves the goals they have set, she disseminates the information through PTA newsletters, principal updates, district newsletters, and the district Web site. The school also stays in constant contact with parents through the use of weekly parent bulletins, which serve as two-way parent-teacher response logs. The staff conducts "Celebrate Our Success" forums in February after the midyear assessments are completed. Parents are invited to hear the good news regarding their students' achievement milestones. The La Mesa Dale school district allows parents great latitude in choosing where they want to send their students within the district. Public confidence in La Mesa Dale is evident in the fact that, despite their Title I status, 39% of the student body chose to transfer into the school this year, and only 4% chose to transfer out.

12.0. Acquire and Sustain Adequate Resources

12.1. Find Alternate Sources of Funding to Support Reading Improvement and Academic Achievement Initiatives

I was always looking for more money to support our reading improvement, reading incentive, and student achievement recognition initiatives. We were a RIF (Reading Is Fundamental) school and received matching funds from our parent-teacher organization and a business partner to fund periodic special events and book giveaways. Several business partners sponsored our A-Team T-Shirt program. Students who received more A's than B's and no C's on their report cards received an A-Team T-shirt at a quarterly assembly. Repeaters received iron-on stars to indicate their continuing achievement. Several small parent-owned businesses funded this program, and we printed the sponsors' names on the backs of the shirts. Soon, other local businesses were lobbying for space on the T-shirts because our students wore them so frequently and proudly around town.

My district's educational foundation sponsored a minigrant program for teachers. They were invited to submit proposals to fund special projects. I worked with teams of teachers to develop proposals that focused specifically on our school goals. For example, a team of primary teachers won a sizable grant to put together theme bags containing books, games, and writing materials for students to take home over weekends and holidays. Another team put together an after-school enrichment program for limited-English-proficient students. Still another developed a parent education program to help parents with developing their children's early literacy skill.

12.2. Find Grant Money to Fund Improvement Initiatives

Many of the schools with whom I have worked in Missouri have written reading improvement grants for staff development as well as the purchase of materials. Don't let a lack of funds stand in your way. Be creative in searching out alternative sources of money.

12.3. Use Zero-Based Budgeting

Build your budget from the ground up every year. Evaluate past expenditures in the light of results rather than automatically transferring the same amount or an even larger one to a program or activity just because "it's always been done that way in the past."

SUMMARIZING CHAPTER 8

There are no easy answers or quick fixes, but there *are* 50 different strategies that have been shown to work in schools and classrooms across the country. In schools where literacy is becoming a reality for thousands of students who formerly fell through the cracks, there is no time for worrying about the inalterable variables. Their teachers, principals, and central office administrators are *teaching them ALL to read*.

CONCLUSION

I hope that your head is bursting with ideas and that you can scarcely wait to talk with your colleagues, principal, or superintendent about where and when you and your team can begin. A word of caution is in order: Change takes careful planning. Change requires adequate resources. Change demands a strong commitment. Change takes time.

If you are a teacher, you may enjoy the autonomy and freedom to change what you are doing in your classroom immediately, but to make your efforts count and sustain themselves, find others with whom to work—most especially, your grade-level teammates and building principal. If you are a building principal, work with your teacher leaders to bring about change in a planned and deliberate way. If you are a central office administrator, focus on principals— not programs. For a quick look at how you are doing in establishing and maintaining a reading culture, take a few minutes to complete the Implementation Questionnaire given in Form E.5 in Resource E.

I invite you to e-mail me at emcewan@mindspring.com with your questions, concerns, and most especially, your success stories. If you are interested in learning more about workshops for administrators and teachers, visit my Web site at www.elainemcewan.com. While at the Web site, you can also enroll in an online, interactive seminar based on this book. I envy you the challenges, excitement, and satisfaction that lie ahead. There is nothing more exhilarating than *teaching them ALL to read!*

Resource A: Phonics Readers

Decodable phonics readers help children to apply newly learned knowledge in a safe context with a high degree of accuracy from the start. It is important for the beginning reader to practice phonics patterns. Easy, short books provide contextual decoding practice in easy patterns. The following list is organized alphabetically by publisher. At the time of this printing, the phone numbers and Web sites were accurate; however, this information often changes without notice.

Academic Therapy Publications
High Noon Books
20 Commercial Boulevard
Novato, CA 94949
(800) 422-7249
www.atpub.com

American Guidance Service
Phonemic Awareness and Sequencing
   (P.A.S.) Stories
Author: Sylvia Hannah
4201 Woodland Road
Circle Pines, MN 55014-1796
(800) 328-2560 (763) 786-4343
www.agsnet.com

Children's Research and Development Co.
Reading Sparkers
216 9th Avenue
Haddon Heights, NJ 08037
(609) 546-9896

Educational Insights
16941 Keegan Avenue
Carson, CA 90746
(800) 995-4436
www.edin.com

Educators Publishing Service, Inc.
Primary Phonics and More Primary
   Phonics
31 Smith Place
Cambridge, MA 02138-1089
(800) 435-7728
www.epsbooks.com

Flyleaf Publishing Co.
Books to Remember
P.O. Box 185
Lyme, NH 03768
(603) 795-2875
www.flyleafpublishing.com

Language!
J and J Readers
4093 Specialty Place
Longmont CO 80504
(303) 651-2829

M. D. Angus & Associates Limited
Poppin Auditory Discrimination
   Reading Series: Sound by Sound
   Stories
Authors: Lorna Smith and Becky
   Stayton

Canadian Address:
2639 Kingsway Avenue, 2nd Floor
Port Coquitlam, BC, CanadaV3C 1T5
United States Address:
1574 Gulf Road
Point Roberts, WA 98281
www.agsnet.com

Modern Curriculum Press
Phonics Practice Readers
P.O. Box 2649
Columbus, OH 43216
(800) 876-5507
www.mcschool.com

Readers at Work
P.O. Box 738
Ridgway, CO 81432
www.readersatwork.com

Rigby Education
Decodable Stories by Rigby
1000 Hart Road
Barrington, Illinois 60010
(800) 822-8661
www.rigby.com

Scholastic, Inc.
Hello Reader Phonics Fun Series
Headquarters and Editorial Office
555 Broadway
New York, NY 10012
(212) 343-6100
www.scholastic.com

Scholastic, Inc.
Bob Books
Available at most major bookstores
www.scholastic.com

SRA/McGraw-Hill
Merrill Linguistic Readers
220 East Danieldale Road
DeSoto, TX 75115-2490
(888) 772-4543
www.sra4kids.com

SRA/McGraw-Hill
Open Court Phonics Minibooks Grades
    1–3
Collections for Young Scholars 1995
220 East Danieldale Road
Desoto, Texas 75115-9960
(888) 772-4543
www.sra4kids.com

SRA/McGraw-Hill
Open Court Decodable Books Grades 1–3
(Orange 2000 version)
220 E. Danieldale Road
Desoto, Texas 75115-9960
(888) 772-4543
www.sra4kids.com

SRA/McGraw-Hill
Merrill Reading Program Student
    Readers Grades 1–3
220 East Danieldale Road
Desoto, Texas 75115-9960
(888) 772-4543
www.sra4kids.com

SRA/McGraw-Hill
SRA Phonics: Grade 1–3
Poetry Posters containing vowels, blends,
    and digraphs
220 East Danieldale Road
Desoto, Texas 75115-9960
(888) 772-4543
www.sra4kids.com

SRA/McGraw-Hill
Independent Readers for Students in
    Reading Mastery I and II: Grade 1–3
220 East Danieldale Road
DeSoto, Texas 75115-9960
(888) 772-4543
www.sra4kids.com

Steck-Vaughn
Phonics Readers
P.O. Box 690789
Orlando, FL 32819-0789
(800) 531-5015
www.steck-vaughn.com

SOURCE: This compilation of Phonics Readers is reprinted by permission of Mary Damer.

Resource B: Brain-Based Reading

*Cognitive Strategies to
Raise Reading Achievement*

Following are detailed descriptions and teaching suggestion for the four essential cognitive strategies: questioning, summarizing, organizing, and monitoring. These strategies have been shown by research to bring about achievement gains when they are consistently modeled, taught, and integrated into content-area instruction (National Reading Panel, 2000, sec. 4, p. 47; Rosenshine, 1997). I have titled my adaptations of the strategies as follows: (a) *Be a Mind Reader*, the questioning strategy; (b) *Get the Gist*, the summarizing strategy; (c) *See the Big Picture*, the organizing strategy; and (d) *Fix Up Your Mix-Ups*, the monitoring strategy.

BE A MIND READER: THE QUESTIONING STRATEGY

What Is Questioning?

Questioning is

- A way that skilled readers interact with the text or the author to construct meaning
- A way that skilled readers predict what is of most importance in the text
- A way that skilled readers engage in learning dialogues with peers and teachers

Materials Needed to Teach the *Be a Mind Reader* Strategy

Select text to use during the modeling portion of the *Be a Mind Reader* strategy lesson presentation. Choose text that will be perceived by your students as challenging for you to read. Also select expository, narrative, or mathematical text for students to read as they learn and practice the *Be a Mind Reader* strategy. Choose text for that purpose that is easier for your students to read. Assemble the following supplies and equipment: overhead transparencies, overhead projector, screen, markers (erasable for use on the overhead and permanent for use on chart paper), easel with chart paper, and a graphic organizer (on either an overhead transparency or chart paper) showing four quadrants into which different types of questions can be written. See Form B.1, The Questioning Quadrant adapted from Raphael (1982).

Teaching the *Be a Mind Reader* Strategy

The Anticipatory Set

Some readers are no doubt too young to remember Karnak the Magnificent, but those of with a few miles on our sneakers remember him well. He was immortalized by comedian Johnny Carson, the late-night predecessor to Jay Leno. Johnny would emerge from behind the curtain sporting a goofy turban, carrying a crystal ball in one hand and a mayonnaise jar in the other. He used his crystal ball, not to peer into the future but to "divine" the "right questions." His questions were certain to be the right ones because he already had the answers; they were stored in a mayonnaise jar on Funk & Wagnall's back porch. It was corny comedy, but Johnny made it work. He would hold the sealed envelopes he retrieved from the jar to his head one by one and presto, he would come up with the right question.

Your mission is to teach students how to read minds like Karnak, *to predict the questions* that you, the teacher, will ask on the quiz as well as to figure out what questions the author was answering when he or she wrote the textbook.

Textbooks, novels, and any other kinds of text that students are given to read contain answers galore. Some of the answers are to important questions —"thick questions" as Harvey and Goudvis (2000, pp. 89–90) call them. Other answers are to unimportant and trivial queries—"thin questions." Like Karnak, students need to be able to divine the big and important questions. To gain meaning and understanding from text, students must be able to ask good questions and also make sure they know the answers.

Your "mind-reading" students will sometimes assume the role of teacher as they read the text by posing the questions they think their teachers would expect them to answer. Or they will try to read the minds of the authors and figure out what questions these individuals intended to answer for their readers when they wrote the textbooks, nonfiction, and novels that students read.

To become mind readers in this way, students must be able to ask four different kinds of questions (Raphael, 1982): (a) questions for which the answer can be found in one specific place in the text; (b) questions for which the answer

Form B.1 The Questioning Quadrant

In the Text: Right There

In Your Head: Use Inference

In the Text: Bring it Together

In Your Head: Use Your Own Experience

can only be found by synthesizing material in the text (pulling together information that is found in several different places in the text), (c) questions for which the answers can only be determined by inferential reasoning or "reading between the lines" of the text, and (d) questions that although related to the text can only be answered from the reader's own prior knowledge and experience. Raphael (1982) labels these four types of questions in this way: (a) In the Text: Right There; (b) In the Text: Pull It Together; (c) In Your Head: Use Inference; and (d) In Your Head: Use Your Own Experience. As you teach your students the *Be a Mind Reader* strategy, you may discover that some students have done the majority of their reading for enjoyment and approach reading with the mind-set that there are no "right" answers—not even for the first three types of questions. You will need to disabuse them of this notion, gently but firmly.

The Importance of Modeling in the Teaching of Cognitive Strategies

The most critical, albeit difficult, aspect of cognitive-strategy instruction is teacher modeling. The *thinking aloud* that is done by the teacher so students can observe *precisely* how skilled readers use a particular strategy as they read is the key to your success as a strategic teacher. You will play the starring role of the skilled reader. After you choose the text you will use to model the *Be a Mind Reader* strategy for your students, rehearse the thinking-aloud process for a colleague or family member. Thinking aloud, as you will soon discover, is not a natural act. Ordinarily, when one is thinking, thoughts are uncensored and unstructured. Teachers often feel awkward about making their thoughts available to students and frequently tend to explain or lecture about the strategy or the content of the text rather than to truly think aloud. Practice repeatedly until you can actually articulate your thinking processes in a relaxed but very specific way to students. Postpone strategy instruction until you are completely comfortable with this aspect of strategy instruction.

Anderson (1991) provides some examples of how teachers might think aloud as they clarify a difficult statement or concept, summarize important information, or think ahead as they model their thinking while reading a piece of text aloud with students.

> Clarifying: *I don't get this. It says that things that are dark look smaller. I know that a white dog looks smaller than a black elephant, so this rule must work for things that are about the same size. Maybe black shoes would make your feet look smaller than white ones would.*
>
> Summarizing: *I'll summarize this part of the article. So far, it tells where the Spanish started in North America and what parts they explored. Since the title is "The Spanish in California," the part about California must be important. I'd sum up by saying that Spanish explorers from Mexico discovered California. They didn't stay in California, but lived in other parts of America. These are the most important ideas so far.*
>
> Thinking Ahead: *So far this has told me that Columbus is poor, the trip will be expensive, and everyone's laughing at his plan. I'd predict that*

Columbus will have trouble getting the money he needs for his exploration.
(Anderson, 1991)

Introducing the Four Kinds of Questions to Students

Show the students an overhead transparency on which you have divided the page into four quadrants, similar to Form B.1, The Questioning Quadrant. Write a heading in each quadrant to correspond to the four types of questions. Write the two types of In the Text Question headings in the quadrants on the left-hand side of the overhead, and write the two types of In the Brain Question headings on the right-hand side of the overhead.

If appropriate to the age level you teach, give students their own copies of the organizer on which to take notes as you explain each category. Briefly describe each of the different types of questions. Tell students not to worry if they don't quite understand the exact differences between the four types of questions yet, because you will be modeling for them exactly how to write the four kinds of questions several times. Prepare an organizer on chart paper on which to write the questions you will write in response to the text you read aloud during your modeling. If you prefer, use two overhead projectors for this project—one for the text and one for the graphic organizer.

Modeling the Be a Mind Reader *Questioning Strategy*

Place the text that you will read aloud on the overhead projector. You may also wish to give the students a copy of the text so they can follow along more easily or take notes as you think aloud. Read two or three sentences of the text aloud, stopping to think aloud in response to what you have read. You may model other cognitive strategies as you think aloud, but be sure to specifically articulate your thinking as you decide what questions to ask. Write one or two questions of each type in the four quadrants of the organizer as you read. Carefully consider your questions ahead of time to be sure they adequately convey the critical attributes of each category of questions to your students. There are three steps to strategy instruction: (a) *I do it* (the teacher models the strategy by thinking aloud for students), (b) *we do it* (the class is divided into cooperative groups to practice using the strategy together with supportive instruction from the teacher), and last, (c) *you do it* (students are expected to use the strategy independently either in the classroom or for a homework assignment). These three steps may take several weeks of instruction and practice, depending on the age and abilities of your students.

Practicing the Be a Mind Reader *Strategy*

The grade level and previous strategy knowledge of your students will dictate the complexity and number of opportunities you provide to practice the strategy, once you have adequately modeled it. When you are ready to practice for the first time, place a copy of the text you will use for practice in the "we do it" segment of instruction on the overhead projector and have either chart paper or a second overhead displaying the four types of questions in their appropriate quadrants. Read the text aloud with the class (choral reading), stopping at appropriate places to ask students for examples of In the Text: Right There questions. Write them on the organizer in the correct quadrant. Always write the questions on the organizer, even if you are writing only one category of question. Students can then begin to associate a type of question with the correct quadrant.

After you have generated a number of appropriate questions with the class as a whole, form cooperative groups of three to five students, and ask each group to write two or three additional In the Text: Right There questions for the remainder of the text. Tell students that you have also written several of your own In the Text : Right There questions for the text they will be reading. Challenge them to see if they can pose the same questions that you do, focusing on asking the big, important questions that get at the main idea or important details. Once students have gained skill in generating questions, you can give computer lab or homework passes to the members of any group able to "read your mind" and come up with one of the same questions that you have written.

Once each cooperative group has generated questions about the text and its members are certain that each one in the group knows the answers to these questions, engage in what I call Round-Robin Questioning. Ask the cooperative groups to number off (e.g., 1–3 or 1–5). Then, number the cooperative groups (e.g., 1–5). Ask the #1 student in each cooperative group to leave his or her group and move to the next group (e.g., Student 1 moves from Group 1 to Group 2; Student 1 from Group 2 moves to Group 3, etc.). On arriving in the new cooperative group, the traveling student asks one question generated by the group they left. Students in the new group are responsible for answering it. If there are questions or disagreements about the answer, the traveling student is responsible for defending, explaining, or justifying his or her group's answer. As time permits, send Student 2 from each group to the next group to pose another question that his or her group generated.

Students in lower grades will need to practice writing In the Text: Right There kinds of questions and answering them on several different occasions and with different types of text before progressing to the other three categories of questions. Older or more sophisticated students may be able to handle practicing both kinds of In the Text questions at the same time. Monitor your students' progress carefully to determine when they are ready to begin working independently to generate questions. The questioning strategy is an ideal way to uncover confusion and misunderstandings that students may have about the content. Encourage students to use different wording in their questions than the wording that is used in the text to make their questions more challenging. Once most students are secure about writing one or two kinds of questions, begin the process of "I do it," "we do it" and "you do it" all over again to model and practice writing the other types of questions. Generating questions in Quadrant 3: In Your Head: Use Inference will prove to the most challenging kind of questions to write. Even more mature students will need to see ample amounts of modeling and have plenty of practice before they will develop the skills to ask good inferential questions.

*The Use of Procedural Prompts or Facilitators in Teaching
the* Be a Mind Reader *Strategy*

Teaching cognitive strategies to students is far different from teaching a skill in which specific steps must be followed and one can teach these steps directly, for instance, a mathematical algorithm, such as addition, or a decoding strategy. At the outset, the words who, what, why, where, when, and how can help students structure questions about the text. King (1990, p. 667) provided the following fill-in-the-blanks questions as prompts to help students write questions about the text:

1. How are _____ and _____ alike?

2. What is the main idea of _____?

3. What do you think would happen if _____?

4. What are the strengths and weaknesses of _____?

5. In what way is _____ related to _____?

6. How does _____ affect _____?

7. Compare _____ and _____ with regard to _____?

8. What do you think causes _____?

9. How does _____ tie in with what we have learned before?

10. Which one is the best _____ and why?

11. What are some possible solutions for the problem of _____?

12. Do you agree or disagree with this statement: _____. Support your answer.

13. What do I (you) still not understand about _____?

Using the *Be a Mind Reader* Strategy in Your Classroom

Once you have taught all aspects of the *Be a Mind Reader* strategy to your students, expect them to write two questions that fit into each of the four categories for each independent-reading homework assignment that you give. At the beginning of class the next day, ask for a volunteer to read one of his or her questions to the class. Ask the students who know the answer to raise their hands. The student who asked the question can then choose someone to answer it. The first individual to answer the question must then pose one of his or her questions. Continue until everyone in the class has asked and answered one question. No one can answer a second question until everyone has answered at least one. Alternate the types of questions that are asked so that all of the questions are not Right There or Pull Together questions. A variation of this questioning strategy is to have students predict what questions they believe will be asked on a unit test. Collect some of the better questions that students generate and use them as part of a weekly quiz (Schoenbach et al., 1999).

Extending Your Students' Mind-Reading Abilities

When students have become skilled at generating the four types of questions suggested by Raphael (1982), introduce them to the questioning typology suggested by Bloom (as cited in Anderson & Krathwohl, 2001): recall, comprehension, analysis, application, synthesis, and evaluation.

GET THE GIST: THE SUMMARIZATION STRATEGY

What Is Summarization?

Summarization is the ability to "get the gist" or figure out the main idea of a segment of text. Summarization is essential to (a) determining what should be remembered about a paragraph, a chapter, or even an entire book; (b) being able to take notes that are needed as a part of research report writing; (c) studying text material or class notes prior to a final examination; and (d) reading confusing or poorly written text and finding the kernels of important information.

Summarization is restating the meaning of what has been read in one's own words—words that are different from those used in the original text. Although summarizing is usually thought of as paraphrasing, it could also include describing, inferring, elaborating, connecting, combining, and synthesizing. A summary can be produced in either a written form (e.g., one word, a sentence, or a paragraph) or a graphic format (e.g., a chart, web, time line, Venn diagram, or continuum). To produce a summary in a graphic format, use the organizing strategy, *See the Big Picture*.

Materials Needed to Teach the *Get the Gist* Strategy

Select text for the teacher to use during the modeling portion of the *Get the Gist* strategy. Also select appropriate expository, narrative, or mathematical text for students to read as they learn and practice the summarizing strategy. Choose short, relatively easy excerpts that do not contain many new concepts or difficult vocabulary. The emphasis during the lesson should be on teaching summarizing, not on mastering difficult content. Assemble the following supplies and equipment: overhead projector, screen, overhead transparencies, markers (erasable ones for use on the overhead and permanent ones for use on chart paper), easel with chart paper, highlighters, and a wall chart listing all of the possible steps that might be followed to *Get the Gist*.

Teaching the *Get the Gist* Strategy

The Anticipatory Set

See if any of your students know the meaning of the phrase *get the gist* and in what context they have heard the phrase. Exactly what is a *gist*? According to the Oxford English Dictionary (Simpson & Weiner, 1989), the word gist was first used during the 1700s as a legal term to mean the real grounds or reason that someone was being charged with a crime. This meaning later evolved into common usage to mean a main idea: "the substance or pith of a matter, the essence or the main part."

Explain to students that you will be teaching them a strategy to help them not only *get the gist* of what they read but which will also give them the skills to construct a written summary of that gist. Emphasize the helpful benefits of being able to *get the gist* that include getting better grades on classroom tests, scoring better on standardized tests, and being able to do research and take notes when they are writing reports and papers. When students *get the gist*, they can understand what they read and explain that understanding to others in either an oral or written form.

Introducing the Steps or Rules of the Get the Gist *Strategy*

Introduce all or some of the following so-called rules or protocols of summarization that a reader might use, depending on the complexity of the text. The age or maturity of your students will dictate which ones and how many you use during your very first lesson. Keeping it simple in the beginning is a good ground rule.

1. Skim through the text to highlight, underline, or make a note of any obvious clues given by the author regarding the main idea(s) and important supporting details.

2. Then, read the selection carefully. If the text is not already divided into sections, chunk it—divide it into smaller parts corresponding to the subpoints or details related to the main idea.

3. Delete trivial (unimportant) information.

4. Delete redundant (repeated) information.

5. Skip information that is difficult to understand, and come back to reread it after you finish reading the entire passage. You may find definitions or explanations later in the text that will help you figure out what you didn't understand, or you may find that you do not need the information that you skipped to complete your summarization.

6. If there is a list of items or a list of actions, collapse the list by choosing a key word that describes the category to which the items or actions belong.

7. Highlight the key supporting ideas or details for the main idea of each chunk of text, and write a summary word or phrase for each.

8. Write a sentence about each supporting detail.

9. Combine the sentences into a paragraph that summarizes the main idea and its supporting information in your own words (Anderson & Hidi, 1989; Brown & Day, 1983; Hare & Borchardt, 1984; Irvin, 1998; Lenz, Ellis, & Scanlon, 1996; Pressley et al., 1995; Rinehart, Stahl, & Erickson, 1986).

Modeling the Get the Gist *Strategy for Your Students*

The first step in teaching a cognitive strategy is to model it for students. Place the text that you will read aloud on the overhead projector. You may also wish to give the students a copy of the text so they can follow along more easily or take notes as you think aloud. Post a chart that contains the *Get the Gist* protocols you have taught and will be using as you think aloud through your text. Although you presented the protocols in a step-by-step fashion, you will use them in an interactive way as you read the text. Make sure you point this out to students. There is an important difference between teaching students a well-structured academic task, such as how to do two-digit multiplication. For those skills, the steps are concrete and visible. Teaching a cognitive strategy is a far-less-structured task, and it cannot be broken down into a fixed sequence of subtasks. That is why teacher modeling of cognitive strategies is so important. You can suggest procedural prompts or possible rules, but they will never be followed in exactly the same order in every piece of text that is read.

Underline or highlight important information on the overhead, and cross out trivial and redundant information. Think aloud for students about how you are making your decisions relative to what to highlight and what to cross out. As you complete each chunk of text, select a key word that describes that chunk.

Using Graphic Organizers to Develop Summaries

A helpful interim step for many students between reading and either writing or giving an oral summary of text that has been read is the preparation of a graphic organizer. Model the development of such an organizer for your students. Segment the text to be summarized into chunks representing the main ideas. Use an organizer similar to Form B.2. It shows a center circle for the main idea and a number of circles around the center circle to correspond with the number of chunks being summarized in the text.

A common problem that students (and many adults) encounter in summarizing a piece of text they have read is putting the author's ideas and words into their own words. They often end up copying from or quoting the author. Choosing a key word or phrase to capture a snapshot of what has been read is a helpful interim step. Once the key words have been written on the organizer, students *must* close the textbook or put away the text they have read. The final step, writing one sentence to describe the main idea embodied in the key word or phrase, is facilitated by the presence of the key word.

Form B.2 Summarization Organizer

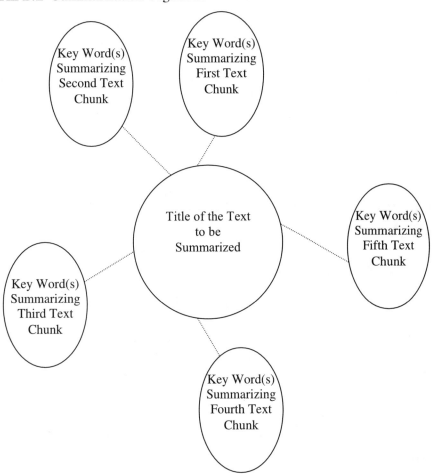

As you model and teach this combination summarizing-organizing strategy, take your time. Make sure that you model this strategy for students at least two or three times using a variety of different texts before you actually lead students through the development of a summary. Use text from an encyclopedia or reference book to show students how the strategy can be used to take notes for research purposes. Students need multiple opportunities for guided practice with the teacher *before* they are placed in small groups to develop a group summary or are expected to write summaries on their own.

Use a prepared script, if necessary, to provide structure to your thinking aloud when you are modeling. Teacher modeling is critical to student understanding and mastery of this strategy. Gradually phase out teacher direction and phase in student independence. Once the summarization of short paragraphs has been mastered, choose a longer selection, and use these same steps to summarize it (Ciborowski, 1992).

Using Cooperative Learning to Evaluate Summaries

When students have read and summarized text independently several times for homework assignments, ask them to exchange summaries with classmates. After reading a classmate's summary, have each student answer the following questions: (a) If you had not read the text yourself, would you be able to understand what it was about from this summary? Why or why not? (b) Is there anything important that should be added to this summary? What is it? (c) Is there anything unimportant that could be left out of the summary? What is it? After students have received feedback from peers, ask them to revise their summaries.

SEE THE BIG PICTURE: THE ORGANIZING STRATEGY

What Is Organizing?

Organizing involves the following steps or skills: (a) reading the text, (b) determining which type of graphic organizer is best suited for constructing a personal schema to understand and remember the information and ideas in the text, and (c) constructing the organizer. A graphic organizer or graphic representation is a visual illustration of a verbal statement (Jones et al., 1988/1989, p. 20).

Materials Needed to Teach the *See the Big Picture* Strategy

Select text to use during the modeling portion of the *See the Big Picture* strategy. Also select appropriate expository, narrative, or mathematical text for students to read as they learn and practice the organizing strategy. Assemble the following supplies and equipment: overhead projector, screen, overhead transparencies, markers (erasable for use on the overhead and permanent for use on chart paper), easel with chart paper, highlighters, and samples of various blank and completed graphic organizers.

Teaching the *See the Big Picture* Strategy

Anticipatory Set

Ask your students what the phrase *big picture* means to them. It is an expression similar to *getting the gist* in that it explains a complex thought process in a few well-chosen words. Sometimes, you will hear someone described as a big-picture kind of person. What does that mean? What is the opposite of seeing the big picture? Have your students heard the expression, "He can't see the forest for the trees"? That kind of person would be the opposite of a big-picture person. Being able to see the big picture is an important skill when it comes to organizing large amounts of information. Explain that you will be teaching students how to construct their own "big pictures" so they can easily visualize and remember important ideas and information. These big pictures are called *graphic organizers*, and there are dozens of different ways to visually represent the big picture (Johns & Lenski, 1997; Jones et al., 1988/1989).

Let them know that you will be introducing the most important organizers to your discipline (or grade level) one at a time throughout the school year. Share the benefits of constructing graphic organizers (either alone or in cooperative groups) that include the abilities to

- Organize large amounts of information into much smaller spaces to make studying easier
- Understand and remember information more readily
- Remember the meanings of new words
- Get better grades on classroom tests
- Organize their thinking before writing reports and papers

Introducing the Organizers You Will Use in Your Class or Grade Level

Choose four to five organizers that best fit your discipline. For example, English teachers might choose the story grammar to organize narrative text; the character map to study a character in depth; a semantic map for vocabulary study; and a Venn diagram to compare works of literature, characters, or genres. Math teachers might choose matrices, flow charts, and pictures. Social studies teachers might choose time lines, continuums, cause-and-effect fishbone diagrams, webs, and concept maps. Science teachers might choose a similar set of organizers with the exception of time lines and continuums.

Lower-elementary teachers might begin strategy instruction with the use of concept maps, webs, Venn diagrams, and simple timelines. Teachers in upper elementary grades would continue to use the organizers selected by teachers in lower grades, and add selected strategies each year, depending on subject matter content.

Framing Graphic Organizers

First, show the students some blank organizers without frames (i.e., the set of questions that must be answered, the labels for the various sections or aspects of the organizer, or the specific categories that must be filled in while reading the text). See Form B.3, Fishbone Diagrams.

Explain that every graphic organizer needs frames. Frames are the labels or categories of information that will be written on the organizer. The frames are never shown on a completed organizer, but the individual who constructed it had to know what they were to select the appropriate information to place in it. Form B. 4 shows the fishbone diagrams that were pictured in Form B.3 with frames added. Point out to your students that although the organizing principle of the fishbone diagram is cause and effect, the kind of text that is being read dictates the frames that are used.

Then, show the same organizer (choose one of the two fishbone diagrams, depending on whether you are using narrative or expository text) filled in with information from your textbook. Or you may choose to use something you

Form B.3 Fishbone Diagrams

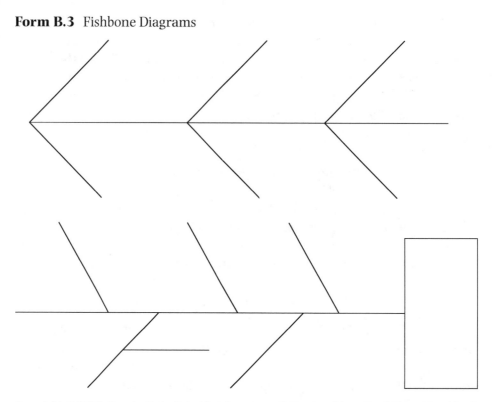

already have prepared. Point out, for example, that a particular organizer could summarize an entire semester of learning or that another organizer could graphically picture a 250-page novel. Tell students that in the beginning of their organizing experiences, you will suggest organizers and frames, but as the semester progresses, they will have the freedom to decide either in a group or on their own how to graphically organize a piece of text.

Modeling the Development of a Graphic Organizer

The first step in teaching any strategy is to model it and think aloud for your students. Place a piece of text on the overhead projector that you will use to model the development of an organizer for your students. You may also wish to give the students a copy of the text so they can follow along more easily or take notes as you think aloud.

Read the text aloud, and as you read, circle or underline important ideas and cross out information on the text that is irrelevant. Tell them as you read and work with the text why you have made a decision to use a certain kind of organizer. Explain once again that every graphic organizer has a frame: a set of questions or categories that are fundamental to understanding a given topic (Jones et al., 1988/1989, pp. 20–21). Meanwhile, begin to develop the organizer on chart paper displayed on an easel. Think aloud for your students as you

Form B.4 Framed Fishbone Diagrams

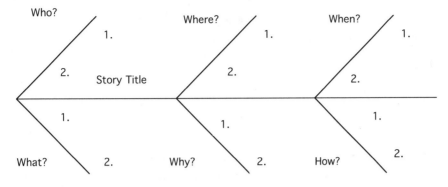

Use this fishbone diagram to organize narrative text or a newspaper article.

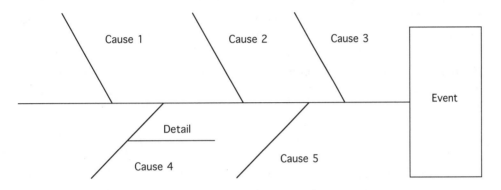

Use this fishbone diagram to organize text that discusses causes leading up to a complex event (e.g., the Civil War). Put the event in the "head" of the fish and the multiple causes on the bones of the internal skeletal structure of the fish. Details related to each cause can be placed on horizontal lines leading from the bones.

move back and forth between the text and the organizer so that students can see how you are making decisions about where on the organizer to place information. Point out to students what you do when you discover "inconsiderate" text that is poorly organized or information that is irrelevant and does not "fit" into the organizer. Remind them to use the summarizing rules and protocols. Explain to students how the author could have benefited from using an organizer as he or she was writing. Discuss the advantages of using organizers when writing an essay.

Take time before beginning a new unit or chapter to preview the text with students. Ask them what organizer they believe would be most appropriate for use with the text. In the beginning, you will need to specify the graphic organizer to be used and supply students with the frame. Later, they will be able to suggest appropriate organizers on their own (Billmeyer & Barton, 1998; Ong & Breneman, 2000).

Organizers for Learning Content-Area Vocabulary

Graphic organizers can also be used to help students understand and remember content-area vocabulary.

Semantic Word Map

Semantic word maps are graphic organizers that are especially useful for teaching a variety of content-related words (Marmolejo, 1991). Figure B.1 shows a semantic word map related to the topic of the brain. To develop this particular word map, participants in my workshop on brain-based reading spent a few moments brainstorming as many words as they could think of related to the central concept of the brain, and then we quickly categorized the words on a blank semantic map. The activity served to introduce the use of graphic organizers as well as learn some new vocabulary related to brain-based reading. Semantic mapping is a well-researched and reliable method of improving students' recall of taught words as well as their comprehension of text that contains the taught words (Johnson, Pittelman, Toms-Bronowski, & Levin 1984; Johnson, Toms-Bronowski, & Pittelman, 1982; Margosein, Pascarella, & Pflaum, 1982).

Semantic Feature Analysis

To construct a semantic feature analysis for students, develop a list of related terms (i.e., names of members of a class of concepts). Write them down the left side of a grid. Then, write all of the possible features of these different members of the group across the top of the page. The analysis can be assigned to students to complete independently or assembled in cooperative groups. Consider each item on the left in terms of each of the features, putting a + (plus) in the appropriate section of the grid if an item is a positive example of the feature and a − (minus) if an item is a negative example of the feature. Figure B.2 shows a semantic feature analysis for a physical education unit on team sports.

FIX UP YOUR MIX-UPS: THE MONITORING STRATEGY

What Is Monitoring?

The monitoring strategy has two aspects. First, it involves the ability to think about how and what one is reading while engaged in the act of reading for purposes of determining if one is comprehending the text, and second, it involves the ability to use a wide variety of strategies to aid in comprehension if needed. Monitoring begins before the reader actually begins reading the text and continues to take place after the reader has completed reading.

Figure B.1 Semantic Word Map: The Brain*

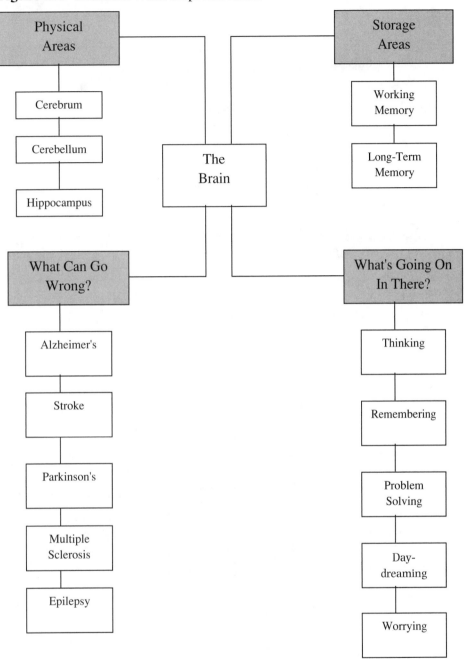

*The entries in this organizer are only suggestive of possible entries. This is not intended to be a conclusive listing.

Figure B.2 Semantic Feature Analysis: Team Sports*

	Played indoors	Referees	Umpires	Coaches	Managers	Fewer than 10 players	More than 10 players	Played with a net	Played with a glove	Played with a puck	Line-up	Fouls	Penalties	Played on grass	Hat trick	Kicking	Hitting	Passing	Dribbling	Blocking	Spiking	Batting	Throwing	Played outdoors	Goals
Football																									
Baseball																									
Rugby																									
Volleyball																									
Soccer																									
Ice Hockey																									
Basketball																									

*This organizer is meant to be illustrative rather than inclusive. Sports enthusiasts will no doubt want to add their own features.

Materials Needed to Teach the *Fix Up Your Mix-Ups* Strategy

Select text for the teacher to use during the modeling part of the *Fix Up Your Mix-Ups* strategy lesson presentation. Also select expository, narrative, or mathematical text for students to read as they learn and practice the monitoring strategy. Assemble the following supplies and equipment: overhead projector, screen, overhead transparencies, markers (erasable for use on the overhead and permanent for use on chart paper), easel with chart paper, highlighters, and chart of monitoring strategies. See Figure B.3, *Fix Up Your Mix-Ups:* The Comprehension Monitoring Checklist.

Teaching Students the *Fix Up Your Mix-Ups* Strategy

The Anticipatory Set

Ask students if they have ever experienced *mix-ups* personally or in their families. Students might describe getting someone else's mail, getting locked out of their houses, getting lost on a vacation. Explain that the mix-ups *you* are talking about are not the ones that occur during daily life but the ones that happen in the course of reading. They happen to every reader at one time or another, and knowing how to use fix-up strategies to straighten out confusion and misunderstandings while reading text is one of the most important things they will learn in your classrooms.

Give some concrete examples of mix-ups that occur in reading: (a) confusing characters in a story, (b) guessing at the meaning of a word and guessing wrong, (c) not being able to figure out what the author is talking about, (d) encountering too many unfamiliar words in the text (lack of vocabulary knowledge), (e) encountering concepts or ideas that are unfamiliar (lack of background knowledge), or (f) getting confused because the text is poorly written.

Giving Students the Reasons Why They Need to Learn the Fix Up Your Mix-Ups *Strategy*

Tell students that you will be teaching them a variety of fix-up strategies to use before, during, and after their reading but especially whenever their understanding falls apart and they are totally mixed up and confused. Explain that everyone encounters text that is difficult for them to understand. Share a personal example of that with your students (e.g., a difficult assignment in a class you are taking or trying to understand directions for your new computer or software). The first response that many readers have when encountering difficult text is to read it once, close the book, and pronounce, "I read it, but I don't get it" (Tovani, 2000).

Tell your students that you will be teaching them a variety of fix-up substrategies but that only they have the power to actually use them during their reading. Share the example of someone who, even though lost, won't stop and

Figure B.3 *Fix Up Your Mix-Ups*: The Comprehension Monitoring Checklist

Is there something specific you don't understand? A word, phrase, concept, idea?

- ☐ Ask someone (e.g., an adult, an expert, a classmate, the author, or your teacher).

- ☐ Look it up: in the dictionary, an encyclopedia, the index, the glossary, or the Internet.

- ☐ Make a prediction: "This must be what the author means. I'm going to keep on reading and see if I'm right."

- ☐ Predict word meaning based on context or word structure.

Is the text poorly written, disorganized, or very long?

- ☐ Chunk it (i.e., divide the text into smaller sections and work on one section at a time).

- ☐ Draw a picture or diagram (i.e., make a graphic organizer).

- ☐ Outline it.

Are you confused about the meaning of the text?

- ☐ Read the back cover copy, the blurb, the preface, a chapter summary, the introduction, a review, or critique it for more clues about the meaning.

- ☐ Connect what you have read to your experience: "This reminds me of the time that . . ."

- ☐ Read the text again and yet again, if necessary.

- ☐ Read the text more slowly.

- ☐ Stop and think out loud to yourself about what you have read.

- ☐ Talk to someone (i.e., think aloud to a friend, family member, or classmate).

- ☐ Ignore the parts you don't understand temporarily and keep reading.

Do you need to remember what you are reading for a test or to write a summary?

- ☐ Form a study group and talk about the text with your classmates.

- ☐ Make a mental picture (i.e., imagine what the text is describing).

- ☐ Write it down (i.e., take notes).

ask for directions. They just keep going around in circles. Using fix-up strategies is a habit of the brain. Explain that the difference between skillful readers and ineffective readers is that good readers recognize when they are lost or mixed up and know what to do about it. Explain that skillful readers have trained their brains to constantly monitor their comprehension by asking the question, "Is it clicking or clunking?" And, skillful readers know that when their reading is clunking rather than clicking, they had better reach for a fix-up strategy immediately.

Modeling the Fix Up Your Mix-Ups *Strategy*

The first step in teaching a cognitive strategy is to model it for your students. Place the text that you will read aloud on the overhead projector. You may also wish to give the students a copy of the text so they can follow along more easily or take notes as you think-aloud. Read the text aloud two to three sentences at a time, and think aloud about showing your students through the words what strategies you are using to figure out the text. Avoid explaining the content or teaching the strategy at this point. That will come later. Now, simply think aloud. Model looking up a word in the dictionary, looking up a name or a subject in the encyclopedia, or putting a phrase into a search engine to see if a short explanation is available. Here are some other possible thought processes for you to model: (a) Make predictions about what you will be reading or what you think the text will be about based on the first few sentences (show how to develop hypotheses), (b) describe any pictures forming in your head while you read, (c) share an analogy (show how you link prior knowledge with new information), or (d) verbalize a confusing point (Schoenbach et al., 1999, p. 97). Use as many of the strategies listed in Figure B. 3 as you can.

After you have modeled as many of the monitoring strategies as practical, give students a challenging piece of text to read. Ask them to read it individually as best they can and determine what monitoring strategies they are using. Then, group students to share their fix-up strategies and discuss the meaning of the text. Have plenty of resources available (books, encyclopedias, dictionaries, a computer, even an expert on the subject, if you want to really make your point) that students can use in their efforts to understand what they are reading (Davey, 1983; Glazer, 1992; Wade, 1990). Younger students may need to learn about and practice only one or at the most two fix-up strategies at a time. For example, what do skilled readers do when they encounter a word they don't know?

Model a variety of vocabulary fix-up strategies to use: (a) Does the unfamiliar word look like or sound like any word you already know? (b) What does that known word mean? (c) Would a similar meaning make sense in the context of what is being read? (d) Is there someone you could ask about the word's meaning? (e) Does your textbook have a glossary you could use to look up the word? (f) Is there a dictionary available? Then, give students a piece of difficult text with a checklist of these strategies, and see how many of them are used by various students. Debrief after this lesson to see if anyone figured out a new strategy to use that you did not have listed.

CONCLUSION

Ideally, every school or district will collaboratively agree on the sequence and approaches to strategy instruction that every teacher will take, thus avoiding what Slavin and Madden (1989) have termed the "cognitive confusion" of multiple instructional approaches to strategy instruction. Presenting cognitive strategies in a disjointed, uncoordinated, and haphazard way is worse than not doing it at all.

Resource C:
Project PRIDE

Project PRIDE is supported by a grant from the United States Department of Education (CFDA 84.324.T). There are four key components to Project PRIDE: (a) a multitiered continuum of reading instruction, (b) curriculum-based assessment, (c) an integrated early-literacy curriculum, and (d) an effective professional development module.

THE MULTITIERED CONTINUUM OF INSTRUCTION

Project PRIDE provides instruction along a continuum of intensities highlighted by general education instruction that is enhanced by instructional strategies effective for at-risk children. The purpose of the tiers is to deliver maximum access to general education programs while at the same time providing more intensive services if they are needed.

The Four Tiers of Instruction

Tier 1: The general education beginning reading program with some teaching methods (enhancements) added that help children who are at risk learn more efficiently

Tier 2: Extra practice (10 minutes, small groups) on the essential word-reading skills that are covered in the school reading series

Tier 3: *Reading Mastery*, an intensive alternative reading program, taught daily for 30 to 40 minutes in small groups; *Reading Mastery* (McGraw Hill) is a phonologically and phonetically based program characterized by a carefully designed instructional sequence with multiple scaffolds to facilitate student learning.

Tier 4: Most intensive instruction, including alternative reading program, smaller group size (1–3), multiple scaffolds (attention to mouth position during articulating; more guided practice and review), and a more deliberate movement through the curriculum.

Supplementary Program Used in Project PRIDE

Language for Learning is a comprehensive, direct-instruction language program that is designed to help develop the at-risk student's language comprehension skills, thus strengthening reading comprehension. All students are given the *Language for Learning* placement test at the beginning of the school year. Students who score below a cut-off level receive 20 to 30 minutes of language instruction per day in addition to the other program components.

Instructional Strategies

These instructional strategies are integrated into all four tiers of the Project PRIDE model.

Advance Organizers

Prior to beginning a lesson, the teacher tells students what they will be doing during the lesson, why the activities are important, and how they are to behave during the lesson. A visual organizer should be presented with a brief verbal description.

Unison Response

The teacher signals all students to answer together to maximize practice and regularly monitor student progress. The teacher asks questions of individual students as an additional check of progress only after the whole group has answered all of the questions.

Judicious Use of Teacher Talk

The teacher presents instruction in concise statements using language the students understand. The teacher does not present information unrelated to the task the students are to complete or provide lengthy explanations.

Perky Pace

There is a brisk presentation of questions or signals made possible by minimizing (a) the amount of time between activities (transition) and (b) the amount of time between a student's answer and the teacher's next question or prompt.

Increased Opportunities for Practice

The teacher maximizes opportunities for student practice by increasing the number of practice items in the text and finding additional time during the school day for practice.

The "I Do It, We Do It, You Do It" Instructional Format

The teacher supports new learning by modeling the correct answer, guiding students to give the correct answer, and then monitoring students as they give correct answers independently. Enhancements involving the "I do it" portion of the lesson help make strategies such as phonemic segmentation and blending more explicit for students. Enhancing a lesson by adding more "you do it" segments provide needed practice on essential sound production skills in both phonemic awareness and letter-sound correspondence tasks.

Systematic Error Correction

The teacher provides immediate corrective feedback to a student by modeling the correct answer, guiding the student to the correct answer as needed, and then asking the student to give the answer independently. The teacher then uses delayed testing by asking the student to repeat the correct answer later in the lesson.

Cumulative Review

The teacher adds examples of previously learned material to examples of newly learned material. Cumulative review teaches students to discriminate between new and old material and helps build student retention of previously learned material.

Example Selection

The teacher uses instructional examples that include common skills students can use to read or write stories. The teacher also selects examples that allow for a high rate (95% accuracy) of student success by including an appropriate blend of new and previous learning.

Motivational Strategies

The teacher strengthens appropriate academic and social behaviors by using positive reinforcement. The teacher increases social behaviors (e.g., staying in seat, raising hand before talking, keeping hands to self) by delivering consistent praise for those behaviors. The goal is to maintain a 3:1 ratio of praise for appropriate behavior to a correction for problem behavior. The teacher also delivers reinforcement to peers who are displaying appropriate behavior. For academic behaviors, the teacher adjusts the level of reinforcement to fit the difficulty level of the task. For example, the teacher provides constant praise when students are working hard on a new and difficult task. For familiar practice tasks, the teacher praises students after they have finished the entire task.

CURRICULUM-BASED ASSESSMENT

Project PRIDE employs curriculum-based assessment (CBA) to regularly monitor student progress on early literacy skills that are particularly difficult for at-risk children to acquire, including phonemic segmentation, blending, letter-sound correspondences, word attack skills, and oral passage reading. CBA enables teachers to identify at-risk students at the first sign of difficulty so that extra support can be provided immediately.

INTEGRATED EARLY-LITERACY CURRICULUM

Project PRIDE stresses the explicit teaching and monitoring of phonemic awareness, word identification, and reading fluency skills within a comprehensive early-literacy program that includes oral language development, reading comprehension, spelling, expressive writing, and the appreciation of literature.

EFFECTIVE PROFESSIONAL DEVELOPMENT

Project PRIDE employs professional development procedures that include after-school and summer workshops as well as extensive classroom practice with a coach and specific feedback. Team-building skills are integrated into workshop sessions.

For more information about Project PRIDE, contact

Bill Bursuck, Professor, Co-Director project PRIDE
Department of Teaching and Learning
147 Gabel Hall
Northern Illinois University
DeKalb, IL 60115
Bursuck @niu.edu

Dennis Munk, Associate Professor, Co-Director project PRIDE
Department of Teaching and Learning
147 Gabel Hall
Northern Illinois University
DeKalb, IL 60115

Resource D: The "I Do It, We Do It, You Do It" Lesson Sequence

Step 1: I Do It

The teacher demonstrates. For example, the teacher introduces the new sound for the letter *p* by showing the letter to the students and saying it for them. The teacher then stops to ask himself or herself this critical question: Are the students ready to move on to Step 2?

Step 2: We Do It

The teacher and students do the activity together, with immediate feedback from the teacher. For example, the teacher practices saying the *p* sound together with the students. If students say the sound incorrectly, the teacher assists them so they say it correctly. The teacher then stops to ask: "Are students ready to move on to Step 3?"

Step 3: You Do It

The students do the activity independently, and the teacher gives feedback about how the students did. This step is a practice phase with the teacher still involved. For example, the teacher asks the students to look at the *p* sound and read it out loud. The teacher then has the students read words in which the students already know all of the letters except for the newly learned *p* sound.[1] The teacher then stops to ask, Are the students ready to move on to Step 4?

Step 4: Apply It

The student applies the skill to a novel problem, cooperative group activity, or real-life situation. For example, the teacher has students play the Oh, No game, where a letter sound is called out. Students point their thumbs down if it's not the sound for *p*. Their thumbs go up in the air whenever a *p* is called out. Several days later, the teacher will have students spell words that contain the letter *p*. Students are assigned to find two pictures of things or people in a magazine at home that begin with the letter p (McEwan & Damer, 2000, p. 143).

NOTE

1. The Project PRIDE lesson format stops here. When Mary Damer and I included this effective teaching sequence in our book, we also included the Apply It part of the sequence. I have left it in for your information.

Resource E: Checklists and Forms to Help You Build a Reading Culture

Form E.1   Fifty Strategies to Build a Reading Culture

1.0   Develop Strong Instructional Leadership and Implement Shared Decision Making by Administrators and Teacher Leaders

_____   1.1   Begin with Principals, Not Programs

_____   1.2   Have a Vision and a Mission Worth Working For

_____   1.3   Follow the Seven Steps to Effective Instructional Leadership

_____   1.4   Develop Teacher Leaders

_____   1.5   Form a Building Leadership Team to Focus on Reading Improvement

2.0   Hold High Expectations, and Make Everyone Accountable for Achievement

_____   2.1   Communicate a Can-Do Attitude to Every Student

_____   2.2   Communicate the Status of Student Performance to Students and Parents

_____   2.3   Apply Ample Amounts of Academic Press

_____   2.4   Hold Classroom Teachers Accountable for the Reading Achievement of Their Students

3.0   Develop a Relentless Commitment to Results Driven by Long- and Short-Term Goals

_____   3.1   Set Meaningful and Measurable Long-Term Goals

_____   3.2   Use the 30-Minute/30-Day Goal-Setting Process to Keep Teachers Focused on Short-Term Goals

4.0   Focus on the Research

_____   4.1   Personally Read the Research

_____   4.2   Conduct Action Research in Your Classroom, School, or District

_____   4.3   Collaboratively Study the Research

_____   4.4   Make Research-Based Decisions

5.0   Develop a Meaningful Instructional Delivery System

_____   5.1   Provide Instructional Diversity

_____   5.2   Provide a Foundation for Success in Kindergarten

_____   5.3   Provide Balanced Literacy in Grades 1 and 2

_____   5.4   Teach Them All to Read to Learn

_____   5.5   Provide *Every* Child with Whole-Group *and* Small-Group Instruction

_____   5.6   Use Research-Based Instructional Strategies

_____   5.7   Teach Less in a More Thorough and Diligent Fashion

_____   5.8   Organize Lesson-Study Groups

6.0   Develop a Comprehensive Monitoring and Assessment System

_____   6.1   Develop an Assessment Mind-Set

_____   6.2   Develop an Assessment Calendar

_____   6.3   Use Frequent Curriculum-Based Assessments

_____   6.4   Know Your Students

_____   6.5   Hit the Ground Running With New Students

7.0   Get Time on Your Side

_____   7.1   Eliminate Time Wasting

_____   7.2   Capture Extracurricular Time for Learning

_____   7.3   Use Time Differently

8.0   Create a Seamless Integration, Coordination, and Continuum of Special Services

_____   8.1   Team Special Education, Remedial Reading, and Speech to Provide Alternative Grouping

_____   8.2   Catch Them in Kindergarten, Before They Fall

RESOURCE E: **165**
CHECKLISTS
AND FORMS
TO HELP YOU
BUILD A
READING
CULTURE

9.0　　Facilitate Teacher Collaboration and Coordination

_____　　9.1　　Provide Teachers With Tools to Assist Them in Planning

_____　　9.2　　Expect Teachers to Coordinate Instruction and Standards on a Vertical Basis

_____　　9.3　　Expect Grade-Level Teams to Meet Regularly to Provide Horizontal Consistency

10.0　　Develop Ongoing and Meaningful Staff Development

_____　　10.1　　Train New Staff Members Intensively

_____　　10.2　　Develop Highly Effective Teachers

_____　　10.3　　Don't Cut Corners on Preimplementation Staff Development

_____　　10.4　　Provide Coaching in the Classrooms

_____　　10.5　　Focus Staff Development on the Mission of the School

_____　　10.6　　Train Your Own Staff Development Cadre

_____　　10.7　　Prioritize Implementation of New Programs

11.0　　Build the Support of Parents and Community for Literacy

_____　　11.1　　Involve Parents in the Writing of School Goals

_____　　11.2　　Make Parents and Community Members Part of Your Team

_____　　11.3　　Get the Word Out Regarding Instruction in the Classrooms

_____　　11.4　　Get the Word Out Regarding Gains in Achievement

12.0　　Acquire and Sustain Adequate Resources

_____　　12.1　　Find Alternate Sources of Funding to Support Reading Improvement Initiatives

_____　　12.2　　Find Grant Money to Fund Improvement Initiatives

_____　　12.3　　Use Zero-Based Budgeting

Figure E.1   Sample Force Field Analysis: To create a pervasive and persuasive reading culture

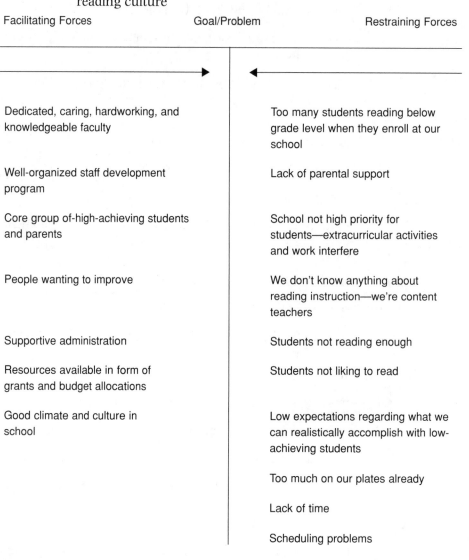

Facilitating Forces   Goal/Problem   Restraining Forces

Dedicated, caring, hardworking, and knowledgeable faculty

Well-organized staff development program

Core group of-high-achieving students and parents

People wanting to improve

Supportive administration

Resources available in form of grants and budget allocations

Good climate and culture in school

Too many students reading below grade level when they enroll at our school

Lack of parental support

School not high priority for students—extracurricular activities and work interfere

We don't know anything about reading instruction—we're content teachers

Students not reading enough

Students not liking to read

Low expectations regarding what we can realistically accomplish with low-achieving students

Too much on our plates already

Lack of time

Scheduling problems

Figure E.2 Neddie's Weekly Newsletter, "Kinder Korner"

Kinder Korner
Week of October 16th, 2000

This Week in School

We delved into our farm unit this week as we read *Rosie's Walk* by Pat Hutchins. This is a wonderful book about a hen who takes a walk around a farm yard (with a fox following her) and gets back (safely) in time for dinner! It is a great book for positional concepts such as over, through, under, past and across. Since Rosie had such a good time walking around the farm yard, we thought Rosie might like to walk around our school! So, we rewrote the book and called it *Rosie's Walk Around Brook Forest*. We can't wait to share it with you!

In math, we made a map of Rosie's walk. This allowed us to practice our positional concepts. We also continued in our chapter on counting, using one-to-one correspondence and the concepts of more and less.

In phonemic awareness, we began isolating the beginning and ending sounds of words (or isolating phonemes) using our second picture word set. The children worked very hard on this! We found out that figuring out the beginning sounds in words is easier than figuring out the ending sounds. But we'll keep working on it! After the children have a firm grasp of the ending sounds, we will move on to isolating middle sounds in words. All the children are working very hard on this and should be very proud of themselves.

Spotlight On... *Phoneme Segmentation and Isolation*

This weeks spotlight is on *phoneme segmentation and isolation*. Phoneme segmentation is the ability to break a word into its sound parts. For example, the word bike has 3 parts- /b/ /i/ /k/. (Keep in mind, we are talking about the SOUNDS, not the letters.) In order to isolate the sounds, the child has to be able to identify WHERE in the word the sound is heard. For example, the beginning sound in the word bike is /b/. The ending sound is /k/. Again, we are not talking about letters at this point, only sounds. To help us with this task, we have been "finger spelling". For each sound we tap our thumb with a finger. For the first sound, we tap it with our index finger. For the second sound, we tap it with our middle finger and for the third sound, we use our ring finger. This really seems to help the children in segmenting and isolating sounds. I have enclosed some picture cards so you can practice isolating beginning and ending sounds in words with your child. Ask him/her to finger spell the words for you!

Centers

Listening Center - Children listened to the book *Inside a Barn in the Country*.
Writing Center - Children free explored.
Art Center - Children painted "spooky" pictures.
Teacher Center - Assessment for upcoming conferences.

Looking Ahead...

Just a reminder...our field trip is Monday! ALL children will come to school at 8:40 and leave at 1:00. We will board the bus at 9:00 to take us to Green Meadows. We will return in time for our 1:00 dismissal. Please make sure you have made arrangements for your child to be picked up if your child is not taking the bus home at 1:00. Also, don't forget we will be eating lunch at Green Meadows! Lunches must be in a paper or plastic disposable bag (no lunchboxes or glass bottles).

Home /School Connection

1.) Please make sure you work on identifying beginning and ending sounds using the picture cards provided.

2.) Scarecrow Happy! We've enclosed the scarecrow version of "Apple Happy". *Your child does not need to return this to school.*

3.) Read, Read, Read!!!

Have a wonderful weekend!
Nettie

Form E.2 30-Minute/30 Day Rapid Results Meeting Agenda,
Grades K and 1

Timekeeper _____ Recorder _____ Facilitator _____

Purpose of this meeting: To set a 30-day team-level reading goal.

List all of the grade-level team's concerns about your students' reading or readiness to read based on running records, Brigance scores, teacher perceptions, other assessments, etc. (5 minutes)

_____

_____

Rate the concerns in order of importance from highest to lowest. (4 minutes)

_____

Write a clear, measurable, attainable, and compelling goal for what your students should be able to do for the one area you have chosen as most important. (5 minutes)

_____

Brainstorm possible solutions to reach this goal. Use the guidelines on the back. (8-10 minutes)

List the best ideas from the brainstorming session. **Describe** how they will be measured. **Set priorities** based on which are perceived to be most effective. (8 minutes)

Best Ideas	Measure	Priority

Team Members Present at Meeting: _____

_____

Next team meeting is on _____ to share results and set a new goal. The recorder is to give a copy of this complete form to principal and team members today. Thank you.

SOURCE: Reprinted by permission of Dr. Christopher Quinn, San Diego County Office of Education.

RESOURCE E: **169**
CHECKLISTS
AND FORMS
TO HELP YOU
BUILD A
READING
CULTURE

Form E.3 30-Minute/30 Day Rapid Results Meeting Agenda, Grades 2
Through 5

Timekeeper ——————— Recorder ——————— Facilitator ———————

Purpose of this meeting: To set a 30-day team-level reading goal.

Rank the grade-level team's reading scores (word study skills, vocabulary or comprehension) on the
SAT-9 *Mastery List Summary* from the highest to lowest using National PR (percentile). (2 minutes)

————————————————————————————————

————————————————————————————————

Identify the lowest score on the *Group Report* (each teacher has one by name) in the *reading* category
listed in the first step. List other areas of concern in reading from other assessments, teacher perceptions
etc. (4 minutes)

————————————————————————————————

Write a clear, measurable, attainable, and compelling goal for what your students should be able to do for
the one area you have chosen as most important. (5 minutes)

————————————————————————————————

Brainstorm possible solutions to reach this goal. Use the guidelines on the back. (8-10 minutes)

List the best ideas from the brainstorming session. **Describe** how they will be measured. **Set priorities**
based on which are perceived to be most effective. (8 minutes)

Best Ideas	Measure	Priority

Team Members Present: _____

————————————————————————————————

Next team meeting is on _____ to share results and set a new goal. The recorder is to give a
copy of this complete form to principal and team members today. Thank you.

SOURCE: Reprinted by permission of D. Christopher Quinn. San Diego County Office of Eudcation.

Form E.4 Sample Reading-Group Planning Form

Name _____

Level: _____   Week of: _____

	Monday	Tuseday	Wednesday	Thursday	Friday
Name of Book					
Skills Addressed					
Vocabulary					
Higher-Level Thinking Skills					

SOURCE: La Mesa Dale School, La Mesa Dale, California. Reprinted by permission.

RESOURCE E: **171**
CHECKLISTS
AND FORMS
TO HELP YOU
BUILD A
READING
CULTURE

Form E.5 Teach Them ALL to Read Implementation Checklist

Scoring Directions: Place one of the following symbols on the line in front of the item to indicate your status with regard to their implementation:

+ Fully implemented

~ A work in progress

– Not implemented

? Need assistance

Use the scores you obtain from this questionnaire to inform your goal-setting, planning, and decision making relative to meeting the needs of the students in your school who are currently falling through the cracks. If you find that you need assistance in one or more of the sections of implementation, consult the must-read resource lists in the chapters to identify materials that can help you.

Phonological Awareness Implementation

_____1. Are all kindergarten students tested upon entrance for phonological awareness skills?

_____2. Do kindergarten students receive at least 25 to 45 minutes of explicit, systematic, supportive instruction per day?

_____3. Are students assessed regularly to determine if time allocation, instructional approaches, or grouping arrangements need to be modified to achieve results?

_____4. Do the most at-risk students receive a booster or tutorial session in addition to in-class instruction?

Phonics Implementation

_____1. Are phonetic skills taught explicitly and systematically?

_____2. Are the 40-plus sound-spelling correspondences taught in grades K through 2?

_____3. Is there an ample supply of decodable books so that students can become fluent?

_____4. Do teachers carefully monitor the in-school and at-home reading of students to ensure that all students are progressing satisfactorily in their decoding abilities?

Spelling Implementation

_____1. Do students write individual letters to correspond to spoken sounds from the beginning of kindergarten?

_____2. Do students write words to correspond to spoken words every day?

_____3. Can students spell; write sentences; punctuate sentences; write notes, letters, and simple stories by the end of first grade?

_____4. Is accurate spelling expected of students?

Fluency Implementation

_____1. Are students given regular assessments of oral reading fluency?

_____2. Do students have daily opportunities to engage in repeated oral reading?

_____3. Are students with low fluency rates put into a systematic program of fluency building?

_____4. Are parents trained to be part of an at-home partnership to build fluency?

Language Implementation

_____1. Is new vocabulary explicitly taught every day?

_____2. Are kindergarten students given language and vocabulary screenings?

_____3. Do students with delayed language development and vocabulary deficiencies receive explicit and systematic language development instruction?

Knowledge Implementation

_____1. Are students introduced to a wide variety of children's literature in a planned and systematic way so as to build domain knowledge on a daily basis?

_____2. Do teachers use science and social studies texts to build domain knowledge?

_____3. Do teachers regularly read aloud expository text to stimulate the acquisition of knowledge and information about the world?

RESOURCE E: **173**
CHECKLISTS
AND FORMS
TO HELP YOU
BUILD A
READING
CULTURE

Cognitive-Strategies Implementation

_____1. Do students have a 30 minute guided and supportive reading period with the teacher every day?

_____2. Do students receive explicit and systematic instruction in the four essential cognitive strategies: summarization, questioning, organizing, and monitoring (including ample amounts of teacher modeling)?

_____3. Are students expected to respond to what they have read every day (orally, in writing, or by drawing pictures)?

_____4. Are students expected to read for meaning immediately and continually?

Reading a Lot Implementation

_____1. Do standards exist for how much time or text students at various grade levels are expected to read?

_____2. Do teachers monitor the achievement of these standards?

_____3. Do teachers engage in motivational techniques and structure programs to encourage students to enjoy books and to read independently?

_____4. Does "real reading" (oral or silent) at the students' independent reading level take place every day?

Reading Culture Implementation

_____1. Do teachers set specific, meaningful, and measurable goals (monthly and yearly) related to the achievement of at-risk students, and are they held accountable for reaching those goals?

_____2. Do teachers have a regular time to meet with the principal to talk about the achievement of at-risk students?

_____3. Do at-risk students receive booster or preteaching sessions every day?

_____4. Do teachers continually monitor the coherence between special programs and the classroom curriculum to eliminate confusion on the part of students?

Glossary

Alphabetic principle

The alphabetic principle is the understanding that spoken words are decomposed into phonemes and that the letters in written words represent the phonemes in spoken words when spoken words are represented in text (Wren, 2001a, p. 2).

Analytic phonics

Analytic phonics denotes phonics instruction that bypasses the teaching of individual sounds and the blending of these sounds to make words and instead focuses on using known words to decode unknown words.

Basal readers

Basal readers are sets of books specifically designed to teach reading. They contain graded selections and are accompanied by comprehensive teachers' manuals and support materials. Basal readers were widely criticized in the past for their formulaic writing and a more recent trend toward teaching students to read using trade books (literature) occurred in response to the poor quality of many basal readers.

Blending

Blending is the rapid combination of individual sounds corresponding to letters in a word that enables a student to decode and thereby "read" a word.

Cognitive apprenticeship

This is a term for the instructional process by which teachers provide and support students with scaffolds as the students develop cognitive strategies (Collins et al., 1991).

Cognitive strategies

Also called *heuristics*, cognitive strategies can be thought of as "procedures that students can use to help them understand and address higher-order tasks in areas such as reading comprehension and writing" (Pressley et al., 1995, p. iii). In the broadest sense, a strategy is a "method or approach that incorporates the steps needed to reach a goal" (Weinstein & Hume, 1998, p. 103).

Contemporary phonics

Contemporary phonics are phonics approaches that were developed in the 1990s, for instance, spelling-based, analogy-based, and embedded-phonics approaches (Stahl, Duffy-Hester, & Stahl, 1998, p. 344).

Content word

A content word is one that has lexical meaning, such as a noun or a verb, as opposed to a function word, which does not have lexical meaning.

Context

According to Webster's definition, *context* is "the parts of a sentence, paragraph, discourse, etc. that occur just before and after a specified word or passage, and determine its exact meaning" (McKechnie, 1983, p. 394). Reading researchers use the term *context* when discussing vocabulary study and have determined that readers with strong background knowledge can generally ascertain the meanings of unfamiliar words from context without direct instruction prior to reading. Many early elementary teachers who use a whole-language approach to reading instruction encourage students to use context as a means of figuring out (identifying) what a new word is. This practice can often lead to what I call the "guessing syndrome" in which novice readers rely too heavily on pictures and other clues and do not use appropriate decoding strategies.

Decodable text

Decodable text is text that does not contain irregular words. Decodable texts are usually designed to reinforce certain "rules" or sounds that have previously been taught in phonics lessons (Wren, 2001a, p. 2). They have been intentionally written to contain only the sound-spelling correspondences that have been taught in a systematic phonics program. Early readers in a reading series should contain a high percentage (at least 75% to 85%) of decodable text. The intent of providing reading material that matches children's letter-sound knowledge is to enable them to experience success in decoding words that follow the patterns they have learned (National Reading Panel, 2000, sec. 2, p. 89). Some states (e.g., Texas and California) have specified the percentage of decodable text that publishers must include in early independent reading books.

Decoding

Decoding is the ability to look at the printed page and translate it into spoken or thought language. Phonics is the methodology used to teach decoding.

Developmental

This word has taken on two meanings in the reading and early childhood literature. The term *developmental* is most commonly used to refer to stages of reading development through which students pass on their way to total reading proficiency (Chall, 1983, 1986). The word has also come to mean "natural," something that will happen gradually over time as a child matures and cannot be taught. In some reading literature, *developmental* is considered to be the opposite of *learned*.

Direct instruction

When written in lower case (i.e., direct instruction), this phrase refers to a style of teaching in which the teacher is "in charge" and has carefully structured the presentation as well as the responses desired from students. When the term appears capitalized (i.e., Direct Instruction), it refers to a specific teaching style originally developed at the University of Oregon.

Discipline

According to Webster's, *discipline* means "anything taught; branch of knowledge or learning" (McKechnie, 1983, p. 520).

Domain

A *domain* is "a sphere or field of influence or activity" (McKechnie, 1983, p. 543).

Encode

To encode is to write the spoken or thought word with accurate spelling.

Exception words

These are words in the English language that cannot be sounded out (e.g., *was*, *the*, *one*, *of*, *shoe*, and *said*) but must be memorized (Wren, 2001b).

Explicit phonics

Explicit phonics is also referred to as *direct code*, *direct phonics*, or *systematic phonics instruction* and is characterized by direct instruction in sound-spelling or spelling-sound correspondences that is provided as a systematic stand-alone component apart from any literature-based activities.

Expository text

Expository text is text written to explain and convey information about a specific topic as opposed to narrative text or nonfiction text.

Fluency

Fluency denotes automaticity and flow in the act of reading. The act of repetitive decoding of a particular word helps to establish the spelling patterns of that word in memory. The most effective way for students to become fluent with a specific word is for them to consciously process both the letter patterns and sounds of the word the first few times it is read (Share & Stanovich, 1995). Some students may need as many as 14 to 20 repetitions to gain total fluency. Fluency is thought by some to be the ability to read connected text "rapidly, smoothly, effortlessly, and automatically with little conscious attention to the mechanics of reading such as decoding" (Meyer & Felton, 1999, p. 284). Others go beyond rapid word identification and include the identification of word meanings as well as the construction of phrase and passage-level meaning in the definition.

Frustration reading level

Frustration reading level is the point at which students' reading skills break down, their fluency disappears, errors in word recognition are numerous, comprehension is faulty, recall is sketchy, and signs of emotional tension and discomfort become evident (Harris & Sipay, 1985).

Function word

A function word is one that does not have lexical meaning and primarily serves to express a grammatical relationship (e.g., *and, of, or, the*) as opposed to a content word (e.g., a noun or verb).

Grapheme

A grapheme is a unit of written language that represents phonemes in the spellings of words (Venezky, 1970, 1999). Graphemes may consist of one letter (e.g., *p, t,* or *m*), two letters (e.g., *ch, ck*), or several letters (e.g., *–igh*).

Guided-process reading

Guided-process reading is the term used by Kathie Dobberteen and her staff to refer to the daily reading groups that teachers have with students. These groups are organized around the reading levels of students determined by an assessment process. Students go to their own specific leveled group during a guided-process reading period. Guided-process reading groups are held in Grades 2 through 5. Students who are in a much higher or lower level than those held in their classrooms travel to another room. In classrooms where the pupil-to-teacher ratio is 20:1, two extra "teachers" come to the room to assist the teacher. In classrooms where the ratio is 33:1, three extra "teachers" come to the classroom to assist the teacher. The following activities take place during guided-process reading, as it is called at La Mesa Dale School: (a) reading of text with support from the teacher, (b) writing in response to reading, (c) vocabulary instruction, (c) higher-level thinking skill instruction, and (d) specific reading skill instruction.

Guided reading

Guided reading in the generic sense takes place when a teacher works with a small group of students who read on a similar level to read and talk about the text together. Students usually read the text orally. Students are supported in their reading by the teacher, as opposed to reading independently. There are a host of conceptions and definitions regarding exactly what guided reading is, but the most prevalent one in most teachers' minds involves "leveled books," "predictable text," and "using context to construct meaning." Teachers will no doubt mention Reading Recovery, Marie Clay (1985), and the work of Lyons (1991) and Pinnell at Ohio State University. Guided reading, as described by Fountas and Pinnell (1996), is a teaching strategy that attempts to provide a bridge or support for students as they develop beginning word-reading skills. The primary materials used in Clay's (1985) model of guided reading are predictable books or books in which words follow very obvious language patterns. During repeated readings of these books, students are encouraged to use context and other cues (mainly the first sound in words) to detect these patterns and read the books accurately and fluently. The assumption is that as children learn to read predictable books, they will intuitively develop word recognition skills that will enable them to read other books, predictable or not.

In Fountas and Pinnell's (1996) guided-reading sessions, students are assumed to develop automatic and fluent word recognition skills through reading connected text and through writing. Students do not receive explicit phonemic decoding instruction. They are thought to learn the phonemic component in the context of writing. Phonological skills are believed to arise incidentally while students are doing "real" reading and writing (Clay, 1985). There is a growing body of research to show that the substitution of explicit phonemic awareness and decoding instruction for the implicit instruction found in the typical guided-reading lesson will result in a more rapid route to reading fluency (Greaney, Tunmer, & Chapman, 1997; Iversen & Tunmer, 1993; Santa & Hoien, 1999; Tunmer & Hoover, 1993).

Independent reading level

Independent reading level denotes the highest level at which students can read easily and fluently —without assistance, with few errors in word recognition, and with good comprehension and recall (Harris & Sipay, 1985).

Instructional reading level

Instructional reading level indicates the highest level at which students can read satisfactorily, provided they receive preparation and supervision from a teacher: few errors in word recognition with adequate comprehension and recall (Harris & Sipay, 1985).

Knowledge

Webster's says that knowledge is the range of understanding; information; acquaintance with facts; practical experience and skills (McKechnie, 1983, p. 1007).

Language

Language includes (a) the speech-and-sound system, (b) the meanings of words (lexicon), (c) how words are put together in utterances to convey a message (semantics and syntax), and (d) how discourse or conversational interaction of various kinds is carried out (Menyuk, 1999, p. 2).

Lexical

Lexical refers to the words or vocabulary of a language.

Literature-based instruction

This term refers to reading from trade books as opposed to basal readers in which selections have often been abridged or written specifically for the textbook using a controlled vocabulary. In most classrooms using literature-based programs, teaching guides have been developed by individual teachers around specific themes or authors.

"Matthew effect"

This is a term with origins in the New Testament parable of the talents in which the rich get richer and the poor get poorer: "For to every one who has will more be given, and he will have abundance; but from him who has not, even what he has will be taken away from him" (Matthew 25:29, Revised Standard Version). The phrase was first coined by sociologist Robert Merton (1968) and later applied by Walberg & Tsai (1983) to education. As used in reading, the term describes the effect of reading deficits in phonemic awareness, vocabulary, or knowledge in kindergarten and first grade from which "poor" students almost never recover (Stanovich, 1986).

Metacognition

Metacognition indicates the process of thinking about one's own thinking. It reflects one's ability to "read" one's own mental state and to assess how that state will affect present and future performance (Meichenbaum & Biemiller, 1998, p. 21).

Morphology

Morphology is "an examination of the morphemic structure of words: an appreciation of the fact that words with common roots share common meanings, and that affixes (i.e., prefixes and suffixes) change words in predictable and consistent ways" (Wren, 2001a, p. 4).

Multisensory phonics

Multisensory phonics refers to phonics programs that include both synthetic and analytic phonics as well as phonology and phonological training, syllables, morphology, syntax, and semantics (McIntyre & Pickering, 1995, p. xi). Examples of multisensory phonics programs include Spalding and Spalding (1990) and Wilson (1988).

Narrative text

Narrative text is written to tell a story or relate a sequence of events; it includes fiction.

Onset-rime

The *onset* is the part of the syllable that precedes the vowel of the syllable. *Rime* is the part of a syllable (not a word) that consists of its vowel and any consonant sounds that comes after it. The phoneme is the smallest sound unit; the word is the biggest sound unit, and an intermediate sound unit is the syllable (called the onset-rime). The onset consists of the initial consonant or consonant cluster in a syllable, and the rime is the vowel and remainder of the syllable. For example, in the word *phonological*, the first syllable or onset-rime is *phon*. The onset is *ph-* and the rime is *-on*.

Orthography

Orthography denotes the spelling of a language.

Phoneme

The phoneme is the most basic element of the language system: a sound.

Phonemic awareness

Phonemic awareness is the ability to hear and manipulate the individual sounds of the language, the ability to recognize individual sounds in words (e.g., rhyming, blending spoken sounds into words, counting phonemes). Phonemic awareness is a critical prerequisite to being able to learn sound-spelling correspondences. The lack of phonemic awareness skills in kindergarten or first grade is now believed by researchers to be the most accurate predictor of a future reading problem. Whole-language proponents sometimes qualify this definition thus: "the ability to detect sounds in speech that are *supposed to be* [italics added] represented by the letters of the alphabet" (Smith, 1994, p. 312).

Phonics

There are two meanings for the word *phonics*. The general meaning of the word is "letters and spelling patterns of a language's alphabet and the speech sounds they represent, i.e. the sounds that the letters make." (Balmuth, 1982, p. 3). Phonics has also come to mean a teaching method "aimed at matching the individual letters of the alphabet with specific sounds of English pronunciation" (Fries, 1963, pp. 143–144).

The term *phonics* has sometimes served as a rallying cry for those who support teaching basic skills in a direct and sequential way as opposed to those who advocate a more developmental approach to reading instruction. Parents sometimes even label schools as "phonics schools" or "whole-language schools," even though phonics instruction at its very best will consume no more than half of the language arts activities time in kindergarten or first grade and for many children, much less. Phonics (stripped of its political baggage) is an instructional method for teaching students to sound out words rather than reading them as a "whole" or guessing what they might be on the basis of context. Smith (1994) defines phonics as "reading instruction based on the *assumption* that reading is decoding to sound and requires learning spelling-to-sound correspondences" (p. 312).

Most parents and many educators do not understand the variety of phonics programs currently in use: synthetic phonics, analytic phonics, embedded phonics, analogy phonics, onset-rime phonics, and phonics through spelling (National Reading Panel, 2000, sec. 2, p. 81). Regardless of the approach taken by the phonics program, "the goal in all phonics programs is to enable learners to acquire sufficient knowledge and use of the alphabetic code so that they can make normal progress in learning to read and comprehend written language (sec. 2, p. 81).

Phonological awareness

Phonological awareness is metalinguistic awareness of all levels of the speech sound system, including word boundaries, stress patterns, syllables, onset-rime units, and phonemes; it is a more encompassing term than phoneme awareness (Moats, 2000, p. 234). *Phonological awareness* as defined by Torgesen and Mathes (2000) is "one's sensitivity to, or explicit awareness of, the phonological structure of words in one's language. In short, it involves the ability to notice, think about, or manipulate the individual sounds in words" (p. 2). To be phonologically aware means (a) knowing that words can be divided into segments of sound smaller than a syllable (phonemes) and (b) knowing how these phonemes sound when they occur in words (Torgesen & Mathes, 2000, p. 2).

Phonological processing

Phonological processing denotes perception, interpretation, recall, and production of language at the level of the speech-sound system, including functions such as pronouncing words, remembering names and lists, identifying words and syllables, giving rhymes, detecting syllable stress, and segmenting and blending phonemes (Moats, 2000, p. 234).

Phonology

Phonology is the ability to hear the difference between different speech sounds, the sounds of a language.

Reading

Reading is a process in which information from the text and the knowledge possessed by the reader act together to produce meaning (National Academy of Education, 1985, p. 8).

Reading culture

A reading cultures is composed of the collective attitudes, beliefs, and behaviors of all of the stakeholders in a school regarding any and all of the activities associated with enabling all students to read at the highest level of attainment possible for both their academic and personal gain.

Repeated reading

Repeated reading occurs when a section of text or a short book is orally read repeatedly to develop accuracy and speed in oral reading. There are two kinds of repeated reading: (a) independent, unassisted reading in which students read the selections on their own either in the classroom or at home and then later read the selection while being assessed for fluency and (b) repeated reading using a prerecorded audio tape of a book with which to orally read along.

Round-Robin reading

Round-Robin reading is "the outmoded practice of calling on students to read orally one after the other" (Harris & Hodges, 1995, p. 222).

Scaffolded instruction

This is instruction in which students are given tasks that are graduated in difficulty, with each one being only slightly more difficult than the last. A scaffold is the temporary support used to assist a learner during initial learning. This support is usually provided by the teacher in the form of prompts, suggestions, and guidance. Scaffolds may also be tools, such as cue cards or checklists. A model of the completed task against which students can compare their work is another example of such support (Rosenshine, 1997).

Segmenting

Segmenting means dividing words into syllables.

Sight words

There are three definitions of *sight words* commonly used in reading instruction: (a) the concept of sight words that originated with the "Look-Say" method of reading instruction in which students were expected to memorize the most common words of the English language (e.g., the Dolch list); (b) words that although originally decoded by the child have been read so frequently, they are eventually read fluently and automatically (but *not* without attention to the letters in the word); and (c) the exception words in the English language that cannot be sounded out (e.g., was, the, one, of, shoe, and said), but must be memorized (Wren, 2001b).

Sound-to-spelling phonics instruction

This is a type of synthetic phonics instruction that first teaches students the sounds and, once the sounds have been learned, teaches the letters (i.e., spelling) that correspond to these sounds.

Spelling

Spelling denotes the ability to recognize, recall, reproduce, or obtain orally or in written form the correct sequence of letters in words (Graham & Miller, 1979, p. 76).

Spelling-to-sound phonics instruction

This is the type of synthetic phonics instruction that begins with teaching students the letters and then teaches the sounds that correspond to those letters.

Strategic learners

Strategic learners are students who approach educational activities or tasks with a high degree of confidence that they can do the tasks, or at least with a sense that they have a good idea of how to try to complete them. Such learners are diligent and resourceful in their efforts and do not give up easily, even in the face of difficulty. (Weinstein & Hume, 1998, p. 10)

Sustained silent reading (SSR)

This denotes a period of time during the school day when classrooms or entire schools lay aside other academic tasks and read.

Syllable

The *Oxford English Dictionary* says that a syllable is a "vocal sound or set of sounds uttered with a single effort of articulation and forming a word or an element of a word" (Simpson & Weiner, 1989, vol. Su-Sz, p. 358).

Synthetic phonics

Synthetic phonics means instruction in either sound-to-spelling or spelling-to-sound correspondences, usually taught in a direct and systematic way.

Systematic instruction

This is instruction that is characterized by a method or plan.

Text

Text is any reading material, whether expository or narrative, that an individual reads.

Three-cueing system

There are two meanings to this term. The first meaning is described in the cognitive-science and reading-instruction literature to indicate the equal importance of the lexical, semantic, and syntactic systems to gaining meaning from text. A fourth system is often included: the pragmatic. The second interpretation is defined by two characteristics: (a) a Venn diagram showing the overlapping of the lexical, semantic, and syntactic cueing systems but with an entire different interpretation as given earlier and (b) three questions that teachers ask their students to help them identify a word they do not know: *Does it make sense? Does it sound right? Does it look right?*

Traditional phonics

Traditional phonics refers to phonics approaches developed and used in the 1960s and 1970s, usually spelling-sound approaches using direct instruction (Stahl et al., 1998, p. 344).

Vocabulary instruction

This is direct instruction in the meanings of unfamiliar words.

Whole language

As described by Ken Goodman (as quoted in Martinez, 1997), one of the principal proponents of the philosophy, whole language is "a pedagogy, or a way that teachers think about teaching; a bringing together [of] everything we've learned about how language works in terms of learning [and] how learning to read and write is an extension of oral language" (p. 11). Frank Smith (1994), a psycholinguist and whole-language advocate, defines whole language as "an educational movement based on the belief that language learning takes place most effectively when learners are engaged collaboratively in meaningful and purposeful uses of language, as opposed to exercises, drills, and tests" (p. 313). It is sometimes referred to as the *naturalistic approach* or as *child-centered learning* and is known in Britain as *real books.*

Word analysis

Word analysis is sometimes called *word attack.* Tests of word analysis measure how well students have mastered consonant sounds and blends, vowel sounds, and polysyllabic words. Older students frequently fool us regarding their knowledge of sound-spelling correspondences because they have memorized so many words. Their poor spelling and inability to read non-words (nonsense words) are usually indicators of deficient word attack skills.

Word identification

Word identification is the ability to visually recognize or "read" words on the printed page.

References

Acheson, K. (1985). *The principal's role in instructional leadership*. Eugene, OR: Oregon School Study Council.

ACT. (2000). *Content validity evidence in support of ACT's educational achievement tests*. Retrieved May, 2000, from www.act.org/news/releases/2000/04-12-00.html

Adams, M. J. (1990). *Beginning to read*. Cambridge: MIT Press.

Adams, M. J. (1991). A talk with Marilyn Adams. *Language Arts, 68*, 206–212.

Adams, M. J. (1998). The three-cueing system. In F. Lehr & J. Osborn (Eds.), *Literacy for all: Issues in teaching and learning* (pp. 73–99). New York: Guilford.

Adams, M. J., Anderson, R. C., & Durkin, D. (1978). Beginning reading: Theory and practice. *Language Arts, 55*, 19–25.

Adams, M. J., & Bruce, B. C. (1982). Background knowledge and reading comprehension. In J. A. Langer & M. T. Smith-Burke (Eds.), *Reader meets author: Bridging the gap* (pp. 2–25). Newark, DE: International Reading Association.

Adams, M. J., & Bruck, M. (1993). Word recognition: The interface of educational policies and scientific research. *Reading and Writing: An Interdisciplinary Journal, 5*, 113–139.

Adams, M., Foorman, B. R., Lundberg, I., & Beeler, T. (1998). *Phonemic awareness in young children: A classroom curriculum*. Baltimore: Brookes.

Adler, M. J., & Van Doren, C. (1972). *How to read a book*. New York: Simon & Schuster.

Advantage Learning Systems. (2001). *Accelerated reader*. Wisconsin Rapids, WI: Author.

Allen-Hagen, B. (1991, January). Children in custody, 1989. *Juvenile Justice Bulletin*, 2–15.

Allington, R. L. (1977). If they don't read much, how they ever gonna get good? *Journal of Reading, 21*, 57–61.

Allington, R. L. (1980). Poor readers don't get to read much in reading groups. *Language Arts, 57*(8), 872–876.

Allington, R. L. (1983). Fluency: The neglected goal. *The Reading Teacher, 36*, 556–561.

Allington, R. L. (1984). Content coverage and contextual reading in reading groups. *Journal of Reading Behavior, 16*, 85–96.

Allington, R. L. (2001). *What really matters for struggling readers*. New York: Longman.

Allington, R. L., & Johnston, P. (2000, April). *Exemplary fourth-grade reading instruction*. Paper presented at the American Educational Research Association, New Orleans.

Allington, R. L., & McGill-Franzen, A. (1989). School response to reading failure: Chapter 1 and special education students in grades 2, 4, and 8. *Elementary School Journal, 89,* 529–542.

Allington, R. L., & Shake, M. C. (1986). Remedial reading and achieving curricular congruence in the classroom. *Reading Teacher, 39*(7), 648–654.

Allred, R. (1977). *Spelling: The application of research findings.* Washington, DC: National Education Association.

Alvermann, D. E., & Phelps, S. F. (1998). *Content reading and literacy: Succeeding in today's diverse classrooms.* Needham Heights, MA: Allyn and Bacon.

amazon. com, (2000). [Reader's commentary on *View from Saturday*]. Retrieved October 2001, from www.amazon.com

Ambrose, S. (1994). *D-day: The climactic battle of World War II.* New York: Simon & Schuster.

Anderson, B. (1981). The missing ingredient: Fluent oral reading. *The Elementary School Journal, 81,* 173–177.

Anderson, L., & Krathwohl, D. R. (2001). *A taxonomy for learning, teaching, and assessing: A revision of Bloom's Taxonomy of Educational Objectives.* New York: Longman.

Anderson, R. C., Wilson, P. T., & Fielding, L. G. (1988). Growth in reading and how children spend their time outside of school. *Reading Research Quarterly, 23,* 285–303.

Anderson, V. (1991, April). *Training teachers to foster active reading strategies in reading-disabled adolescents.* Paper presented at the annual meeting of the American Educational Research Association, Chicago.

Anderson, V., & Hidi, S. (1989). Teaching students to summarize. *Educational Leadership, 46*(4), 26–28.

Ansara, A. (1969). Maturational readiness for school tasks. *Bulletin of the Orton Society, 19,* 51–59.

Antrim, J. (2001). *Summaries of test scores at Eureka School.* Unpublished report. Eureka School, Rockwood School District, Eureka, MO.

Aram, D. M., & Hall, N. E. (1989). Longitudinal follow-up of children with preschool communication disorders: Treatment implications. *School Psychology Review, 18*(4), 487–501.

Armbruster, B. B., Anderson, T. H., & Ostertag, J. (1987). Does text structure/summarization instruction facilitate learning from expository text? *Reading Research Quarterly, 22,* 331–346.

Armor, D., Conry-Oseguera, P., Cox, M., King, N., McDonnell, L., Pascal, A., Pauly, E., & Zellman, G. (1976). *Analysis of the School Preferred Reading Program in selected Los Angeles minority schools* (Report No. R-2007-LAUSD). Santa Monica, CA: RAND. (ERIC Document Reproduction Service No. ED 130 243)

Ashton, P. T., & Webb, R. B. (1986). *Making a difference: Teachers' sense of efficacy and student achievement.* New York: Longman.

Atwell, N. (1998). *In the middle: New understandings about writing, reading and learning.* Portsmouth, NH: Heinemann.

Baker, L., Serpell, R., & Sonnenschein, S. (1995). Opportunities for literacy learning in the homes of urban preschoolers. In L. M. Morrow (Ed.), *Family literacy: Connections in schools and communities* (pp. 236–252). Newark, DE: International Reading Association.

Ball, E. W., & Blachman, B. A. (1991). Does phoneme awareness training in kindergarten make a difference in early word recognition and developmental spelling? *Reading Research Quarterly, 24*(1), 49–66.

Balmuth, M. (1982). *The roots of phonics.* New York: McGraw-Hill.

Bashir, A. S., & Scavuzzo, A. (1992). Children with language disorders: Natural history and academic success. *Journal of Learning Disabilities, 25*(1), 53–65.

Becker, W., & Engelmann, S. (1983). *Reading Mastery.* Chicago: SRA/McGraw-Hill.

Bell, N. (1991a). Gestalt imagery: A critical factor in language comprehension. *Annals of Dyslexia, 41,* 246–260.

Bell, N. (1991b). *Visualizing and verbalizing for language comprehension and thinking.* Paso Robles, CA: Academy of Reading. (Original work published 1986)

Bell, N. (1997). *Seeing stars: Symbol imagery for sight words and spelling.* San Luis Obispo, CA: Gander.

Berkowitz, S. J. (1986). Effects of instruction in text organization on sixth-grade students' memory for expository reading. *Reading Research Quarterly, 21,* 161–178.

Berliner, D. C. (1981). Academic learning time and reading achievement. In J. Guthrie (Ed.), *Comprehension and teaching: Research reviews* (pp. 203–225). Newark, DE: International Reading Association.

Biemiller, A. (1999). *Language and reading success.* Cambridge, MA: Brookline.

Billmeyer, R., & Barton, M. L. (1998). *Teaching reading in the content areas: If not me, then who?* Aurora, CO: McRel.

Bird, T. D., & Little, J. W. (1985). *Instructional leadership in eight secondary schools. Final report.* Boulder, CO: Center for Action Research.

Blachowicz, C. (1987). Vocabulary instruction: What goes on in the classroom? *Reading Teacher, 41*(2), 132–137.

Block, F. L. (1998). *I was a teen-age fairy.* New York: HarperCollins.

Bloom, A. (1987). *The closing of the American mind.* New York: Simon & Schuster.

Bloom, B. S. (1980). The new direction in educational research: Alterable variables. *Phi Delta Kappan, 61,* 382–385.

Blow, B. (1976, April). Individualized reading. *Arizona English Bulletin, 18,* 151–53.

Bond, G. L., & Dykstra, R. (1967). The cooperative research program in first-grade reading instruction. *Reading Research Quarterly, 2*(4), 10–89.

Bowers, P. G. (1995). Tracing symbol naming speed's unique contributions to reading disability over time. *Reading and Writing: An Interdisciplinary Journal, 7,* 1–28.

Bowers, P. G., Golden, J., Kennedy, A., & Young, A. (1994). Limits upon orthographic knowledge due to processes indexed by naming speed. In V. W. Berninger (Ed.), *The varieties of orthographic knowledge: I. Theoretical and developmental issues* (pp. 173–218). Dordrecht, The Netherlands: Kluwer.

Bowers, P. G., & Wolf, M. (1993). Theoretical links among naming speed, precise timing mechanisms, and orthographic knowledge. *Reading and Writing: An Interdisciplinary Journal, 5,* 69–85.

Bridge, C. A., Winograd, P. N., & Haley, D. (1983). Using predictable materials vs. preprimers to teach beginning sight words. *The Reading Teacher, 36,* 84–91.

Brophy, J. (Ed.). (1989). *Advances in research on teaching* (vol. 1). Greenwich, CT: JAI.

Brophy, J. E., & Good, T. L. (1986). Teacher behavior and student achievement. In M. C. Wittrock (Ed.), *Handbook of research on teaching* (3rd ed., pp. 328–375). Upper Saddle River, NJ: Merrill/Prentice Hall.

Brown, A. L., & Day, J. D. (1983). Macrorules for summarizing texts: The development of expertise. *Journal of Verbal Learning and Verbal Behavior, 22*, 1–14.

Brown, A. L., Day, J. D., & Jones, R. S. (1983). The development of plans for summarizing texts. *Child Development, 54*, 968–979.

Brown, R., Pressley, M., Van Meter, P., & Schuder, T. (1996). A quasi-experimental validation of transactional strategies instruction with low-achieving second-grade readers. *Journal of Educational Psychology, 88*(1), 18–37.

Bruck, M. (1990). Word recognition skills of adults with childhood diagnoses of dyslexia. *Developmental Psychology, 26*, 439–454.

Bruck, M. (1992). Persistence of dyslexics' phonological awareness deficits. *Developmental Psychology, 28*, 874–886.

Bryant, P., & Bradley, L. (1985). *Children's reading problems: Psychology and education.* Oxford, UK: Basil Blackwell.

Burns, M. S., Griffin, P., & Snow, C. (Eds.). (1999). *Starting out right: A guide to promoting children's reading success.* Washington, DC: National Academy Press.

Byrne, B., & Fielding-Barnsley, R. (1989). Phonemic awareness and letter knowledge in the child's acquisition of the alphabetic principle. *Journal of Educational Psychology, 81*, 313–321.

Calfee, R. C. (1998). Phonics and phonemes: Learning to decode in a literature-based program. In J. Metsala & L. Ehri (Eds.), *Word recognition in beginning literacy* (pp. 315–340). Mahwah, NJ: Lawrence Erlbaum.

Calfee, R. C, & Piontkowski, D. C. (1981). The reading diary: Acquisition of decoding. *Reading Research Quarterly, 16*, 346–373.

California Department of Education. (2001). *Criteria for 2002 language arts adoption.* Retrieved May 28, 2001, from www.cde.ca.gov/cilbranch/eltdiv/2002lacriteria.html

California Early Literacy Learning Project. (1996). *CELL Training Manual* (in CELL training materials). San Bernadino: California State University, Reading Recovery Center.

Cameron, J., & Pierce, W. E. (1994). Reinforcement, reward, and intrinsic motivation: A meta-analysis. *Review of Educational Research, 64*, 363–423.

Campbell, R., & Butterworth, B. (1985). Phonological dyslexia and dysgraphia in a highly literate subject: A developmental case with associated deficits in phonemic processing and awareness. *Quarterly Journal of Experimental Psychology, 37*, 375–396.

Carbo, M. (1988). Debunking the great phonics myth. *Phi Delta Kappan, 70*, 226–240.

Carbo, M. (1996). Whole language or phonics? Use both. *Education Digest, 61*, 60–64.

Carnine, D. W., Silbert, J., & Kame'enui, E. J. (1997). *Direct instruction reading* (3rd ed.). Upper Saddle River, NJ: Merrill.

Carr, E., & Wixon, K. K. (1986). Guidelines for evaluating vocabulary instruction. *Journal of Reading, 29*(7), 588–595.

Carter, S. C. (1999). *No excuses: Seven principals of low-income schools who set the standard for high achievement.* Washington, DC: Heritage Foundation.

Chall, J. S. (1983). *Learning to read: The great debate.* New York: McGraw-Hill. (Original work published 1967)

Chall, J. S. (1986). *Stages of reading development.* New York: Harcourt Brace. (Original work published 1983)

Chall, J. S. (1989). Learning to read: The great debate 20 years later—A response to "Debunking the Great Phonics Myth." *Phi Delta Kappan, 70,* 521–537.

Chall, J. S. (1996). *Learning to read: The great debate.* Fort Worth, TX: Harcourt Brace.

Chall, J. S. (1999). Some thoughts on reading research: Revisiting the first-grade studies. *Reading Research Quarterly, 34*(1), 8–10.

Chall, J. S., & Dale, E. (1995). *Readability revisited: The new Dale-Chall Readability Formula.* Cambridge, MA: Brookline.

Chall, J. S., Jacobs, V. A., & Baldwin, L. E. (1990). *The reading crisis: Why poor children fall behind.* Cambridge, MA: Harvard University Press.

Chall, J. S., & Popp, H. M. (1996). *Teaching and assessing phonics: A guide for teachers.* Cambridge, MA: Educators Publishing Service.

Chapman, J. W., Tunmer, W. E., & Prochnow, J. E. (2001). Does success in the Reading Recovery program depend on developing proficiency in phonological-processing skills? A longitudinal study in whole language instructional context. *Scientific Studies of Reading, 5*(2), 141–176.

Ciborowski, J. (1992). *Textbooks and the students who can't read them.* Cambridge, MA: Brookline.

Clay, M. M. (1985). *The early detection of complex behavior.* Auckland, New Zealand: Heinemann.

Cognitive Concepts. (2001). *Earobics.* Evanston, IL: Author.

Coleman, J. (1966). *Equality of educational opportunity.* Washington, DC: United States Department of Health Education and Welfare, Office of Education.

Coles, G. S. (1997, April 2). Phonics findings discounted as part of flawed research [Letter to the editor]. *Education Week,* 45.

Coles, G. S. (2000a). *A reply to Louise Spear-Swerling's review of Misreading Reading: The Bad Science That Hurts Children.* Retrieved March 20, 2001, from www.education-news.org/a_reply–to_louise_spear.htm

Coles, G. S. (2000b). *Misreading reading: The bad science that hurts children.* Portsmouth, NH: Heinemann.

Collins, A., Brown, J. S., & Holum, A. (1991). Cognitive apprenticeship: Making thinking visible. *American Educator, 15,* 6–11, 38–41.

Conrad, R. (1979). *The deaf school child.* London: Harper & Row.

Cook, S. A., & Page, C. A. (1994). *Books, battles & bees.* Chicago: American Library Association.

Cook, T. D., & Campbell, D. T. (1979). *Quasi-experimentation: Design and analysis issues for field studies.* Chicago: Rand McNally.

Coyne, M. D., Kame'enui, E. J., & Simmons, D. C. (2001). Prevention and intervention in beginning reading: Two complex systems. *Learning Disabilities Research and Practice, 16*(2), 62–72.

Craik, F. I. M., & Tulving, E. (1975). Depth of processing and the retention of words in episodic memory. *Journal of Experimental Psychology: General, 104,* 268–294.

Cronnell, B. (1978). Phonics for reading vs. phonics for spelling. *Reading Teacher, 32,* 337–340.

Cubberly, E. P. (1909). *Changing conceptions of education.* New York: Houghton Mifflin.

Cunningham, A. E. (1990). Explicit versus implicit instruction in phonemic awareness. *Journal of Experimental Child Psychology, 50,* 429–444.

Cunningham, P. M. (1995). *Phonics they use: Words for reading and writing.* New York: Longman.

Curtis, M. E., & Longo, A. M. (1999). *When adolescents can't read: Methods and materials that work.* Cambridge, MA: Brookline Books.

Davey, B. (1983). Think-aloud: Modeling the cognitive process of reading comprehension. *Journal of Reading, 26,* 44–47.

Davidson, M. (2000). *Intervention manual in reading: Research based instructional strategies to accompany the Reading Screening Test* (RST). Bellingham: Western Washington University, Applied Research and Development Center.

Delpit, L. (1995). *Other people's children: Cultural conflict in the classroom.* New York: New Press.

Dickinson, D. K., & Smith, M. W. (1994). Long-term effects of preschool teachers' book readings on low-income children's vocabulary, story comprehension, and print skills. *Reading Research Quarterly, 29*(2), 104–122.

Dixon, R., Carnine, D., & Kame'enui, E. (1992). *Curriculum guidelines for diverse learners* (Monograph for National Center to Improve the Tools of Educators). Eugene: University of Oregon.

Dobberteen, C. (1999). *California School Recognition Program, 2000 Elementary School Application* (La Mesa Dale Elementary School, La Mesa, CA). Unpublished document.

Dobberteen, C. (2000). *Application for Title I Distinguished School* (La Mesa Dale Elementary School, La Mesa, CA). Unpublished document.

Dobberteen, C. (2001). *Second Annual Chase Change Award: Essay* (La Mesa Dale Elementary School, La Mesa, CA). Unpublished document.

Dole, J. (2000). Explicit and implicit instruction in comprehension. In B. M. Taylor, M. F. Graves, & P. van den Broek (Eds.), *Reading for meaning: Fostering comprehension in the middle grades* (pp. 52–69). New York: Teachers College Press.

Donahue, P., Voelkl, K., Campbell, J., & Mazzeo, J. (1999). *NAEP 1998 reading report card for the nation and states.* Washington, DC: U.S. Department of Education, Office of Educational Research and Improvement. Retrieved April 5, 2000, from http://nces.ed.gov/pubs99/quarterlyapr/4-elementary/4-esq11-a.html]

Dowhower, S. L. (1989). Repeated reading: Research into practice. *The Reading Teacher, 42*(7), 502–506.

Duffy, G. G. (1993). Rethinking strategy instruction: Four teachers' development and their low achievers' understandings. *Elementary School Journal, 93*(3), 231–247.

Duffy, G. G., & Roehler, L. R. (1987). Teaching reading skills as strategies. *The Reading Teacher, 40,* 414–418.

Duffy, G. G., Roehler, L. R., Sivan, E., Rackliffe, G., Book, C., Meloth, M., Varus, L., Weselman, R., Putnam, J., & Basiri, D. (1987). The effects of explaining the reasoning associated with using reading strategies. *Reading Research Quarterly, 16,* 403–411.

Duin, J. (1999, December 17). Youth fiction takes a stark, eerie turn: Literature for teens is full of images of rape, demons, torture and more. *Washington Times.* Retrieved December 19, 1999, from www.washtimes.com

Dunkin, M. J., & Biddle, B. J. (1974). *The study of teaching.* New York: Holt, Rinehart & Winston.

Durkin, D. (1966). *Children who read early.* New York: Teachers College Press.

Editorial Projects in Education (2000). *Quality counts 2000.* Washington, DC: Author.

Edmonds, R. (1981). Making public schools effective. *Social Policy, 12,* 53–60.

Educational Research Service (1998). *Reading at the middle and high school levels.* Arlington, VA: Author.

Egoff, S. (1972). If that don't do no good, that won't do no harm: The uses and dangers of mediocrity in children's reading. *School Library Journal, 19*(10), 93–97.

Ehri, L. C. (1991). Learning to read and spell words. In L. Rieben & C. A. Perfetti (Eds.), *Learning to read: Basic research and its implications* (pp. 57–73). Hillsdale, NJ: Lawrence Erlbaum.

Ehri, L. C. (1998). Grapheme-phoneme knowledge is essential for learning to read words in English. In J. L. Metsala & L. C. Ehri (Eds.), *Word recognition in beginning literacy* (pp. 3–40). Hillsdale, NJ: Lawrence Erlbaum.

Elley, W. B. (1992). *How in the world do students read?* Hamburg, Germany: International Association for the Evaluation of Educational Achievement.

Elley, W. B. (1999). *Raising literacy levels in third world countries: A method that works.* Culver City, CA: Language Education Associates.

English, F. (1992). *Deciding what to teach and test: Developing, aligning, and auditing the curriculum.* Thousand Oaks, CA: Corwin.

Ennis, C. D. (1998). Shared expectations: Creating a joint vision for urban schools. In J. Brophy (Ed.), *Advances in research on teaching: Expectations in the classroom* (pp. 151–182). Greenwich, CT: JAI.

Farr, R. (1998). *Strengthening reading comprehension: Developing critical thinking and problem-solving skills.* Unpublished materials provided in a workshop.

Fawcett, A. J., & Nicolson, R. I. (2001). Speed and temporal processing in dyslexia. In M. Wolf, (Ed.), *Dyslexia, fluency, and the brain* (pp. 24–40). Timonium, MD: York.

Feitelson, D., Kita, B., & Goldstein, Z. (1986). Effects of listening to series stories on first graders' comprehension and use of language. *Research in the Teaching of English, 20,* 339–356.

Felton, R. S. (1993). Effects of instruction on the decoding skills of children with phonological-processing problems. *Journal of Learning Disabilities, 26*(9), 583–589.

Fine, M. (1991). *Framing dropouts: Notes on the politics of an urban public high school.* New York: State University of New York Press.

Finn, C. E., Rotherham, A. J., & Hokanson, C. R. (Eds.). (2001). *Rethinking special education for a new century.* Washington, DC: Thomas B. Fordham Foundation and Progressive Policy Institute. Retrieved June 13, 2002, from www.edexcellence.net

Fisher, C. W., & Berliner, D. C. (1985). *Perspectives on instructional time.* New York: Longman.

Foorman, B. R. (1995). Research on the great debate: Code-oriented versus whole language approaches to reading instruction. *School Psychology Review, 24*(3), 376–392.

Foorman, B. R., Fletcher, J. M., & Francis, D. J. (1998). Preventing reading failure by ensuring effective reading instruction. In S. Patton, & M. Holmes (Eds.), *The keys to literacy* (pp. 29–37). Washington, DC: Council for Basic Education.

Foorman, B. R., Fletcher, J. M., Francis, D. J., & Schatschneider, C. (2000). Response: Misrepresentation of research by other researchers. *Educational Research, 29*(6), 27–37.

Foorman, B. R., Fletcher, J. M., Francis, D. J., Schatschneider, C., & Mehta, P. (1998). The role of instruction in learning to read: Preventing reading failure in at-risk children. *Journal of Educational Psychology, 90*(1), 37–55.

Fountas, I. C., & Pinnell, G. S. (1996). *Guided reading: Good first teaching for all children.* Portsmouth, NH: Heinemann.

Francis, D. J., Shaywitz, S. E., Stuebing, K. K., Shaywitz, B. A., & Fletcher, J. M. (1996). Developmental lag versus deficit models of reading disability: A longitudinal, individual growth curve analysis. *Journal of Educational Psychology, 88*(1), 3–17.

Fries, C. C. (1963). *Linguistics and reading.* New York: Holt, Rinehart & Winston.

Fry, E. B., Kress, J. E., & Fountoukidis, D. L. (2000). *The reading teacher's book of lists* (4th ed.). Upper Saddle River, NJ: Prentice Hall.

Fuchs, L. S., Fuchs, D., Hops, M. K., & Jenkins, J. R. (2001). Oral reading fluency as an indicator of reading competence: A theoretical, empirical, and historical analysis. *Scientific Studies of Reading, 5*(3), 239–245.

Fuchs, L. S., Fuchs, D., & Maxwell, L. (1988). The validity of informal measures of reading comprehension. *Remedial and Special Education, 9*(2), 20–28.

Fullan, M. (1990). Staff development, innovation and institutional development. In B. Joyce (Ed.), *Changing school culture through staff development* (pp. 3–25). Alexandria, VA: Association for Supervision and Curriculum Development.

Gaskins, I. W. (1998a). *Benchmark word identification program.* Media, PA: Benchmark School.

Gaskins, I. W. (1998b). There's more to teaching at-risk and delayed readers than good reading instruction. *The Reading Teacher, 51*(7), 534–547.

Gaskins, I. W., & Elliot, T. T. (1991). *Implementing cognitive strategy instruction across the school: The Benchmark manual for teachers.* Cambridge, MA: Brookline.

Gaskins, I. W., Satlow, E., Hyson, D., Ostertag, J., & Six, L. (1994). Classroom talk about text: Learning in science class. *Journal of Reading, 3*(7), 558–565.

Gilbar, S. (Ed.). (1990). *The reader's quotation book: A literary companion.* Wainscott, NY: Pushcart.

Glazer, S. M. (1992). *Reading comprehension: Self-monitoring strategies to develop independent readers.* New York: Scholastic.

Glickman, C. D. (1993). *Renewing America's schools: A guide for school-based action.* San Francisco: Jossey-Bass.

Goldberg, M. (2000). *Bee season.* New York: Doubleday.

Goldenberg, C., Reese, L., & Gallimore, R. (1992). Effects of school literacy materials on Latino children's home experiences and early reading achievement. *American Journal of Education, 100*, 497–536.

Good, R. H. (2000). *Dynamic indicators of basic early literacy (DIBELS)*. Eugene: University of Oregon. Retrieved September 8, 2001, from http://dibels.uoregon.edu

Good, R. H., III, Simmons, D. C., & Kame'enui, E. J. (2001). The importance and decision-making utility of a continuum of fluency-based indicators of foundational reading skills for third-grade high-stakes outcomes. *Scientific Studies of Reading, 5*(3), 257–288.

Goodman, K. (1967). Reading: A psycholinguistic guessing game. *Journal of the Reading Specialist, 6*, 126–135.

Goodman, K. (1986). *What's whole in whole language?* Richmond Hill, Ontario, Canada: Scholastic.

Goodman, K. (1996). *On reading.* Portsmouth, NH: Heinemann.

Goodman, Y. M., & Burke, C. L. (1972). *Reading miscue inventory manual: Procedure for diagnosis and evaluation.* New York: Macmillan.

Goodman, Y. M., Watson, D. J., & Burke, C. L. (1987). *Reading miscue inventory: Alternative procedures.* New York: R. C. Owen.

Gough, P. B. (1983). Context, form and interaction. In K. Raynor (Ed.), *Eye movements in reading.* New York: Academic Press.

Gough, P. B., & Hillinger, M. L. (1980). Learning to read: An unnatural act. *Bulletin of the Orton Society, 30*, 179–196.

Graham, S., & Miller, L. (1979). Spelling research and practice: A unified approach. *Focus on Exceptional Children, 12*(2), 75–91.

Greaney, K., Tunmer, W., & Chapman, J. (1997). Effects of rime-based orthographic analogy training on the word recognition skills of children with reading disability. *Journal of Educational Psychology, 89*, 645–651.

Gunning, T. G. (1998). *Assessing and correcting reading and writing difficulties.* Boston: Allyn and Bacon.

Haifiz, F., & Tudor, I. (1989) Extensive reading and the development of language skills. *English Language Teaching Journal, 43*, 4–11.

Hall, G. S. (1900). Child study and its relation to education. *The Forum, 29*, 691.

Hall, S., & Moats, L. (1998). *Straight talk about reading.* New York: McGraw-Hill.

Hare, V., & Borchardt, K. M. (1984). Direct instruction of summarization skills. *Reading Research Quarterly, 21*, 62–78.

Harris, A. J., & Sipay, E. R. (1985). *How to increase reading ability: A guide to developmental and remedial methods.* New York: Longman.

Harris, T., & Hodges, R. (Eds.). (1995). *The literacy dictionary.* Newark, DE: International Reading Association.

Hart, B., & Risley, T. R. (1995). *Meaningful differences in the everyday experience of young American children.* Baltimore: Brookes.

Harvey, S., & Goudvis, A. (2000). *Strategies that work: Teaching comprehension to enhance understanding.* York, ME: Stenhouse.

Hasbrouck, J. E., Ihnot, C., & Rogers, G. (1999). Read naturally: A strategy to increase oral reading fluency. *Reading Research Instruction, 39*(1), 27–37.

Hasbrouck, J. E., Ihnot, C., & Woldbeck, T. (1997). One teacher's use of curriculum-based measurement: A changed opinion. *Learning Disabilities, Research and Practice, 14*(2), 118–126.

Hasbrouck, J. E., & Tindal, G. (1992). Curriculum based oral reading fluency for students in grades 2 through 5. *Teaching Exceptional Children, 24,* 41–44.

Heath, S. B. (1983). *Ways with words: Language, life, and work in communities and classrooms.* Cambridge, UK: Cambridge University Press.

Hecht, S. A., Burgess, S. A., Torgesen, J. K., Wagner, R. K., & Rashotte, C. A. (2000). Explaining social class differences in growth of reading skills from beginning kindergarten through fourth-grade: The role of phonological awareness, rate of access, and print knowledge. *Reading and Writing: An Interdisciplinary Journal, 12*(1–2), 99–127.

Heckelman, R. G. (1969). A neurological-impress method of remedial reading instruction. *Academic Therapy, 4*(4), 277–282.

Heward, W. L., & Dardig, J. C. (2001, Spring). What matters most in special education. *Education Connection,* 41–44.

Hiebert, E. H. (1994). Reading Recovery in the United States: What difference does it make to an age cohort? *Educational Researcher, 23*(9), 15–25.

Hirsch, E. D., Jr. (Ed.). (1989). *A first dictionary of cultural literacy.* Boston: Houghton Mifflin.

Hirsch, E. D., Jr. (1996). *The schools we need and why we don't have them.* New York: Doubleday.

Hirsch, E. D., Jr. (2001a). Breadth versus depth: A premature polarity. *Common Knowledge: The Newsletter of the Core Knowledge Foundation, 14*(4), 3–4.

Hirsch, E. D., Jr. (2001b). Make better use of the literacy time block. *American Educator, 25*(2), 4, 6–7.

Holt, J. (1964). *How children fail.* New York: Pitman.

Honig, B. (1996). *Teaching our children to read: The role of skills in a comprehensive reading program.* Thousand Oaks, CA: Corwin.

Howell, K. W., Zucker, S. H., & Morehead, M. K. (1994). *The multilevel academic skills inventory.* Paradise Valley, AZ: H & Z.

Ihnot, C. (1995). A plan to attack fluency problems. *Research/Practice, 3*(1). Minneapolis: University of Minnesota Center for Applied Research and Educational Improvement. Retrieved July 14, 2001, from http://carei.coled.umn.edu/Rpractice/Winter95/fluency.htm

Ihnot, C. (2001). *Read naturally.* Retrieved September 9, 2001, from www.readnaturally.com

Institute for Multisensory Education. (1998). *Sensational strategies for teaching beginning readers.* Retrieved January 9, 2002, from www.ortongillingham.com

Irvin, J. L. (1998). *Reading and the middle school student: Strategies to enhance literacy.* Boston: Allyn & Bacon.

Iversen, S., & Tunmer, W. (1993). Phonological processing skills and the Reading Recovery program. *Journal of Educational Psychology, 8,* 112–126.

Jenkins, J. R., Fuchs, L. S., Espin, C., van den Broek, P., & Deno, S. L. (2000, February). *Effects of task format and performance dimension on word reading measures: Criterion validity, sensitivity to impairment, and context facilitation.* Paper presented at Pacific Coast Research Conference, San Diego, CA.

Jewett, K. (2000). Review of *Jip: His Story* from *The New York Times Book Review*. Retrieved July 14, 2000, from www.amazon.com

Johns, J., & Lenski, S. D. (1997). *Improving reading: A handbook of strategies*. Dubuque, IA: Kendall-Hunt.

Johnson, D. D., Pittelman, S. D., Toms-Bronowski, S., & Levin, K. M. (1984). *An investigation of the effects of prior knowledge and vocabulary acquisition on passage comprehension* (Program Report 84–5). Madison: University of Wisconsin, Wisconsin Center for Educational Research.

Johnson, D. D., Toms-Bronowski, S., & Pittelman, S. D. (1982). *An investigation of the effectiveness of semantic mapping and semantic feature analysis with intermediate grade children* (Program Report 83–3). Madison: University of Wisconsin, Wisconsin Center for Educational Research.

Johnson, D. W., Maruyama, G., Johnson, R. G., Nelson, D., & Skon, I. (1981). Effects of cooperative, competitive, and individualistic goal structures on achievement: A meta-analysis. *Psychological Bulletin, 89*, 47–62.

Johnston, F. R. (1998). The reader, the text, and the task: Learning words in first grade. *The Reading Teacher, 51*(8), 666–675.

Jones, B. F., Pierce, J., & Hunter, B. (1988/1989). Teaching students to construct graphic representations. *Educational Leadership, 46*(4), 20–25.

Juel, C. (1994). *Learning to read and write in one elementary school*. New York: Springer-Verlag.

Juel, C., & Roper-Schneider, D. (1985). The influence of basal readers on first grade reading. *Reading Research Quarterly, 20*, 134–152.

Just, M. A., & Carpenter, P. A. (1987). *The psychology of reading and language comprehension*. Boston: Allyn & Bacon.

Kame'enui, E. J., & Carnine, D. (Eds.). (1998). *Effective teaching strategies that accommodate diverse learners*. Upper Saddle River, NJ: Prentice Hall.

Kame'enui, E. J., & Simmons, D. C. (2001). Introduction to this special issue: The DNA of reading fluency. *Scientific Studies of Reading, 5*(3), 203–210.

Kame'enui, E. J., Simmons, D. C., Good, R. H., & Harn, B. (2001). The use of fluency-based measures in early identification and evaluation of intervention efficacy in schools. In M. Wolf, (Ed.), *Dyslexia, fluency, and the brain* (pp. 307–331). Timonium, MD: York.

Kaminski, R. A., & Good, R. H., III. (1996). Toward a technology for assessing basic early literacy skills. *School Psychology Review, 25*(2), 215–227.

Karchmer, M. A. (1978, March). *Early manual communication, parental hearing status, and the academic achievement of deaf students*. Paper presented at the American Education Research Association Annual Meeting. Toronto, Ontario, Canada.

Keene, E. O., & Zimmermann, S. (1997). *Mosaic of thought: Teaching comprehension in a reader's workshop*. Portsmouth, NH: Heinemann.

Kerman, S. (1979). Teacher expectations and student achievement. *Phi Delta Kappan, 60*, 28–31.

Kibby, M. W. (1993). What reading teachers should know about reading proficiency in the U. S. *Journal of Reading, 27*(1), 48–51.

King, A. (1990). Enhancing peer interaction and learning in the classroom through reciprocal peer questioning. *American Educational Research Journal, 27*, 664–687.

King, S. R., & Torgesen, J. K. (2000). *Improving the effectiveness of reading instruction in one elementary school: A description of the process.* Unpublished manuscript.

Kiss, G. R., & Savage, J. E. (1977). Processing power and delay—limits on human performance. *Journal of Mathematical Psychology, 16,* 68–90.

Klinger, J. K., Vaughn, S., Hughes, M. T., Schumm, J. S., & Elbaum, B. (1998). Outcomes for students with and without learning disabilities in inclusive classrooms. *Learning Disabilities Research & Practice, 13*(3), 153–161.

Kohn, A. (1999, October). The trouble with 'back-to-basics' and 'tougher standards.' *Wisconsin School News,* pp. 17–18.

Kollars, D. (1999, June 25). City schools improve in statewide reading, math tests. *Sacramento Bee.* Retrieved July 20, 1999, from www. sacbee. com

Konigsburg, E. L. (1996). *The view from Saturday.* New York: Atheneum.

Koskinen, P. S., & Blum, I. H. (1986). Paired repeated reading: A classroom strategy for developing fluent reading. *The Reading Teacher, 40*(1), 70–75.

Kozol, J. (1985). *Illiterate America.* New York: Anchor Press/Doubleday.

Krashen, S. (1993). *The power of reading.* Englewood, CO: Libraries Unlimited.

Labbo, L. D., & Teale, W. H. (1990). Cross-age reading: A strategy for helping poor readers. *The Reading Teacher, 43,* 362–369.

LaBerge, D., & Samuels, S. J. (1974). Toward a theory of automatic information processing in reading. *Cognitive Psychology, 6,* 293–323.

Lee, V., Brooks-Gunn, J., Schnur, E., & Liaw, F. (1990). Are Head Start effects sustained? A longitudinal follow-up comparison of disadvantaged children attending Head Start, no preschool, and other pre-school programs. *Child Development, 61,* 495–507.

Lenz, B. K., Ellis, E. S., & Scanlon, D. (1996). *Teaching learning strategies to adolescents and adults with learning disabilities.* Austin, TX: PRO-ED.

Levy, B. A. (2001). Moving the bottom: Improving reading fluency. In M. Wolf, (Ed.), *Dyslexia, fluency, and the brain* (pp. 357–379). Timonium, MD: York.

Levy, B. A., Abello, B., & Lysynchuk, L. (1997). Transfer from word training to reading in context: Gains in reading fluency and comprehension. *Learning Disability Quarterly, 20,* 173–188.

Liberman, I. Y., & Shankweiler, D. (1985). Phonology and the problems of learning to read and write. *Remedial and Special Education, 6*(6), 8–17.

Lie, A. (1991). Effects of a training program for stimulating skills in word analysis for first-grade children. *Reading Research Quarterly, 26*(3), 263–284.

Lieberman, L. M. (2001, January 17). The death of special education. *Education Week,* pp. 60, 41.

Lindamood, C. H., & Lindamood, P. C. (1979). *Lindamood auditory conceptualization test.* Austin: TX: PRO-ED.

Lindamood, P. C., & Lindamood, P. (1998). *Lindamood phoneme sequencing program.* San Luis Obispo, CA: Gander.

Lionni, L. (1971). *Leo, the late bloomer.* New York: Windmill.

Lovett, M. W., Steinbach, K. A., & Frijters, J. C. (2000). Remediating the core deficits of development reading disability: A double-deficit perspective. *Journal of Learning Disabilities, 33*(4), 334–358.

Lovitt, T. C., & Hansen, C. L. (1976). The contingent use of skipping and drilling to improve oral reading and comprehension. *Journal of Learning Disabilities*, *9*(8), 486.

Lundberg, I., Frost, J., & Peterson, O. (1988). Effects of an extensive program for stimulating phonological awareness in pre-school children. *Reading Research Quarterly*, *23*, 263–284.

Lyon, G. R. (1995). Towards a definition of dyslexia. *Annals of Dyslexia*, *45*, 3–27.

Lyon, G. R. (1997). Quoted in P. G. Mathes and J. K. Torgesen. A call for equity in reading instruction for all students: A response to Allington and Woodside-Jiron, (p. 6). *Educational Researcher*, *29*(6), 4–14.

Lyon, G. R., Fletcher, J. M., Shaywitz, S. E., Shaywitz, B. A., Torgesen, J. K., Wood, F. B., Schulte, A., & Olson, R. (2000). Rethinking learning disabilities. In C. E. Finn, Rotherham, A. J., & C. R. Hokanson (Eds.), *Rethinking special education for a new century* (pp. 259–287). Washington, DC: Thomas B. Fordham Foundation and Progressive Policy Institute. Retrieved June 13, 2001, from www.edexcellence.net

Lyons, C. A. (1991). Reading Recovery: A viable prevention of learning disability. *Reading Horizons*, *31*(5), 384–308.

Manis, F. R., & Freedman, L. (2001). The relationship of naming speed to multiple reading measures in disabled and normal readers. In M. Wolf (Ed.), *Dyslexia, fluency and the brain* (pp. 66–92). Timonium, MD: York.

Manzo, K. K. (1998, April 29). More states moving to make phonics law. *Education Week*. Retrieved June 10, 2001, from www.edweek.org

Margosein, C. M., Pascarella, E., & Pflaum, S. (1982, April). *The effects of instruction using semantic mapping on vocabulary and comprehension*. Paper presented at annual Meeting of the American Educational Research Association, Chicago, IL.

Marmolejo, A. (1991, April). *The effects of vocabulary instruction with poor readers*. Paper presented at annual meeting, American Education Research Association, Chicago, IL.

Marshall, J. D. (1987). The effects of writing on students' understanding of literary texts. *Research in the Teaching of English*, *21*(1), 30–63.

Marston, D., & Magnusson, D. (1988). *Curriculum based measurement: District level implementation*. Washington, DC: National Association of School Psychologists.

Martin, A. M. (1996). *Bad-luck mystery* (Babysitter's Club Book). New York: Scholastic.

Martinez, P. (1997, February 16). Universities' reading ethos shuns extremes. *Arizona Daily Star*, p. A11.

Mason, B., & Krashen, S. (1997). Extensive reading in English as a foreign language. *System*, *25*, 91–102.

Mathes, P. G., & Torgesen, J. K. (2000). A call for equity in reading instruction for all students: A response to Allington and Woodside-Jiron. *Educational Researcher*, *29*(6), 4–14.

Mathews, M. (1966). *Teaching to read*. Chicago: University of Chicago Press.

McCormick, C. (2000). *Decodable little books*. New York: Goodyear.

McEwan, E. K. (1998a). *The principal's guide to raising reading achievement*. Thousand Oaks, CA: Corwin.

McEwan, E. K. (1998b). *Seven steps to effective instructional leadership*. Thousand Oaks, CA.

McEwan, E. K. (1999). *How to raise a reader* (2nd ed.). Grand Rapids, MI: Baker Book House.

McEwan, E. K. (2001a). *Raising reading achievement in middle and high schools: Five simple-to-follow strategies for principals.* Thousand Oaks, CA: Corwin.

McEwan, E. K. (2001b). *Ten traits of highly effective teachers: How to hire, mentor, and coach successful teachers.* Thousand Oaks, CA: Corwin.

McEwan, E. K., & Damer, M. (2000). *Managing unmanageable students: Practical solutions for administrators.* Thousand Oaks, CA: Corwin.

McGuinness, C., & McGuinness, G. (1998). *Reading reflex.* New York: Simon & Schuster.

McGuinness, D. (1985). *When children don't learn: Understanding the biology and psychology of learning disabilities.* New York: Basic Books.

McIntyre, C., & Pickering, J. S. (Eds.). (1995). *Clinical studies of multisensory structured language education for students with dyslexia and related disorders.* Salem, OR: International Multisensory Structured Language Education Council.

McKechnie, J. L. (Ed.). (1983). *Webster's new universal unabridged dictionary* (2nd ed.). New York: Simon & Schuster.

McMahon, S. (1992). *Student-led book clubs: What will children discuss when given opportunity to interact among themselves?* Paper presented at the annual meeting of the National Reading Conference. San Antonio, TX.

Meichenbaum, D., & Biemiller, A. (1998). *Nurturing independent learners.* Cambridge, MA: Brookline.

Menyuk, P. (1999). *Reading and linguistic development.* Cambridge, MA: Brookline.

Mercer, C. D., & Campbell, K. U. (2001). *Great leaps.* Gainseville, FL: Diarmuid. Retrieved September 21, 2001, from www.greatleaps.com/default.asp

Mercer, C. D., Campbell, K. U., Miller, M. D., Mercer, K. D., & Lane, H. B. (2000). Effects of a reading fluency intervention for middle schoolers with specific learning disabilities. *Learning Disabilities Research and Practice, 15*(4), 179–189.

Merton, R. (1968). The Matthew effect in science. *Science, 160,* 56–63.

MetaMetrics, Inc. (1998). *About the Lexile framework.* Durham, NC: MetaMetrics. Retrieved December 5, 1998, from www.lexile.com/about_lex/about_lexile.asp

Meyer, L. A., Stahl, S. A., Wardrop, J. L., & Linn, R. L. (1999). Reading *to* or *with* children? *Effective School Practices, 17*(3), 56–64.

Meyer, M. S., & Felton, R. H. (1999). Repeated reading to enhance fluency: Old approaches and new directions. *Annals of Dyslexia, 49,* 283–306.

Miccinati, J. (1985). Using prosodic cues to teach oral reading fluency. *The Reading Teacher, 39,* 206–212.

Missouri Council of School Administrators. (2001). *Evaluation reports of Readership Academy participants.* Jefferson City, MO: Author. Unpublished document.

Moats, L. C. (1995). *Spelling: Development, disability, and instruction.* Baltimore: York.

Moats, L. C. (1998). Teaching decoding. *American Educator, 22*(1–2), 42–49, 95–96.

Moats, L. C. (1999, June). *Teaching reading is rocket science: What expert teachers of reading should know and be able to do.* Washington, DC: American Federation of Teachers. Retrieved August 9, 2001, from www.aft.org/edissues/rocketscience.htm

Moats, L. C. (2000). *Speech to print: Language essentials for teachers.* Baltimore: Brookes.

Moats, L. C. (2001). Overcoming the language gap: Invest generously in teacher professional development. *American Educator, 25*(2), 5, 8–9.

Morissey, B. (1985, July 14). A cartoonist can't worry about the good of the country. *Washington Post*, p. B3.

Mosteller, F., Light, R., & Sachs, J. (1996). Sustained inquiry in education: Lessons from skill grouping and class size. *Harvard Educational Review, 66*(4), 797–828.

Nagy, W. E., & Anderson, R. C. (1984). How many words are there in printed school English? *Reading Research Quarterly, 19*, 304–330.

National Academy of Education, Commission on Reading. (1985). *Becoming a nation of readers: The report of the Commission on Reading* (Prepared by R. C. Anderson, E. H. Hiebert, J. A. Scot, & I. A. G. Wilkinson). Washington, DC: National Academy of Education, National Institute of Education, Center for the Study of Reading.

National Center for Education Statistics. (2001). *NAEP data for 2000*. Washington, DC: Author. Retrieved August 9, 2001, from www.nces.ed.gov/nationsreportcard/tables

National Literacy Secretariat of Canada. (1997). *International adult literacy survey (1997)*. Retrieved June 10, 2001, from www.nald.ca/nls/ials/introduc.htm

National Reading Panel. (2000). *Report of the National Reading Panel: Teaching children to read: An evidence-based assessment of the scientific research literature on reading and its implications for reading instruction. Reports of the Subgroups*. Rockville, MD: National Institute of Child Health and Human Development.

Neil, A. S. (1960). *Summerhill: A radical approach to child rearing*. New York: Hart.

O'Connor, R. E., Jenkins, J. R., & Slocum, T. A. (1993). *Unpacking phonological awareness: Two treatments for low-skilled kindergarten children*. Unpublished manuscript.

O'Connor, R. E., Notari-Syverson, A., & Vadasy, P. (1997). *Ladders to literacy: A kindergarten activity book*. Baltimore: Brookes.

Ong, F., & Breneman, B. (Eds.). (2000). *Strategic teaching and learning: Standards-based instruction to promote content literacy in grades four through twelve*. Sacramento, CA: California Department of Education.

Open Court Reading. (1995). *Collection for young scholars*. Chicago and Peru, IL: SRA/McGraw-Hill.

Opitz, M. F., & Rasinski, T. V. (1998). *Good-bye Round Robin: 25 effective oral reading strategies*. Portsmouth, NH: Heinemann.

Packard, E. (1998). *Fugitive* (Choose Your Own Adventure series). New York: Bantam.

Palinscar, A. S., & Brown, A. L. (1984). Reciprocal teaching of comprehension-fostering and comprehension-monitoring activities. *Cognition and Instruction, 2*, 117–175.

Pascal, F. (1995). *Jessica + Jessica = trouble* (Sweet Valley Kids, No. 59). New York: Bantam.

Pascal, F. (2001). *Where we belong* (Sweet Valley Sr. Year, No. 29). New York: Skylark.

Paterson, K. (1996). *Jip: His story*. New York: Lodestar.

Patterson, K. E., & Coltheart, V. (1987). Phonological processes in reading: A tutorial review. In M. Coltheart (Ed.), *Attention and performance: Vol. 12. The psychology of reading* (pp. 421–447). Hillsdale, NJ: Lawrence Erlbaum.

Pearson, P. D. (1976). The psycholinguistic model of reading. *Language Arts, 53*(3), 309, 314.

Pearson, P. D., & Fielding, L. (1991). Comprehension instruction. In R. Barr, M. L. Kamil, P. Mosenthal, & P. D. Pearson (Eds.), *Handbook of reading research* (pp. 815–860). White Plains, NY: Longman.

Perfetti, C. A. (1985). *Reading ability*. New York: Oxford University Press.

Perfetti, C. A. (1989). There are generalized abilities and one of them is reading. In L. Resnick (Ed.), *Knowing, learning and instruction: Essays in honor of Robert Glaser* (pp. 307–335). Hillsdale, NJ: Lawrence Erlbaum.

Perfetti, C. A. (1995). Cognitive research can inform reading education. *Journal of Research in Reading*, *18*(2), 106–115.

Perfetti, C. A., Marron, M. A., & Foltz, P. W. (1996). Sources of comprehension failure: Theoretical perspectives and case studies. In C. Cornoldi & J. Oakhill (Eds.), *Reading comprehension difficulties: Processes and intervention* (pp. 137–165). Mahwah, NJ: Lawrence Erlbaum.

Personke, C., & Yee, A. (1971). *Comprehensive spelling instruction: Theory, research, and application*. Scranton, PA: Intext Educational Publishers.

Peterson, R., & Eeds, M. (1990). *Grand conversations: Literature groups in action*. New York: Scholastic.

Petty, W., Herold, C., & Stoll, E. (1967). *The state of knowledge about the teaching of vocabulary*. Champaign, IL: National Council of Teachers of English.

Pilgreen, J. L. (2000). *The SSR handbook: How to organize and manage a sustained silent reading program*. Portsmouth, NH: Boyton/Cook.

Pilgreen, J., & Krashen, S. (1993). Sustained silent reading with English as a second language high school students: Impact on reading comprehension, reading frequency, and reading enjoyment. *School Library Media Quarterly*, *22*(1), 21–23.

Pinnell, G. S., Pikulski, J. J., Wixson, K. K., Campbell, J. R., Gough, P. B., & Beatty, A. S. (1995). *Listening to children read aloud*. Washington, DC: U. S. Department of Education, Office of Educational Research and Improvement.

Postlewaite, N. T., & Ross, K. N. (1992). *Effective schools in reading: Implications for educational planners. An exploratory study*. Amsterdam, The Netherlands: International Association for the Evaluation of Educational Achievement.

Pressley, M. (1998). *Reading instruction that works: The case for balanced teaching*. New York: Guilford.

Pressley, M., Burkell, J., Cariglia-Bull, T., Lysynchuk, L., McGoldrick, J. A., Schneider, B., Snyder, B., Symons, S., & Woloshyn, V. E. (1995). *Cognitive strategy instruction that really improves children's academic performance*. Cambridge, MA: Brookline.

Pressley, M., Wharton-McDonald, R., & Mistretta, J. (1998). Effective beginning literacy instruction: Dialectical, scaffolded, and contextualized. In J. L. Metsala & L. C. Ehri. (Eds.), *Word recognition in beginning literacy* (pp. 357–373.). Mahwah, NJ: Lawrence Erlbaum.

Quindlen, A. (1998). *How reading changed my life*. New York: Ballantine.

Raphael, T. (1982). Question-answering strategies for children. *The Reading Teacher*, *36*(2), 186–190.

Rasinski, T. V., Padak, N., Linke, W., & Sturdevant, E. (1994). The effects of fluency development instruction on urban second graders. *Journal of Education Research*, *87*, 158–164.

Ravitch, D. (2000). *Left back: A century of battles over school reform.* New York: Simon & Schuster.

Rayner, K., & Pollatsek, A. (1989). *The psychology of reading.* Englewood Cliffs, NJ: Prentice Hall.

Raywid, M. (1993). Finding time for collaboration. *Educational Leadership, 51*(1), 30, 34.

Reder, S. (2001). *The state of literacy in America: Synthetic estimates of adult literacy proficiency at the local, state and national levels.* Washington: DC: National Institute for Literacy. Retrieved June 14, 2001, from http://novel.nifl.gov/reders/reder.htm

Reutzel, R. (1999). Organizing literacy instruction: effective grouping strategies and organizational plans. In L. Gambrell, L. M. Morrow, S. B. Neuman, & M. Pressley (Eds.), *Best practices in literacy instruction* (pp. 271–291). New York: Guilford.

Reutzel, R., & Cooter, R. B., Jr. (1996). *Teaching children to read: From basals to books.* Columbus, OH: Merrill, Prentice Hall.

Rinehart, S. D., Stahl, S. A., & Erickson, L. G. (1986). Some effects of summarizing on reading and studying. *Reading Research Quarterly, 21*(4), 422–436.

Robbins, C., & Ehri, L. C. (1994). Reading storybooks to kindergartners helps them learn new vocabulary words. *Journal of Educational Psychology, 86*(1), 54–64.

Rosenshine, B. (1971). *Teaching behaviors and student achievement.* London: National Foundation for Education Research in England and Wales.

Rosenshine, B. (1997). Advances in research on instruction. In J. W. Lloyd, E. J. Kame'enui, & D. Chard (Eds.), *Issues in educating students with disabilities* (pp. 197–221). Mahwah, NJ: Lawrence Erlbaum.

Rosenshine, B. (1997, March). *The case for explicit, teacher-led, cognitive strategy instruction.* A paper presented at the annual meeting of the American Educational Research Association, Chicago, IL.

Rosenshine, B., Meister, C., & Chapman, S. (1996). Teaching students to generate questions: A review of the intervention studies. *Review of Educational Research, 66*(2), 181–221.

Routman, R. (1988). *Transitions: From literature to literacy.* Portsmouth, NH: Heinemann.

Russell, D. H., & Fea, H. (1963). Research on teaching reading. In N. L. Gage (Ed.), *Handbook of research on teaching* (pp. 865–928). Chicago: Rand McNally.

Sadker, M., Sadker, D., & Klein, S. (1991). The issue of gender in elementary and secondary education. *Review of Research in Education, 17,* 269–334.

Samuels, S. J. (1976). Automatic decoding and reading comprehension. *Language Arts, 53,* 323–325.

Samuels, S. J. (1979). The method of repeated readings. *The Reading Teacher, 32,* 403–408.

Sandal, I. (2001, 18 June). PCC puts new focus on remedial education. *Arizona Daily Star,* pp. A1, A7.

Santa, C. M., & Hoien, T. (1999). An assessment of Early Steps: A program for early intervention of reading problems. *Reading Research Quarterly, 34*(1), 54–79.

Savage, J. (2000). *Sound it out! Phonics in a balanced reading program.* New York: McGraw-Hill.

Scarborough, H. S., & Dobrich, W. (1990). Development of children with early language delays. *Journal of Speech and Hearing Research, 33*, 70–83.

Scarborough, H. S., & Dobrich, W. (1994). On the efficacy of reading to preschoolers. *Developmental Review, 14*, 245–302.

Schmoker, M. (1999). *Results: The key to continuous school improvement* (2nd ed.). Alexandria, VA: Association for Supervision and Curriculum Development.

Schmoker, M. (2001, October 24). The "crayola curriculum." *Education Week, 42*, 44.

Schoenbach, R., Greenleaf, C., Cziko, C., & Hurwitz, L. (1999). *Reading for understanding: A guide to improving reading in middle and high school classrooms.* San Francisco: Jossey-Bass.

Scholastic. (2001a). *Reading counts.* New York: Author.

Scholastic. (2001b). *Scholastic reading inventory.* New York: Author.

Searfoss, L. (1975). Radio reading. *The Reading Teacher, 29*, 295–296.

Segal, D., & Wolf, M. (1993). Automaticity, word retrieval, and vocabulary development in children with reading disabilities. In L. Meltzer (Ed.), *Cognitive linguistic and developmental perspectives on learning disorders* (pp. 141–165). Boston: Little, Brown.

Senechal, M. (1997). The differential effect of storybook reading on preschoolers' acquisition of expressive and receptive vocabulary. *Journal of Child Language, 24*(1), 123–138.

Shanker, J. L., Ekwall, H. E., Ekwall, E. E. (1993). *Ekwall-Shanker reading inventory.* Boston: Allyn & Bacon.

Shankweiler, D. (1996). Reading and spelling difficulties in high school students: Causes and consequences. *Reading and Writing: An Interdisciplinary Journal, 8*, 267–294.

Shankweiler, D., Lundquist, E., Katz, L., Stuebing, K. K., Fletcher, J. M., Brady, S., Fowler, A., Dreyer, L. G., Marchione, K. E., Shaywitz, S. E., & Shaywitz, B. A. (1999). Comprehension and decoding: Patterns of association in children with reading difficulties. *Scientific Studies of Reading, 3*(1), 69–94.

Share, D. L., & Stanovich, K. E. (1995). Cognitive processes in early reading development: Accommodating individual differences into a model of acquisition. *Issues in Education: Contributions from Educational Psychology, 1*, 1–57.

Shaywitz, S. E., Shaywitz, B. A., Fletcher, J. M., & Escobar, M. D. (1990). Prevalence of reading disabilities in boys and girls: Results of the Connecticut study. *Journal of the American Medical Association, 264*, 998–1001.

Shefelbine, J. (1999). Reading voluminously and voluntarily. In *Scholastic Reading Counts Research.* New York: Scholastic. Retrieved June 12, 1999, from http://apps.scholsatic.com/readingcounts/research/voluminouslky/Voluntarily.

Shinn, M., Good, R. H., Knutson, N., Tilly, W. D., & Collins, V. (1992). Curriculum-based measurement of oral reading fluency: A confirmatory analysis of its relation to reading. *School Psychology Review, 21*(3), 459–479.

Simpson, J. A., & Weiner, E. S. C. (Eds.). (1989). *The Oxford English dictionary.* Oxford, UK: Clarendon. Retrieved September 21, 2001, from http:dictionary. oed. com

Slavin, R. E. (1988). Cooperative learning and student achievement. *Educational Leadership, 45*(2), 31–33.

Slavin, R. E. (1991). Are cooperative learning and "untracking" hurting the gifted? *Educational Leadership, 48*(6), 68–71.

Slavin, R. E., & Madden, N. (1989). What works for students at risk: A research synthesis. *Educational Leadership, 64,* 4–13.

Slavin, R. E., Madden, N. A., Dolan, L. J., & Wasik, B. A. (1996). *Every child, every school: Success for all.* Thousand Oaks, CA: Corwin.

Smith, F. (1971). *Understanding reading: A psycholinguistic analysis of reading and learning to read.* New York: Holt, Rinehart & Winston.

Smith, F. (1994). *Understanding reading: A psycholinguistic analysis of reading and learning to read.* New York: Holt, Rinehart & Winston.

Smith, S. B., Simmons, D. C., & Kame'enui, E. J. (1996). *Synthesis of research on phonological awareness: Principles and implications for reading acquisition* (Technical Report No. 21). Eugene, OR: National Center to Improve the Tools of Educators.

Smylie, M. A. (1989). Teachers' views of the effectiveness of the sources of learning to teach. *Elementary School Journal, 89*(5), 543–558.

Snow, C. E., Barnes, W. S., Chandler, J., Goodman, J. F., & Hemphill, L. (1991). *Unfulfilled expectations: Home and school influences on literacy.* Cambridge, MA: Harvard University Press.

Snow, C. E., Burns, M. S., & Griffin, P. (Eds.). (1998). *Preventing reading difficulties in young children.* Washington, DC: National Academy Press, Committee on the Prevention of Reading Difficulties in Young Children, Commission on Behavioral and Social Sciences and Education, National Research Council.

Spalding, R. B., & Spalding, W. T. (1990). *The writing road to reading: The Spalding Method of phonics for teaching speech, writing & reading* (4th rev. ed.). New York: William Morrow.

Spear-Swerling, L. (2000). Straw men and very misleading reading: A review of *Misreading Reading.* Retrieved March 25, 2000, from www.ldonline.org/ld_store/reviews/swerling_coles.html

Spear-Swerling, L., & Sternberg, R. J. (1998). *Off track: When poor readers become "reading disabled."* Boulder, CO: Westview.

Spiegel, D. L. (1999). Meeting each child's literacy needs. In L. Gambrell, L. M. Morrow, S. B. Neuman, & M. Pressley, M. (Eds.), *Best practices in literacy instruction* (pp. 245–270). New York: Guilford.

Spinelli, J. (1990). *Maniac Magee.* Boston: Little, Brown.

Spinelli, J. (1994). *Who put that hair in my toothbrush?* Boston: Little, Brown.

Stahl, S. A. (1999a). *Vocabulary development.* Cambridge, MA: Brookline.

Stahl, S. A. (1999b). Why innovations come and go (and mostly go): The case of whole language. *Educational Researcher, 28*(8), 13–22.

Stahl, S. A., Duffy-Hester, A. M., & Stahl, K. A. (1998). Everything you wanted to know about phonics (but were afraid to ask). *Reading Research Quarterly, 33*(3), 338–355.

Stahl, S. A., & Fairbanks, M. M. (1986). The effects of vocabulary instruction: A model-based meta-analysis. *Review of Educational Research, 56*(1), 72–110.

Stahl, S. A., Pagnucco, J. R., & Suttles, C. W. (1996). First graders' reading and writing instruction in traditional and process-oriented classes. *Journal of Educational Research, 89*(3), 131–144.

Stanovich, K. E. (1986). Matthew effects in reading: Some consequences of individual differences in the acquisition of literacy. *Reading Research Quarterly, 21*, 360–407.

Stanovich, K. E., & Cunningham, A. E. (1993). Where does knowledge come from? Specific associations between print exposure and information acquisition. *Journal of Educational Psychology, 85*, 211–229.

Stein, J. F. (2001). The neurobiology of reading difficulties. In M. Wolf, (Ed.), *Dyslexia, fluency, and the brain* (pp. 4–21). Timonium, MD: York.

Stein, M., Johnson, B., & Gutlohn, L. (1998). Analyzing beginning reading programs: The relationship between decoding instruction and text. *Remedial and Special Education, 20*(5), 275–287.

Stein, J. F., & Talcott, J. B. (1999). The magnocellular theory of dyslexia. *Dyslexia, 5*, 59–78.

Stein, J. F., & Walsh, V. (1997). To see but not to read: The magnocellular theory of dyslexia. *TINS, 20*, 147–152.

Stenner, A. J. (1996, February). *Measuring reading comprehension with the Lexile framework*. Paper presented at the Fourth North American Conference on Adolescent/Adult Literacy, Washington, DC. Retrieved December 12, 1998, from www.lexile.com

Sternberg, R. J. (1987). Most vocabulary is learned from context. In M. G. McKeown & M. E. Curtis (Eds.), *Nature of vocabulary acquisition*. Hillsdale, NJ: Lawrence Erlbaum.

Stevenson, R. L. (1911). *Treasure island*. New York: Scribner.

Stine, R. L. (1996). *Forbidden secrets* (Fear Street Saga). New York: Archway.

Stine, R. L. (1998). *The werewolf of twisted tree lodge* (Give Yourself Goosebumps series). New York: Scholastic.

Stotsky, S. (1999). *Losing our language: How multicultural classroom instruction is undermining our children's ability to read, write, and reason*. New York: Free Press.

Sulzby, E., & Teale, W. (1991). Emergent literacy. In R. Barr, M. Kamil, P. Mosenthal, & P. D. Pearson (Eds.), *Handbook of reading research* (Vol. 2, pp. 727–757). White Plains, NY: Longman.

Tan, A., & Nicholson, T. (1997). Flashcards revisited: Training poor readers to read words faster improves their comprehension in text. *Journal of Educational Psychology, 89*, 276–288.

Taylor, B. M., Anderson, R. C., Au, K. H., & Raphael, T. E. (2000). Discretion in the translation of research to policy: A case from beginning reading. *Educational Researcher, 29*(6), 16–26.

Taylor, B. M., & Beach, R. W. (1984). The effects of text structure instruction on middle-grade students' comprehension and production of expository text. *Reading Research Quarterly, 19*, 134–146.

Teddlie, C., & Stringfield, S. (1993). *Schools make a difference: Lessons learned from a 10-year study of school effects*. New York: Teachers College Press.

Thomas, L. (2000). *Decoding instruction for beginning readers: Phonics versus the cueing systems*. Unpublished paper, San Diego State University, San Diego, CA.

Tompkins, G. (1998). *Fifty literacy strategies step by step*. Upper Saddle River, NJ: Merrill.

Topping, K. (1987). Paired reading: A powerful technique for parent use. *The Reading Teacher, 40*, 608–614.

Torgesen, J. K. (2000). Individual differences in response to early interventions in reading: The lingering problem of treatment results. *Learning Disabilities and Research Practice, 15*(1), 55–64.

Torgesen, J. K., Alexander, A. W., Wagner, R. K., Rashotte, C. A., Voeller, K., Conway, T., & Rose, E. (2001). Intensive remedial instruction for children with severe reading disabilities: Immediate and long-term outcomes from two instructional approaches. *Journal of Learning Disabilities, 34,* 33–58.

Torgesen, J. K., & Bryant, B. R. (1993). *Phonological awareness training for reading.* Austin, TX: PRO-ED.

Torgesen, J. K., & Mathes, P. G. (2000). *A basic guide to understanding, assessing, and teaching phonological awareness.* Austin, TX: PRO-ED.

Torgesen, J. K., Rashotte, C. A., & Alexander, A. W. (2001). Principles of fluency instruction in reading: Relationships with established empirical outcomes. In M. Wolf (Ed.), *Dyslexia, fluency, and the brain* (pp. 333–355). Timonium, MD: York.

Torgesen, J. K., Wagner, R., & Rashotte, C. (1997). The prevention and remediation of severe reading disabilities: Keeping the end in mind. *Scientific Studies of Reading, 1,* 217–234.

Torgesen, J. K., Wagner, R., & Rashotte, C. (1999). *TOWRE: Test of word reading efficiency.* Austin, TX: PRO-ED.

Tosi, A. (1979). Bilingualism and immigration: A sociolinguistic view of the European plan for the maintenance of national languages in immigrant communities. *Rassegna Italiana di Linguistica Applicata, 11,* 243–263.

Tovani, C. (2000). *I read it, but I don't get it: Comprehension strategies for adolescent readers.* Portland, ME: Stenhouse.

Treiman, R. (1993). *Beginning to spell.* Oxford, UK: Oxford University Press.

Trelease, J. (2001, September 9). The quick Q & A: Benefit by being book-friendly. *Chicago Tribune,* sec. 13, p. 5.

Tsang, W. K. (1996). Comparing the effects of reading and writing on writing performance. *Applied Linguistics, 17*(2), 210–233.

Tunmer, W., & Hoover, W. (1993). Phonological recoding skill and beginning reading. *Reading and Writing: An Interdisciplinary Journal, 5,* 161–179.

Tynan, W. D., & Latsha, R. (1999, November). *Minutes from the quarterly joint meeting on coordination of services of Central Susquehanna Special Educators and the Department of Pediatrics.* Danville, PA: Geisinger Medical Center.

U. S. Department of Education, Office of Special Education Programs. *21st annual report to Congress on the implementation of the Individuals with Disabilities Education Act.* Washington, DC: Author.

Van Patten, J. R., Chao, C. I., & Reigeluth, C. M. (1986). A review of strategies for sequencing and synthesizing information. *Review of Educational Research, 43,* 203–215.

Vellutino, F., & Scanlon, P. (1987). Phonological coding, phonological awareness, and reading ability: Evidence from a longitudinal and experimental study. *Merrill-Palmer Quarterly, 33,* 321–363.

Vellutino, F. R., Scanlon, D. M., & Lyon, G. R. (2000). Differentiating between difficult-to-remediate and readily remediated poor readers: More evidence against the IQ-achievement discrepancy definition of reading disability. *Journal of Reading Disabilities, 33*(3), 223–238.

Venezky, R. (1970). *The structure of English orthography.* The Hague, The Netherlands: Mouton.

Venezky, R. (1999). *The American way of spelling.* New York: Guilford.

Venezky, R. L., Kaestle, C. F., & Sum, A. M. (1987, January). *The subtle danger: Reflections on the literacy abilities of America's young adults* (Report No. 16-CAEP-01). Princeton, NJ: Center for the Assessment of Educational Progress, Educational Testing Service.

Vogel, S. (1990). Gender difference in intelligence, language, visual-motor abilities, and academic achievement in students with learning disabilities: A review of the literature. *Journal of Learning Disabilities, 23,* 44–52.

Wade, S. E. (1990). Using think alouds to assess comprehension. *The Reading Teacher, 43*(7), 442–451.

Wagner, R. K., & Torgesen, J. K. (1987). The nature of phonological processing and its causal role in the acquisition of reading skills. *Psychological Bulletin, 101*(2), 192–212.

Wagner, R. K., Torgesen, J. K., & Rashotte, C. A. (1994). Development of reading-related phonological processing abilities: New evidence of bidirectional causality from a latent variable longitudinal study. *Developmental Psychology, 30*(1), 73–87.

Wagner, R. K., Torgesen, J. K., Rashotte, C. A., Hecht, S. A., Barker, T. A., Burgess, S. R., Donahue, J., & Garon, T. (1997). Changing causal relations between phonological processing abilities and word-level reading as children develop from beginning to fluent readers. A five-year longitudinal study. *Developmental Psychology, 33,* 468–479.

Wahl, G. (2001, March 21). My three sons. *Sports Illustrated, 49*(4), 36–39.

Walberg, H. (1986). Syntheses of research on teaching. In M. C. Wittrock (Ed.), *Handbook of research on teaching* (pp. 214–229). Upper Saddle River, NJ: Merrill/Prentice Hall.

Walberg, H. J., & Tsai, S. L. (1983, Fall). Matthew effects in education. *Educational Research Quarterly, 20,* 359–373.

Wallace, I. F., & Hooper, S. R. (1997). Otitis media and its impact on cognitive, academic, and behavioral outcomes: A review and interpretation of the findings. In J. E. Roberts, I. F. Wallace, & F. W. Henderson (Eds.), *Otitis media in young children* (pp. 163–194). Baltimore: Brookes.

Walter, J. (1998). *Making up megaboy.* New York: Dorling Kindersley.

Waters, G. D., & Doehring, D. G. (1990). Reading acquisition in congenitally deaf children who communicate orally: Insights from an analysis of component reading, language, and memory skills. In T. Carr & B. A. Levy (Eds.), *Reading and its development: Component skills approaches* (pp. 323–373). San Diego: Academic Press.

Weaver, C. (1988). *Reading process and practice: From socio-psycholinguistics to whole language.* Portsmouth, NH: Heinemann.

Weaver, C. (1994). *Reading process and practice: From socio-linguistics to whole language* (2nd ed.). Portsmouth, NH: Heinemann.

Weber, J. (1987). *Instructional leadership: contexts and challenges.* Eugene, OR: Oregon School Study Council.

Weeks, L. (2001, May 14). A survey shows Americans are reading less. *Washington Post,* p. C1.

Weinstein, C. E., & Hume, L. M. (1998). *Study strategies for lifelong learning.* Washington, DC: American Psychological Association.

Weinstein, C. E., & Mayer, R. E. (1986). The teaching of learning strategies. In M. C. Wittrock (Ed.), *Handbook of research on teaching* (pp. 315–327). New York: Macmillan.

Wells, C. G. (1985). *Language development in the preschool years.* New York: Cambridge University Press.

White, B. L., & Watts, J. C. (1973). *Experience and environment.* Englewood Cliffs, NJ: Prentice Hall.

Wilkinson, G. S. (1995). *The Wide Range Achievement Test-Third Edition.* Wilmington, DE: Jastak.

Wilson, B. (1988). *Wilson reading system.* Millbury, MA: Wilson Language Training.

Wise, B. W., Ring, J., & Olson, R. K. (1999). Training phonological awareness with and without explicit attention to articulation. *Journal of Experimental Child Psychology, 72,* 271–304.

Wolf, M. (1991). Naming speed and reading: The contribution of cognitive neuro-sciences. *Reading Research Quarterly, 26,* 123–141.

Wolf, M. (2001). (Ed.). *Dyslexia, fluency, and the brain.* Timonium, MD: York.

Wolf, M., & Bowers, P. G. (1999). The double-deficit hypothesis for developmental dyslexias. *Journal of Educational Psychology, 91,* 415–438.

Wolf, M., & Bowers, P. G. (2000). Naming-speed processes and developmental reading disabilities: An introduction to the special issue on the double-deficit hypothesis. *Journal of Learning Disabilities, 33*(4), 322–324.

Wolf, M., Miller, L., & Donnelly, K. (2000). Retrieval, automaticity, vocabulary elaboration, orthography (RAVE-O): A comprehensive, fluency-based reading intervention program. *Journal of Learning Disabilities, 33*(4), 375–386.

Wolf, M., & Segal, D. (1992). Word finding and reading in the development dyslexias. *Topics in Language Disorders, 13*(1), 51–65.

Wood, F. B., Flowers, L., & Grigorenko, E. (2001). On the functional neuroanatomy of fluency or why walking is just as important to reading as talking is. In M. Wolf (Ed.), *Dyslexia, fluency and the brain* (pp. 235–244). Timonium, MD: York.

Wood, E., Woloshyn, V. E., & Willoughby, T. (1995). *Cognitive strategy instruction for middle and high schools.* Cambridge, MA: Brookline.

Woodcock, R. W. (1987). *Woodcock Reading Mastery Tests-Revised.* Circle Pines, MN: American Guidance Service.

Wren, S. (2001a). *A glossary of reading-related terms* (Reading Coherence Initiative). Retrieved June 13, 2001, from www.sedl.org/reading/topics.html

Wren, S. (2001b). *Reading by sight* (Reading Coherence Initiative). Retrieved June 13, 2001, from www.sedl.org/reading/topics.html

Yopp, H. K. (1995). A test for assessing phonemic awareness in young children. *The Reading Teacher, 49,* 20–29.

Yoshida, M. (1999). *Lesson study: An ethnographic investigation of school-based teacher development in Japan.* Doctoral dissertation, University of Chicago, Chicago, IL.

Zigmond, N., & Baker, J. M. (1996). Full inclusion for students with learning disabilities: Too much of a good thing. *Theory Into Practice, 35*(1), 26–34.

Index

CORWIN
PRESS

Spooky Friends

Scarlet and Igor

by **JANE FEDER**

illustrated by **JULIE DOWNING**

SCHOLASTIC INC.

For Neal who inspired it, Julie who brought it to life,

and Dianne who made it happen — J.F.

To Jane, Dianne, and Marijka with thanks — J.D.

Library of Congress Cataloging-in-Publication Data
Feder, Jane. Spooky friends / by Jane Feder ; illustrated by Julie Downing.
— 1st ed. p. cm. — (Spooky friends)
Summary: Scarlet the vampire and Igor the mummy are best friends, even though they can never agree
on anything. But when they cooperate, wonderful things begin to happen.

ISBN 978-0-545-47815-1 (hardcover : alk. paper) — ISBN 978-0-545-47816-8 (pbk. : alk. paper)
1. Vampires—Juvenile fiction. 2. Mummies—Juvenile fiction. 3. Best friends—Juvenile fiction.
4. Friendship—Juvenile fiction. [1. Vampires—Fiction. 2. Mummies—Fiction. 3. Best friends—Fiction.
4. Friendship—Fiction.] I. Downing, Julie, ill. II. Title. PZ7.F2997Spo 2013[E]—dc23   2012014786

10 9 8 7 6 5 4 3 2 1   13 14 15 16 17
Printed in the U.S.A.   40
First paperback printing, August 2013

The display type was set in Brickhouse. The text was set in Adobe Garamond Pro Regular. The art was
created with ballpoint pen, watercolor, and digital artwork. Book design by Marijka Kostiw